THE ANALECTS OF CONFUCIUS

论语

今译（汉英对照）

编注：孙芝斋

浙江大学出版社
ZHEJIANG UNIVERSITY PRESS

怎样读《论语》？

出一本新书，总得有个序言以作介绍，如果请名家来写序言，更可引起读者的重视，提高这本书的分量。但我想，作为历史如此悠久的儒家经典——《论语》，现在有人称它谓"东方的圣经"，它在人们心目中的地位，是可想而知的。根据当前国内乃至海外出现的"孔子热"，和年轻一代新起之秀想读《论语》的需要，谈一点个人的认知和建议可能更切合实际。何况编写这本书的目的也是为了面向年轻一代，作普及《论语》之用。

什么是《论语》？它不是一本宗教书，也不是一本什么专业的理论书。东汉班固的《汉书·艺文志》说："论语者，孔子应答弟子、时人，及弟子相与言而闻于夫子之语也。当时弟子各有所记，夫子既卒，门人相与辑而论纂，故谓之论语。"它成书于战国初期，距今约两千四五百年。当时有几种简本，后经西汉安昌侯张禹以《鲁论语》为基础，采纳《齐论语》等可取部分完成校勘本，称《张侯论》。现在通行的就是这一版本。

孔子何许人也？他是中国古代（春秋后期）的一位很了不起的思想家、政治家、教育家，是儒家学说的创始人。孔子名丘，字仲尼。公元前551年出生于鲁国鄹邑（今山东曲阜附近）。幼时家贫，据他自己说："少也贱，故多能鄙事"，"十有五而志于学"。好古敏求；及长，做过一些小吏，去周问礼于老聃。三十岁左右创设平民教育，开始授徒。三十五岁时鲁昭公奔齐，鲁乱；孔子也至齐求仕，景公不用。遂返鲁，退而修诗、书、礼、乐，凡十五年，其时学益进，弟子滋众。五十一岁至五十四岁出仕，任鲁中都宰、司空，继任大司寇，摄行相事，在内政和外交上政绩显著，鲁大治。终因齐惧，馈女乐至鲁以沮之。孔子谏不听，遂行。开始周游列国，凡十四年，途中险遭宋司马桓魋杀害，又绝粮于陈、蔡之间。六十八岁时应季康子召，返鲁；康子卒，鲁终不能用孔子，孔子也不求仕，悉心于教育和文献工作，叙《书》、《礼》，删

《诗》，正《乐》，序《易》，修《春秋》；弟子盖三千，通六艺者七十二人，培养出相当一批贤哲和从政者。公元前479年，孔子七十三岁，卒。

孔子的一生仕途并不得意，也没有机会实现其理想，但他的思想、学说，对中国的历史发展，无论在政治思想、伦理道德，还是教育文化等领域，都产生了极大的影响。自汉武帝刘彻（公元前140年至公元前88年）采纳了董仲舒的建议，提出"罢黜百家，独尊儒术"的方针始，儒家学说作为治国的指导理论，上升到统治地位。两千多年来，孔子和儒家学说，一直受到人们的尊重。元延祐开始，《论语》等经典陆续译成拉丁文、法文、英文等流传海外。然而近百年来，孔子和儒家学说却遭到严重冲击，有人将中国积弱归咎到受孔子的影响；以民族虚无主义的态度，喊出"全盘西化"和"打倒孔家店"的口号；其在"文革"中所遭受到的诬侮、祸殃，甚至严重到了无以复加的地步。今天，经过拨乱反正，人们痛定思痛，重新拾起老祖宗遗留下来的传统文化精华，出现了"孔子热"。这种反弹现象，不但是一种社会规律，亦可以看到人心之向背。

《论语》是儒家学说中最重要的经典，全书原文约一万六千字，分二十篇，内容十分丰富，不但有反映儒家早期思想的基本面貌和它的宇宙观，而且涉及现实生活——大到如何治国安邦、德治仁政，小到每个人如何安身立命、处世为人。对应人生、社会问题，《论语》蕴涵有无穷的智慧，确是很值得学习、研究的文献，有其现实意义。

今读《论语》，关键在于认知它的精义，学以致用，而不是去搞复古，也不是去赶潮流。有人写文章说，读了这本古书，竟感到如此贴切，面对人生、社会问题的智慧近在咫尺。这正是读书联系实际的体会。但要有此体会也不太容易，毕竟《论语》成书距今已两千多年了，时代在变，人们的生产、生活习惯，认知和观念，乃至语言、文学等都在改变。

《论语》，虽然篇幅不大，言语简朴，没有矫揉造作的虚伪劲儿，非常务实，但读起来有时还是会有些困难。所以，本书对古汉语原文加以注释，有的还交代了背景，并用白话文作译。为满足国内年轻学子读《论语》以加强对外交流的需要，也为外国人读《论语》提供方便，故选择了国际上多数学者公认的、由英国 James Legge 翻译的《中国经典》（*The Chinese Classics*）的英文本，逐条列出对照，并将人名、地名和某些音译专用名词，改成中国大陆通行的汉语拼音，以飨读者。

《论语》原文有些章句的解释，历来有争议；也有个别章句，用现代的认知和观点来看，难以理解；另外还有发现原来刻简的字位置可能有误。而现在有些解读《论语》的版本，自行加以改动；也有的就干脆违避、删舍了这些章句原文。不过我们并不苟同这样的做法。相反，本书仍用繁体字，按原来的篇目一字不动地列出了所有原文章句，有不同解读者，亦在"注释"中列出。要允许"和而不同"，让读者见仁见智，有思考、讨论的空间。

宋大儒程颐说："读《论语》，有读了全然无事者；有读了后，其中得有一两句喜者；有读了后，知好之者；有读了后，直有不知手之舞之，足之蹈之者。"又说："如读《论语》，未读时是此等人，读了后又只是此等人，便是不曾读。"所以，首先要端正学习的态度，静下心来，虚心去读，从识文义到求精义，联系实际，学以致用。

我不是一个学研哲学、历史、文学、社会学等的专业者，只是从事医学、卫生学的"小器"而已。正因为数十年所经历和所看到的实际，深感"夫子之言不可侮"，夫子书不可不读，人们亟须补上这一课。所以不揣浅陋，花了几年时间编写这本书。因为水平低，肯定会有不少错误，竭诚希望得到各位专家、学者和读者们的帮助、指导。我怀着惴惴之心，翘首以待。

此书稿在编写过程中，得到早年毕业于复旦大学中文系的佼佼者、现年 94 岁的徐微老师的指导，又得到美国的两位同学姐妹——Christine 和 Sunny 在英译方面的帮助，特此致谢。

孙芝斋
2008 年 2 月于美国加州

目　录

学而第一

本篇取"学而时习之"的"学而"二字为题,用以与其他各篇之区别,别无他义。以下各篇同。本篇凡十六章(1—1～1—16)。

1—1

子曰^①:"學而時習之,不亦説^②乎? 有朋^③自遠方來,不亦樂乎? 人不知而不愠^④,不亦君子^⑤乎?"

[注释]

①子:何晏《论语集解》引马融谓:"子者,男子之通称。"沈知方《论语新解》按:"春秋时称卿大夫皆曰'子'、曰'夫子'。孔子曾为鲁大夫,故弟子亦称之曰'子'、曰'夫子'。私人聚弟子讲学,以孔子为最早,故此后相沿,遂称曰'夫子'。"事实上古代对学术上独树一帜,成为体系,有著书立说者亦都称之为"子"。《论语》中"子曰"的"子",都是孔子的弟子对孔子的称呼。　②说:同"悦",读 yuè,喜悦的意思。　③朋:《集解》包咸曰"同门曰朋"。《史记·孔子世家》称:"孔子不仕,退而修诗书礼乐;弟子弥众至自远方。"故此"朋"字当指来自远方的求学弟子们。朱熹《集注》曰:"朋,同类也。"现一般都将"朋"释为"朋友",似过于泛指。　④愠:读 yùn,怒的意思。⑤君子:指地位高的人,也指人格高尚的人。朱熹《集注》有"君子,成德之名"之释。

[白话文]

孔子说:"学习了之后,又经常去复习它,常常会有新的领会,这不是令人高兴的事吗? 有志同道合的朋友从远方来,不也是令人快乐的吗? 别人不了解我,我也不因生气而怨恨人家,这不也是有修养的君子吗?"

[英译文]

The Master said, "Is it not pleasant to learn with a constant perseverance and application? Is it not delightful to have friends coming from distant quarters? Is he not a man of complete virtue, who feels no discomposure though men may take note of him?"

1—2

有子^①曰:"其爲人也孝弟^②,而好犯上者鮮^③矣! 不好犯上,而好作亂者,未之有也。君子務^④本,本立而道生。孝弟也者,其爲仁^⑤之本與^⑥。"

[注释]

①有子:孔子的弟子。姓有名若,鲁国人。《论语》中对孔子的弟子一般都称他的字。唯闵损、冉求二人各在一处(参阅先进篇、子路篇)称子,而曾参、有若二人在各处皆称为子。故后人据此推断《论语》是他二人的再传弟子参与编写的,故而尊此二人。　②弟:即悌。朱熹曰:"善事父母为孝,善事兄长为弟(悌)。"③鲜:同"少"。　④务:专心致志。　⑤为仁:仁,指仁爱、同情,爱护,帮助人的思想、感情。为仁,即实行仁。《论语新解》注:"为仁,犹言行仁。欲仁而志于仁,用力于仁以求仁,是谓'为仁'。"⑥与:即欤,助词,表示感叹,跟"啊"相同;亦可表示疑

问,跟"吗"、"呢"相同。《论语》中"欤"均写成"与"。

[白话文]

有子说:"如果能够孝顺父母,尊敬兄长,而还喜好冒犯上位的人,那是很少的。不喜好冒犯上位而喜好作乱的人,那是不会有的。君子专心致力于事物的根本,根本建立了,'道'就从此而生。孝悌就是'仁'的根本啊!"

[英译文]

The philosopher You said, "They are few who, being filial and fraternal, are fond of offending against their superiors. There have been none, who, not liking to offend against their superiors, have been fond of stirring up confusion. The superior man bends his attention to what is radical. That being established, all practical courses naturally grow up. Filial piety and fraternal submission! Are they not the root of all benevolent actions?"

1－3

子曰:"巧言令色,鲜矣仁。"

[白话文]

孔子说:"花言巧语,话说得好听,又装着一副讨人喜欢的脸色去奉承人家,这种人是很少有仁德的。"

[英译文]

The Master said, "Fine words and an insinuating appearance are seldom associated with ture virtue."

1－4

曾子①曰:"吾日三省②吾身:爲人謀而不忠乎③? 與朋友交而不信乎? 傳④,不習乎?"

[注释]

①曾子:孔子的弟子,姓曾名参,字子与,南武城人。比孔子小四十六岁。《四书》中的《大学》,经一章为孔子之言,由曾子所述,传十章则为曾子之意,由其门人记之。宋朱熹对他的评价很高,称孔子的三千弟子中,"曾氏之传独得其宗,于是作为传义,以发见意"。(参阅朱熹《大学章句序》) ②省:读 xǐng。检查自己的思想行为。 ③不忠乎:指是否尽心尽力。 ④传:郑康成云:"鲁读传为'专'。"《说文解字》称:"专,六寸簿也。"按当时所用六寸的竹简作簿,记录所述。今多译为老师所传授给我的、记录在竹简簿上的(学问技艺等)。

[白话文]

曾子说:"我每日以三件事自我反省:为他人办事有没有尽心尽力? 与朋友交

往，有没有不信实之处？老师传授给我的东西有没有复习熟悉它？"

[英译文]

The philosopher Zeng said, "I daily examine myself on three points: whether, in transacting business for others, I may have been not faithful; whether, in intercourse with friends, I may have been not sincere; whether I may have not mastered and practised the instructions of my teacher."

1－5

子曰："道①千乘之國②，敬事③而信，節用④而愛人，使民以時⑤。"

[注释]

①道：作"治"字解。　②千乘之国：古时用四匹马拉的一辆车为一乘。当时拥有一千辆这样的兵车的诸侯国，称千乘之国，算大国。　③敬事：敬，谨慎，郑重意；事，指政事。如果不敬事，玩忽职守，朝令暮改，人民如何能信任？　④用：指财用。　⑤使民以时：要使用人民劳动力来兴建国家工程或进行其他劳役，必须选择在合适的时候。

[白话文]

孔子说："治理一个拥有千辆兵车的大国，就要谨慎认真地对待政事并取信于民，节省财用而爱护人民，役使人民要安排在合适的时候。"

[英译文]

The Master said, "To rule a country of a thousand chariots, there must be reverent attention to business, and sincerity; economy in expenditure, and love for men; and the employment of the people at the proper seasons."

1－6

子曰："弟子①入則孝，出則弟②，謹而信，汎③愛眾，而親仁④；行有餘力，則以學文。"

[注释]

①弟子：指为人子、为人弟者。一说孔子称学生们。　②弟：即悌，敬爱兄长。　③汎："泛"的异体字，广泛的意思。　④亲仁：亲，亲近；仁，指有仁德的人。

[白话文]

孔子说："弟子在家要孝顺父母，外出要敬爱兄长，办事要很谨慎，说话要守信用，博爱众人，亲近有仁德的人。做到这些之后，有余力的话，就再去学习文化知识。"

[英译文]

The Master said, "A youth, when at home, should be filial, and, abroad, respectful to his elders. He should be earnest and truthful. He should overflow in love to all, and cultivate the friendship of the good. When he has time and opportunity, after the performance of there things, he should employ them in polite studies."

1-7

子夏①曰:"賢賢易色②;事父母,能竭其力;事君,能致其身;與朋友交,言而有信。雖曰未學,吾必謂之學矣!"

[注释]

①子夏:孔子的弟子,姓卜名商,子夏是他的字。 ②贤贤易色:第一个贤字作动词,看重敬重的意思;第二个贤字为名词,指贤人。易,改换的意思。色,容貌。朱熹注曰:"贤人之贤,而易其好色之心。"一说,指配偶要看重其是否贤德,而不是以容貌为重。

[白话文]

子夏说:"一个人能改变好色之心为敬重贤人;奉养父母能尽心尽力;为代表国家和人民的君主服务于工作,有献身忘我精神;与朋友交往,说话有信用。这样的人虽然说未曾受过教育,我必定说他是很有教养的。"

[英译文]

Zi-xia said, "If a man withdraws his mind from the love of beauty, and applies it as sincerely to the love of the virtuous; if, in serving his parents, he can exert his utmost strength; if, in serving his prince, he can devote his life; if, in his intercourse with his friends, his words are sincere—although men say that he has not learned, I will certainly say that he has."

1-8

子曰:"君子不重①則不威,學則不固。主忠信②,無友不如己者③。過則勿憚④改。"

[注释]

①重:旧多作"庄重"解,指外表容貌,难免有装模作样之嫌,求的是外表形象。近代学者桂裕撰《论语新说》注为"自重","君子不重"乃指君子如不自重。后者较确切。 ②主忠信:主,亲的意思。主忠信,即亲忠信的人。 ③无友不如己者:历来较多释为"不要结交不如自己者",朱熹又注:"无,即毋。"一说,"无"为形容词,没有的意思;"毋"为动词,不要的意思。"无友不如己者"释读为"没有一个朋友不如自己的",其内涵是人各有长处,要尊重别人。芝斋按:交友颇有学问,近朱者赤,近墨者黑,慎重交友,此乃古训。对缺乏社会经验的青少年来说,尤为重要。择道德、学问好,为人忠信如己的人为友,何"势利"之有?如果专择地位高于己、有权有势者为友,

更有谄媚之嫌，或别有用心。这不是交友划算不划算的问题，而是德育和社会风尚的问题。故从前说为宜。 ④惮：惧怕的意思。

[白话文]

孔子说："君子如果不自重，则威望不立，在学习知识和道德行为上也不能扎实巩固；为人处世要以忠信为本；交朋友，不要和道德行为不如自己、不忠信者为友。朋友间要互尊、互重、互诤，如有缺点或过错，不要怕改过。"

[英译文]

The Master said, "If the scholar be not grave, he will not call forth any veneration, and his learning will not be solid. Hold faithfulness and sincerity as first principles. Have no friends not equal to yourself. When you have faults, do not fear to abandon them."

1-9

曾子曰："慎終①追②遠，民德歸厚矣！"

[注释]

①终：人去世，或称寿终。 ②追：追悼，怀念（去世者）的过去（一般都追念其德行）。

[白话文]

曾子说："慎重办理去世者的丧葬事宜，并追念他以往的德行。这样可使民风道德归向淳厚。"

[英译文]

The philosopher Zeng said, "Let there be a careful attention to perform the funeral rites to parents, and let them be followed when long gone with the ceremonies of sacrifice; then the virtue of the people will resume its proper excellence."

1-10

子禽①問於子貢②曰："夫子至於是邦也，必聞其政。求之與？抑與之與③？"子貢曰："夫子溫、良、恭、儉、讓以得之。夫子之求之也，其諸異乎人之求之與！"

[注释]

①子禽：孔子的弟子。姓陈，名亢，又字子元，齐国人，比孔子小四十岁。 ②子贡：姓端木，名赐，子贡是他的字，卫国人，是孔子的弟子中的出色者。 ③与："之与"的"与"，置于句末，都同"欤"，表示疑问，跟"吗"或"呢"意思相同；亦可表示感叹，跟"啊"同。"与之"的"与"，给予、交往、赞许、等待，亦用作介词"跟"、连词"和"。这里，作"告诉给孔子"解。

[白话文]

子禽问子贡说:"老师每到一个邦国,必闻知该国的政治情况,是他自己去向别人求得的呢? 还是人家主动告诉他的?"子贡说:"老师是以他的温和、善良、恭敬、节俭、谦让的美德而获得的。他和别人之求不同。"

[英译文]

Zi-qin asked Zi-gong, "When our master comes to any country, he does not fail to learn all about its government. Does he ask his information; or is it given to him?"

Zi-gong said, "Our master is benign, upright, courteous, temperate, and complaisant, and thus he gets his information. The master's mode of asking information! Is it not different from that of other men?"

1－11

子曰:"父在觀其志①;父没,觀其行;三年無改於父之道,可謂孝矣。"

[注释]

①志:历代儒者都释为"志向"。亦有指是"意志",包括思想、态度;延伸到"行",乃指不论父母在或不在,观察其言行是否一致。至于"无改于父之道",其前提是要看其父兄所从事业和行为是否符合"道"。《集注》引尹氏注曰:"如其道,虽终身无改可也;如其非道,何待三年?"近人沈知方《四书广解》曰:"何以不改也,为其为道也。若其非道,虽朝没而夕改可也。"可见"父之道"重点在于其理念、人格、品行。

[白话文]

孔子说:"父亲在的时候,要看这孩子的志向和从学、从事的意志;父亲不在或去世了,就要看这孩子的行为、言行是否一致,以较长期间看这孩子是否守持着父辈良好的理念、人格和行事。把好的传统继承下来,对得起先人,这样可以算是孝了。"

[英译文]

The Master said, "While a man's father is alive, look at the bent of his will; when his father is dead, look at his conduct. If for three years he does not alter from the way of his father, he may be called filial."

1－12

有子曰:"禮①之用,和爲貴②;先王之道,斯③爲美,小大由之。有所不行,知和而和,不以禮節之,亦不可行也。"

[注释]

①礼:就是礼制规矩,表现于妥善处理人际关系,尊敬人的思想、态度、言语、动作,共同遵守伦理道德、风尚、秩序,以及礼仪、礼节、礼貌等。离开了礼,就会坏伦纪、泯是非、茫荣耻、乱秩序,发生各种争端。　②和为贵:遇事以礼为规范,协调各种矛盾,分清是非,平息争端,待人以礼,使之和谐共处于统一体中,保持事物的发展和稳定,这是礼的作用最为可贵之处。　③斯:这里指礼。

[白话文]

有子说:"礼的功用,贵在人和。先王之道,以礼为美,无论大事小事,大小人物,都得遵照礼而行为。然而知礼之用在和,而一味和气,为和而和,不以礼来节制,亦不可行。"

[英译文]

The philosopher You said, "In practising the rules of propriety, a natural ease is to be prized. In the ways prescribed by the ancient kings, this is the excellent quality, and in thing small and great we follow them. Yet it is not to be observed in all cases. If one, knowing how such ease should be prized, manifests it, without regulating it by the rules of propriety, this likewise is not to be done."

1－13

有了口:"信近①於義,言可復②也;恭近於禮,遠耻辱也。因③不失其親,亦可宗④也。"

[注释]

①近:符合。　②復:兑现的意思。　③因不失其亲:因,作"亲近"解。因不失其亲,就是亲近不失其所当亲的人,如本篇第六章(1-6)所说的"亲仁"——亲近有仁德者。　④宗:众人所师法的人。

[白话文]

有子说:"守信,就合于义,所说的诺言能兑现;恭敬,符合于礼,就可远离耻辱〔'恭而无礼则劳'(参阅《礼记·表记》),且易被旁人看作谄谀取媚而带来耻辱〕;亲近所当亲近的仁人,尊敬而效法他。"

[英译文]

The philosopher You said, "When agreements are made according to what is right, what is spoken can be made good. When respect is shown according to what is proper, one keeps far from shame and disgrace. When the parties upon whom a man leans are proper persons to be intimate with, he can make them his guides and masters."

1-14

子曰:"君子食無求飽,居無求安,敏於事而慎於言,就有道而正焉,可謂好學也已。"

[白话文]

孔子说:"君子对于饮食不强求饱足,对居住不强求安逸,勤快做事,谨慎说话,就教于有道德学问的人来纠正自己的错误。这样,就可以说是好学的了。"

[英译文]

The Master said, "He who aims to be a man of complete virtue in his food does not seek to gratify his appetite, nor in his dwelling-place does he seek the appliances of ease; he is earnest in what he is doing, and careful in his speech; he frequents the company of men of principle that he may be rectified—such a person may be said indeed to love to learn."

1-15

子貢曰:"貧而無諂①,富而無驕,何如?"子曰:"可也。未若貧而樂,富而好禮者也。"子貢曰:"《詩》云:'如切如磋,如琢如磨②。'其斯之謂與?"子曰:"賜也,始可與言《詩》已矣,告諸往而知來者。"

[注释]

①谄:读 chǎn,谄媚,用卑贱的态度去讨好人。 ②如切如磋,如琢如磨:句出《诗经·卫风·淇奥》。将骨头加工成器物的工艺过程叫切,加工象牙叫磋,加工玉叫琢,加工石叫磨。切磋琢磨用来比喻探讨、研究学问,学习长处,纠正缺点。

[白话文]

子贡说:"贫而不谄谀,富而不骄傲,如何?"孔子说:"可以,但不如贫而乐,富而好礼!"子贡说:"《诗经》中说:'如切如磋,如琢如磨。'这两句话比喻(要精益求精)就是这个意思吧!"孔子说:"赐呀! 现在可以和你谈论《诗经》了! 因为告诉你一些道理,你能进而思考,悟出其他未曾告诉你的道理来!"

[英译文]

Zi-gong said, "What do you pronounce concerning the poor man who yet does not flatter, and the rich man who is not proud?" The Master replied, "They will do; but they are not equal to him, who though poor, is yet cheerful, and to him, who, though rich, loves the rules of propriety."

Zi-gong replied, "It is said in the Book of Poetry, 'As you cut and then file, as you carve and then polish.' The meaning is the same, I apprehend, as that which you have, just expressed."

The Master said, "With one like Ci, I can begin to talk about the Odes. I told him one point, and he knew its proper sequence."

1 – 16

子曰："不患人之不己知，患不知人也。"

[白话文]

孔子说："不怕别人不了解自己，只怕自己不了解别人。"

[英译文]

The Master said, "I will not be afflicted at men's not knowing me; I will be afflicted that I do not know men."

为政第二

本篇凡二十四章(2—1~2—24)。

2-1

子曰:"爲政以德①,譬如北辰②,居其所,而衆星共③之。"

[注释]

①为政以德:治理国政,重在德治,执政者以身作则,依靠道德来感化、教育人民,规范生活秩序,容德于各行各业。 ②北辰:即北极星。 ③共:同"拱"。

[白话文]

孔子说:"用道德来治理国政,执政者就好似北极星,位于天之中枢,众星都围绕着它。"

[英译文]

The Master said, "He who exercises government by means of his virtue may be compared to the north polar star, which keeps its place and all the stars turn towards it."

2-2

子曰:"《詩》三百①,一言以蔽之,曰:'思無邪②。'"

[注释]

①《诗》三百:《诗经》三百篇。实际上,《诗经》中除了有目无辞的以外,共有诗三百零五篇。这里说三百,是说个大概数。 ②思无邪:《集注》引程子曰:"思无邪者,诚也。"《诗经》各篇,大到赞美或批评朝廷政治,小到抒发男女情感,都是至情至诚的流露,没有虚假。

[白话文]

孔子说:"《诗经》三百篇,用一句话来概括,那就是至情至性,真诚地流露。"

[英译文]

The Master said, "In the Book of Poetry are three hundred pieces, but the design of them all may be embraced in one sentence—having no depraved thoughts."

2-3

子曰:"道①之以政,齊②之以刑,民免而無恥③。道之以德,齊之以禮,有恥且格④。"

[注释]

①道:同"导",教导。 ②齐:整饬的意思。 ③民免而无耻:民众但求避免刑罚,而不知犯罪是羞耻的。 ④有耻且格:对犯罪感到羞耻,且归于正。

[白话文]

孔子说:"用政令、法律来教导百姓,用刑罚来加以整饬,这样,民众但求避免刑罚而无羞耻之心;如果用道德来教导民众,用礼来教化整治,则民众自知罪恶可耻,而归至于正。"

[英译文]

The Master said, "If the people are led by laws, and uniformity sought to be given them by punishment, they will try to avoid the punishment, but have no sense of shame. If they are led by virtue, and uniformity sought to be given them by the rules of propriety, they will have the sense of shame, and moreover will become good."

2 - 4

子曰:"吾十有五而志於學,三十而立①,四十而不惑,五十而知天命②,六十而耳順③,七十而從心所欲④,不踰矩。"

[注释]

①立:立于礼。〔参阅尧曰篇第三章(20-3)、泰伯篇第八章(8-8)、季氏篇第十三章(16-13)〕②天命:《集注》曰:"即天道之流行而赋于物者。乃事物所以当然之故也。"用现代的话说,宇宙间一切事物的发展变化,都有它的自然规律和社会规律。 ③耳顺:听得进去别人所讲的话,并能知言。〔参阅尧曰篇第三章(20-3)〕 ④从心所欲:从,随。主观意志和客观实际得以统一,办事多能成功。

[白话文]

孔子说:"我十五岁时就立志于学习;三十岁说话、做事能够合于礼,故能立足于社会;四十岁能辨明是非,分析问题,不受迷惑;五十岁能了解事物发展的自然规律和社会规律;六十岁能听得进别人所说的话,知言并能知人;七十岁能做到主客观统一,办事随心所欲,所想所做的一切不会越规。"

[英译文]

The Master said, "At fifteen, I had my mind bent on learning. At thirty, I stood firm. At forty, I had no doubts. At fifty, I know the decrees of Heaven. At sixty, my ear was an obedient organ for the reception of truth. At seventy, I could follow what my heart desired, without transgressing what was right."

2 - 5

孟懿子①問孝。子曰:"無違②。"樊遲御③,子告之曰:"孟孫問孝於我,我對曰'無違'。"樊遲曰:"何謂也?"子曰:"生,事之以禮;死,葬之以禮,祭之以禮。"

[注释]

①孟懿子:鲁国三桓之一,即仲孙何忌。出于桓公子庆父。庆父为鲁庄公庶兄,故称孟(庶长曰孟);以非嫡长,又称仲。名保忌,懿是谥号。 ②无违:不要违背礼。 ③樊迟御:樊迟,人名。孔子的弟子,姓樊,名须,字子迟,齐国人(一说鲁国人),比孔子小三十六岁。御,驾车。樊迟御,樊迟替孔子驾车。

[白话文]

孟懿子问孔子什么是孝。孔子说:"不要违背礼。"有一次,樊迟替孔子驾车,孔子告诉他说:"孟孙(即孟懿子)问我什么叫作孝,我回答他'不要违背礼'。"樊迟问:"这是什么意思呢?"孔子说:"父母在世时,要按照礼来奉养;父母去世,也要按照礼来安葬,按照礼来祭祀。"

[英译文]

Meng Yi-zi asked what filial piety was. The Master said, "It is not being disobedient." Soon after, as Fan-chi was driving him, the Master told him, "Meng-sun asked me what filial piety was, and I answered him—not being disobedient." Fan-chi said, "What did you mean?" The Master replied, "That parents, when alive, should be served according to propriety; that, when dead, they should be buried according to propriety; and that they should be sacrificed to according to propriety."

2 - 6

孟武伯①問孝。子曰:"父母唯其疾之憂②。"

[注释]

①孟武伯:孟懿子(参阅上一章注)的儿子,名彘,武是谥号。 ②父母唯其疾之忧:《集注》曰:"言父母爱子之心,无所不至,唯恐其有疾病,常以为忧也。人子体此,而以父母之心为心,则凡所以守其身者,不容不谨矣。"讲的是父母忧孩子患病之心,做孩子的要体会父母之心,保重自身,不使父母担忧。然而《孝经·孝行章》云:"孝子之事亲也,疾则致其忧。"乃言子忧父母之疾为孝。两说皆通,现从后说。唯,同"惟"。

[白话文]

孟武伯问什么是孝。孔子说:"做儿女的,唯独担心的是父母有了疾病。"

[英译文]

Meng Wu-bo asked what filial piety was. The Master said, "Parents are anxious lest their children should be sick."

2－7

子游①問孝。子曰："今之孝者,是謂能養。至於犬馬,皆能有養。不敬,何以別乎?"

[注释]

①子游:孔子的弟子。姓言,名偃,字子游,吴国人(一说鲁国人)。比孔子小四十五岁。

[白话文]

子游问怎样才是孝。孔子说:"现在一般人所谓的孝,只知能供养父母就算孝了。可是狗与马也能得到人的饲养。如果没有真心孝敬父母,那么和养犬马又有什么区别呢?"

[英译文]

Zi-you asked what filial piety was. The Master said, "The filial piety of now-adays means the support of one's parents. But dogs and horses likewise are able to do something in the way of support; without reverence, what is there to distinguish he one support given from the other?"

2－8

子夏問孝。子曰："色難①。有事,弟子服其勞;有酒食,先生②饌③,曾④是以爲孝乎?"

[注释]

①色难:色,指脸色、态度。色难,谓奉侍父母,须和颜悦色,有好的态度。脸色、态度不好,就是色难。　②先生:古代对上一辈人尊称为先生。这里指父母。　③饌:读 zhuàn,吃喝。④曾:读 céng,何尝、难道。

[白话文]

子夏问怎么做到孝。孔子说:"难在事亲之际,有好的脸色和态度。虽在平时长辈有事,子弟出其劳力去做;有酒食时请父母先吃喝,这是叫作孝吗?"(言下之意,最要紧的是要和颜悦色、态度好。)

[英译文]

Zi-xia asked what filial piety was. The Master said, "The difficulty is with the countenance. If, when their elders have any troublesome affairs, the young take the toil of them; and if, when the young have wine and food, they set them before their elders, is this be considered filial piety?"

2－9

子曰："吾與回①言終日,不違,如愚②。退而省其私,亦足以發,回也不愚。"

[注释]

①回：即颜渊。名回，字子渊，鲁国人，是孔子最得意的弟子。好学而安贫乐道，道德学问在孔子门下首屈一指。《论语》中多处提到孔子对他的称赞，惜乎英年早逝。 ②不违，如愚：指和颜回言谈整天，他只是听受，没有提出和我见解相违背的问题，好像个愚人一般。

[白话文]

孔子说："我和颜回言谈整天，他只是听受，从不提出和我见解相违背的意思，好像个愚人一般。等他退出去之后，我考察他私下的议论，识见很高，对我所讲的都能予以发挥，颜回一点也不笨。"

[英译文]

The Master said, "I have talked with Hui for a whole day, and he has not made any objection to anything I said; as if he were stupid. He has retired, and I have examined his conduct when away from me, and found him able to illustrate my teachings. Hui—he is not stupid."

2－10

子曰："视其所以，观其所由，察其所安①。人焉廋②哉！人焉廋哉！"

[注释]

①视其所以，观其所由，察其所安："常视口视，非常曰观"，仔细看为察。故视、观、察同为看的意思，有粗细深浅之不同。以，朱注"为也"，指所做的事。由，指事的原因、动机。安，指从事的心态，安与不安。 ②廋：读 sōu，隐藏、隐匿。

[白话文]

孔子说："看他所做的事的过程、性质、后果，判断是好事还是坏事；再看他做事的原因、动机；细察他行事时的心态是否安心乐意。用这种方法观察一个人的为人处世，可以发现其真面目。怎么能掩藏得住呢？怎么能掩藏得住呢？"

[英译文]

The Master said, "See what a man does; mark his motives; examine in what things he rests. How can a man conceal his character? How can a man conceal his character?"

2－11

子曰："温故而知新，可以为师矣！"

[白话文]

孔子说："温习过去学过的东西（可以有新的体会），不断学习新知识。这样就可以为人师。"

[英译文]

The Master said, "If a man keeps cherishing his old knowledge, so as continually to be acquiring new, he may be a teacher of others."

2 – 12

子曰:"君子不器①。"

[注释]

①器:指器具、器皿、器物,也指才能。《三字经》有"玉不琢,不成器",喻人是要经过琢磨锤炼,才可成为一个对社会、对国家有用之人。本章所说的"不器",并不是不要成为有才能技艺、各有专长、各适其用的人。对一个有仁德的为政者来说,要求他所发挥的作用,不是像一器一皿的作用,应该是用无不适的,故曰君子不器。〔学习本章,可同时阅读公冶长篇第三章(5-3)〕

[白话文]

孔子说:"君子不要像个器物,只局限于一种用途。"

[英译文]

The Master said, "The accomplished scholar is not a utensil."

2 – 13

子貢問君子。子曰:"先行其言,而後從之。"

[白话文]

子贡向孔子请问怎样才能做一个君子。孔子说:"君子应该在没有说以前先做,做到了以后再说出来。"

[英译文]

Zi-gong asked what constituted the superior man. The Master said, "He acts before he speaks, and afterwards speaks according to his actions."

2 – 14

子曰:"君子周而不比,小人比而不周①。"

[注释]

①周:亲和、调和。比:依附、勾结,如朋比为奸。周和比的区别在于公私义利。

[白话文]

孔子说:"君子与人亲和,不与少数人勾结;小人结党营私,不能普遍与人亲和。"

[英译文]

The Master said, "The superior man is catholic and no partisan. The mean man is a partisan and not catholic."

2－15

子曰："學而不思則罔①，思而不學則殆②。"

[注释]

①罔：同"惘"，迷惑、蒙蔽。　②殆：读 dài，危险。

[白话文]

孔子说："只读书，不加思考，便会陷于迷惘；只思索，不读书，有时会失去方向，那就危险了。"

[英译文]

The Master said, "Learning without thought is labour lost; thought without learning is perilous."

2－16

子曰："攻乎異端①，斯害也已②。"

[注释]

①攻乎异端：攻，指责、驳斥。异端，不同于孔子学说的异端邪说。　②斯害也已：斯，此、这。已，终止、完结。

[白话文]

孔子说："批驳那些异端邪说，其祸害自然可以停止。"

[英译文]

The Master said, "The study of strange doctrines is injurious indeed!"

2－17

子曰："由①！誨②女③知之乎？知之爲知之，不知爲不知，是知④也。"

[注释]

①由：孔子的弟子，姓仲，名由，字子路或季路，季是行辈，比孔子小九岁。好勇过人而个性急，常挨孔子的批评。在《论语》中出现次数最多（高达四十二次）。　②诲：教导。　③女：同"汝"，你的意思。　④知：同"智"。

[白话文]

孔子说："由啊！我教你什么叫'知之'的道理吧！学问的态度贵于笃实，知道就是知道，不知道就是不知道，这才是一个聪明人。"

[英译文]

The Master said, "You! Shall I teach you what knowledge is? When you know a thing, to hold that you know it; and when you do not know a thing, to allow that you do not know it—this is knowledge."

2-18

子張①學干祿②。子曰:"多聞闕疑③。慎言其餘,則寡④尤⑤;多見闕殆⑥,慎行其餘,則寡悔。言寡尤,行寡悔,祿在其中矣。"

[注释]

①子张:孔子的弟子,姓颛孙,名师,子张是字,陈国人,比孔子小四十八岁。 ②干禄:干,求;禄,官爵的薪俸。 ③阙疑:阙,同"缺"。阙疑,把疑难问题留着,不下判断,如"暂作阙疑"。④寡:少的意思。 ⑤尤:错误。 ⑥阙殆:见有疑而感到不妥者,暂搁置不做。

[白话文]

子张想学求官得禄的方法。孔子告知他:"多听各方面的意见。有疑惑的地方,就暂作保留,不下判断;至于其余没有疑惑的部分,也要谨慎地阐述,这样说话就少犯过失。还要多方面观察,对于有疑问而感到不妥的事搁置不做;其余稳妥而有把握的事,做起来也要很谨慎。这样行事就少于后悔。说话少过失,行事少后悔,官禄也就在其中了。"

[英译文]

Zi-zhang was learning with a view to official emolument. The Master said, "Hear much and put aside the points of which you stand in doubt, while you speak cautiously at the same time of the others; then you will afford few occasions for blame. See much and put aside the things which seem perilous, while you are cautious at the same time in carrying the others into practice; then you will have few occasions for repentance. When one gives few occasions for blame in his words, and few occasions for repentance in his conduct, he is in the way to get emolument."

2-19

哀公①問曰:"何爲則民服?"孔子對曰:"舉直錯諸枉②,則民服;舉枉錯諸直,則民不服。"

[注释]

①哀公:鲁国的国君,姓姬,名蒋,定公之子,哀是谥号。在位于公元前494年至公元前468年。 ②举直错诸枉:举,举用、提拔。直,正直,这里指正直的人。错,错开,这里直接指废置、

不用。诸，"之于"的合音。枉，指弯曲、歪斜，这里指邪曲、不正直的人。

[白话文]

鲁哀公问孔子说："怎样做才可以使老百姓顺服？"孔子对答说（《论语》中凡臣对君主的回答，都用"对曰"二字）："举用正直的人，废置那些邪曲的人，老百姓便会顺服。如果举用那些邪曲的人，让正直的人闲置起来，老百姓就不会顺服。"

[英译文]

The duke Ai asked, "What should be done in order to secure the submission of the people?" Confucius replied, "Advance the upright and set aside the crooked, then the people will submit. Advance the crooked and set aside the upright, then the people will not submit."

2－20

季康子^①问："使民敬、忠以劝^②，如之何？"子曰："临之以庄则敬，孝慈则忠，举善而教不能则劝。"

[注释]

①季康子：季孙氏，名肥，康是谥号。鲁哀公时正卿，为当时鲁国三家权臣势力最大的一家。他任用较多的孔子弟子，请教孔子的问题也较多（参阅为政篇、八佾篇、雍也篇、颜渊篇、先进篇、乡党篇、宪问篇等）。　②使民敬、忠以劝：这是季康子所提的问题——怎样使人民能敬上、忠上，并相互劝勉？

[白话文]

季康子问孔子说："要想使民众尊敬我、忠于我，且能相互劝勉，怎样才能做到呢？"孔子说："作为一个在上位的人，临近下属臣民，态度庄重认真，言语举止不要随便和轻浮，人们自然也会对你恭敬；你要真心实意地孝顺父母，慈爱人民，人们也就会忠诚；举用优秀的人，教导能力差的人，并作出示范，人们也会相互劝勉。"

[英译文]

Ji Kang-zi asked how to cause the people to reverence their ruler, to be faithful to him, and to go on to nerve themselves to virtue. The Master said, "Let him preside over them with gravity; then they will reverence him. Let him be filial and kind to all; then they will be faithful to him. Let him advance the good and teach the incompetent; then they will eagerly seek to be virtuous."

2－21

或谓孔子曰："子奚^①不为政？"子曰："《书》^②云：'孝乎，惟孝友于兄弟，施于有政^③。'是亦为政，奚其为为政？"

[注释]

①奚：疑问词，即何。　②《书》：指《尚书》。　③孝乎，惟孝友于兄弟，施于有政：出自《尚书·周书·君陈》，乃周成王命君陈治理洛邑东郊的成周时所说的话。"君陈，惟尔令德孝恭。惟孝友于兄弟，克施有政。"意思是说，你君陈有这种孝顺父母、友爱兄弟的品德，是能够转而用于政事的。其意与孔子所说的"是亦为政"同。

[白话文]

有人对孔子说："夫子为什么不出仕做官，参与政事？"孔子说："《尚书》说：'惟有孝顺父母、友爱兄弟的品德，施行于齐家，转而推及治国。'这就是参与政事，为何要做官才算参与政事呢？"

[英译文]

Some one addressed Confucius, "Sir, why are you not engaged in the government?" The Master said, "What does the Shu-shang say of filial piety: 'You are filial, you discharge your brotherly duties. These qualities are displayed in government.' This then also constitutes the exercise of government. Why must there be that—making one be in the government?"

2－22

子曰："人而無信，不知其可也。大車無輗，小車無軏①，其何以行之哉。"

[注释]

①輗、軏：古代车前驾牲畜的部分有两根直木称辕木，辕木与横木相接处的榫，大车称輗（读 ní），小车称軏（读 yuè）。驾车时，牲口在辕木里，輗或軏必须扣上，车子才可平衡拉动。这里用来比喻如果人无信用，就如车无輗或軏而无法行车。

[白话文]

孔子说："一个人如果不讲信用，不知他怎样立身处世。这就好像大车没有輗、小车没有軏，怎么能行车呢？"

[英译文]

The Master said, "I do not know how a man without truthfulness is to get on. How can a large carriage be made to go without the crossbar for yoking the oxen to, or a small carriage without the arrangement for yoking the horses?"

2－23

子張問："十世可知也①？"子曰："殷因②於夏禮，所損益③可知也；周因於殷禮，所損益可知也。其或繼周者，雖百世可知也。"

[注释]

①十世可知也：世，指朝代。也，这里作疑问词"吗"用。可知什么？据下文说的是礼仪，包括一切典章、制度、政令、仪式和民间习俗。子张问的全句是："今后十代的礼仪制度可以预知吗？" ②因：沿袭。 ③损益：损，减少。益，增加。这里指沿袭前代的礼仪制度有所增添或删减。

[白话文]

子张问："今后十代的（礼仪制度）可以知道吗？"孔子说："商（殷）朝沿袭夏朝的礼仪制度，其中有所增减的；周朝沿袭商朝的，其中有所增减的，大部分是沿袭了前代的，是可以预见的。如果将来有继周而起的朝代，不用说十代，就是一百代所行的，也是可以预先知道的。"

[英译文]

Zi-zhang asked whether the affairs of ten ages after could be known. The Master said, "The Yin dynasty followed the regulations of the Xia; wherein it took from or added to them may be known. The Zhou dynasty has followed the regulations of the Yin; wherein it took from or added to them may be known. Some other may follow the Zhou, but though it should be at the distance of a hundred ages, its affairs may be known."

2-24

子曰："非其鬼①而祭之，諂也。見義不爲，無勇也。"

[注释]

①鬼：古代，人死称鬼，这里指已亡故的祖先。

[白话文]

孔子说："不是自己应该祭拜的祖先而去祭拜他，这是谄媚。看到符合正义的事，不挺身而出，这是无勇。"

[英译文]

The Master said, "For a man to sacrifice to a spirit which does not belong to him is flattery. To see what is right and not to do it is want of courage."

八佾第三

本篇凡二十六章(3-1~3-26)。

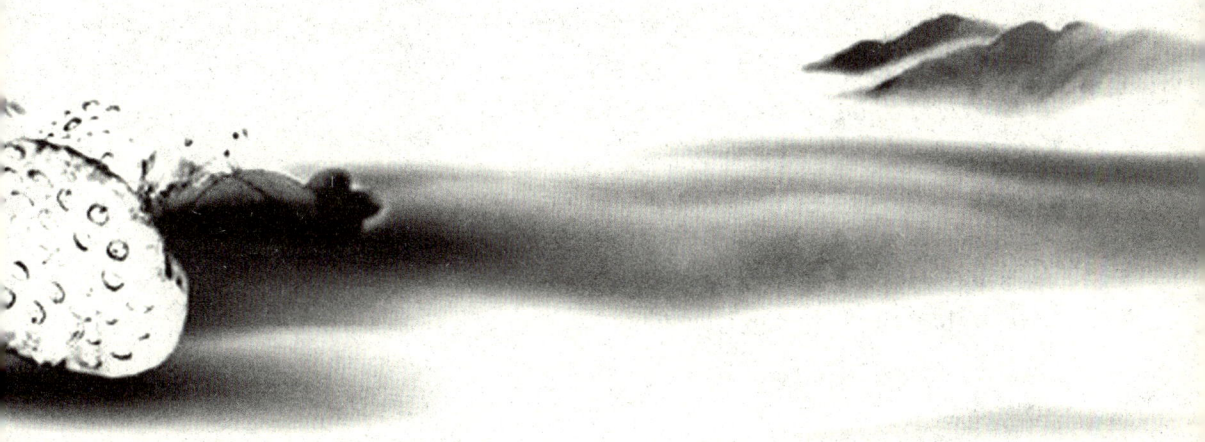

3－1

孔子謂季氏①："八佾②舞於庭，是可忍也，孰不可忍③也？"

[注释]

①季氏：指鲁国大夫季孙氏，是鲁国三桓中权力最大的一家。　②八佾：佾，读 yì，指古代舞蹈的行列。古礼制规定：天子之舞乐，以八人为一排，共八排；诸侯用六排，每排六人；卿大夫用四排，每排四人。八佾，是天子舞乐的行列。　③忍：容忍。

[白话文]

孔子谈到季氏说："他在厅堂中用了八佾的舞乐，这是僭越礼制的行为。如果这件事可以容忍的话，还有什么事不可以容忍呢？"

[英译文]

Confucius said of the head of the Ji family, who had eight rows of pantomimes in his area, "If he can bear to do this, what may he not bear to do?"

3－2

三家①者以《雍》②徹③。子曰："'相維辟公，天子穆穆④'，奚取於三家之堂？"

[注释]

①三家：即鲁大夫孟孙氏（也叫仲孙氏）、叔孙氏、季孙氏，为当时鲁国权臣，又称"三桓"〔参阅季氏篇第三章(16-3)注〕。　②《雍》：《诗经·颂·周颂》中的诗篇，是武王祭文王的乐章。后来沿用于天子祭宗庙。　③彻：同"撤"，这里指撤祭品。　④相维辟公，天子穆穆：这是《雍》诗中的句子。相，助祭的人。维，是、由的意思。辟公，指诸侯。穆穆，仪态貌，庄重、肃静。

[白话文]

鲁国大夫孟孙、叔孙、季孙三家在家祭祀时，也唱着《雍》撤下祭品。孔子说："《雍》诗中'四方的诸侯都来助祭，天子仪态庄重肃穆'的句子是天子祭祀宗庙时所唱的，怎么可以在三家祭祖的庙堂上取用呢？"

[英译文]

The three families used the Yong ode, while the vessels were being removed, at the conclusion of the sacrifice. The Master said, "'Assisting are the princes; the son of Heaven looks profound and grave', what application can these words have in the hall of the three families?"

3－3

子曰："人而不仁，如禮何？ 人而不仁，如樂何①？"

[注释]

①礼、乐是人类文化的表现，也能感化、熏陶人的思想、感情，影响行为，促进生活有序、社会和谐，其根本在于仁。《集注》引程子曰："仁者，天下之正理，失正理，则无序而不和。"礼乐终究只会沦于形式，或产生不良影响。所以孔子说这一段话，意谓失去仁的人，怎么能用礼乐呢？朱子认为本章在"八佾，《雍》彻之后，疑其为僭越礼乐者发也"。

[白话文]

孔子说："作为一个人，都失去了仁，那怎么能用礼？作为一个不仁的人，又怎么能用乐呢？"

[英译文]

The Master said, "If a man be without the virtues proper to humanity, what he to do with the rites of propriety? If a man be without the virtues proper to humanity, what has he to do with music?"

3-4

林放问禮之本①。子曰："大哉問！ 禮，與其奢也，寧儉；喪，與其易②也，寧戚③。"

[注释]

①林放问礼之本：林放，鲁国人，是否孔子弟子，未见记载。他见当时有的礼节过于繁文缛节，怀疑其本意而发问。 ②易：治的意思。 ③与其易也，宁戚：言丧礼节文习熟，而无哀痛惨怛之实也，不若悲戚于心。

[白话文]

林放向孔子请教礼的本意。孔子说："这是个重大的问题（指有普遍意义）。礼仪，若过于奢侈，不如俭朴些比较好；丧事，与其办理得尽善尽美，不如在心里真诚地哀戚悼念。"

[英译文]

Lin-fang asked what was the first thing to be attended to in ceremonies. The Master said, "A great question indeed! In festive ceremonies, it is better to be sparing than extravagant. In the ceremonies of mourning, it is better that there be deep sorrow than a minute attention to observances."

3-5

子曰："夷狄①之有君，不如諸夏②之亡③也④。"

[注释]

①夷狄：我国古代东方和北方的民族。夷，也泛指周边地区民族。 ②诸夏：华夏，中国的

古称。诸夏,即华夏的诸侯各国。　③亡:同"无"。　④夷狄之有君,不如诸夏之亡也:对全句解释有相反之说。一说是边远地区落后民族有君主,还比不上华夏各诸侯国没有君主。而程颐曰:"夷狄且有君长,而诸夏之乱,反不如夷狄之有君臣之分。"按此章前后各章所述,以及在春秋之世发生弑君三十六、亡国五十二之实,故当从程说。

[白话文]

孔子说:"东夷、北狄这些边陲地区少数民族国家,犹有君主,不像华夏诸侯各国,有的形同虚设,名存实亡,礼崩乐坏,僭乱纷争。"

[英译文]

The Master said,"The rude tribes of the east and north have their princes, and are not like the States of our great land which are without them."

3－6

季氏①旅於泰山②,子謂冉有③曰:"女弗能救與④?"對曰:"不能。"子曰:"嗚呼!曾謂泰山不如林放乎⑤?"

[注释]

①季氏:即季孙氏。　②旅于泰山:旅,祭山。当时礼制只有天子才可以祭祀名山大川。季氏是卿大夫,他去祭泰山是越礼行为。　③冉有:孔子的弟子,姓冉名求,字子有,当时为季氏的家臣。　④女弗能救与:女,即汝、你。救,劝止。与,同"欤",作疑问词"吗"解。　⑤曾谓泰山不如林放乎:难道说泰山之神不如问礼的林放〔参阅本篇第四章(3-4)〕知礼,竟接受越礼的祭祀吗?

[白话文]

季孙氏要去祭泰山。孔子对冉有说:"你不能劝止这件事吗?"冉有说:"不能。"孔子叹道:"难道说泰山之神还不如林放懂礼吗?"

[英译文]

The chief of the Ji family was about to sacrifice to the Tai mountain. The Master said to Ran-you,"Can you not save him from this?"He answered,"I cannot."The Master said,"Alas! Will you say that the Tai mountain is not so discerning as Lin-fang?"

3－7

子曰:"君子無所爭。必也射乎!揖讓而升,下而飲,其争也君子!"

[白话文]

孔子说:"君子对人没什么争的。若是有争,也只是在射箭比赛的时候。比赛前,互相作揖礼让,然后升堂比赛。赛毕,又互相作揖下堂,饮酒互相作贺。(这样雍容有礼的竞争)可说是君子之争。"

[英译文]

The Master said, "The student of virtue has no contentions. If it be said he cannot avoid them, shall this be in archery? But he bows complaisantly to his competitors; thus he ascends the hall, descends, and exacts the forfeit of drinking. In his contention, he is still the Jun-zi."

3-8

子夏問曰:"'巧笑倩兮,美目盼兮①,素以爲絢兮②。'何謂也?"子曰:"繪事後素③。"曰:"禮後乎?"子曰:"起予者商也,始可與言《詩》已矣!"

[注释]

①巧笑倩兮,美目盼兮:《诗经·卫风·硕人》中的句子。倩,酒靥之美。兮,助词,相当于"啊",古诗歌中常用。盼,眼睛黑白分明。　②素以为绚兮:《诗经》无此句,朱熹认为是逸诗。素,白色的粉底。绚,读 xuàn,色彩华丽。素以为绚,即在白色粉底上施以色彩。　③绘事后素:朱注:"绘事,绘画之事也。后素,后于素也。"又注:"谓先以粉底为质,而后施五彩,犹人有美质,然后可加文饰。""礼必以忠信为质,犹绘事必以粉素为先。"

[白话文]

子夏问孔子说:"诗句'巧笑倩兮,美目盼兮,素以为绚兮'是什么意思?"孔子说:"先以白色的粉底为质,然后绘画。"子夏又问:"由此看来,人是要以仁德为质,然后用礼来修饰吗?"孔子说:"启发我者是商(子夏)呀!像你这样颖悟的人,现在可以与你谈《诗》了。"

[英译文]

Zi-xia asked, "What is the meaning of the passage—the pretty dimples of her artful smile! The well-defined black and white of her eye! The plain ground for the colours?" The Master said, "The business of laying on the colours follows (the preparation of) the plain ground."

"Ceremonies then are a subsequent thing?" The Master said, "It is Shang who can bring out my meaning. Now I can begin to talk about the Odes with him."

3-9

子曰:"夏禮,吾能言之,杞①不足徵②也;殷禮,吾能言之,宋③不足徵也。文獻④不足故也。足,則吾能徵之矣。"

[注释]

①杞:周武王为天子后,封夏朝的后代为杞国,故城在今河南杞县。　②征:证明。

③宋：故国名，殷朝后代的封国，亦为周武王所封。故城在今河南商丘一带。 ④文献：文，指典册。献，贤者。

[白话文]

孔子说："夏代的礼制，我能说出来，但夏代的后代杞国已经不足以作证了。商代的礼制，我也能说出来，但商的后代宋国也已经不足以作证了。这是因为这两国的历史典籍和贤者缺乏的缘故，如果文献充足，我就能用来作证。"

[英译文]

The Master said, "I could describe the ceremonies of the Xia dynasty, but Qi cannot sufficiently attest my words. I could describe the ceremonies of the Yin dynasty, but Song cannot sufficiently attest my words. (They cannot do so) because of the insufficiency of their records and wise men. If those were sufficient, I could adduce them in support of my words."

3-10

子曰："禘①，自既灌②而往者，吾不欲观③之矣。"

[注释]

①禘：读 dì，古代一种很隆重的祭祀，只有天子才能用这种禘礼。 ②灌：祭祀开始后第一次献酒洒地。 ③不欲观：不想看。孔子不想看鲁国举行禘礼的原因，一说这是鲁国的越礼行为；一说因木主位的排列将禧公排在闵公之上。闵、禧原是庶弟兄，闵公为君，禧公为臣，后来禧公弑君，自立为君。故孔子大不以为然，春秋亦认为是逆祀。

[白话文]

孔子说："鲁举行禘祭，从开始献酒洒地，我就不想看了。"

[英译文]

The Master said, "At the great sacrifice, after the pouring out of the libation, I have no wish to look on."

3-11

或问禘之说。子曰："不知也。知其说者之於天下也①，其如示诸斯乎②！"指其掌。

[注释]

①知其说者之于天下也：知禘之说的人来治理天下。朱熹谓："盖知禘之说，则理无不明，诚无不格，而治天下不难矣。" ②其如示诸斯乎：一说"示"是"置"的假借字，放、摆的意思。解释为"就像把东西摆放在手掌上那么容易"。一说根据《中庸》第十九章有"明乎郊社之礼，禘尝之义，其如示诸掌乎"句，解释为："知禘者治理天下，就像看自己手掌那么容易。"当从此。

[白话文]

有人向孔子请教禘礼之说。孔子说:"我不晓得呀! 如果有人知道,那么他来治理天下,就同看自己的手掌(那么容易)。"一边说,一边指手掌。

[英译文]

Some one asked the meaning of the great sacrifice. The Master said, "I do not know. He who knew its meaning would find it as easy to govern the kingdom as to look on this."—pointing to his palm.

3 - 12

祭如在,祭神如神在①。子曰:"吾不與②祭,如不祭。"

[注释]

①祭如在,祭神如神在:《集注》引程子曰:"祭,祭先祖也。祭神,祭外神也。祭先祖主于孝,祭神主于敬。"自古以来,人们每用祭祀的方式来缅怀先祖和造福人民、功德卓著、死后被奉为神者,好像他们仍在世,以继承其爱和美德。　②与:参与。

[白话文]

任何人祭祀先祖时,好像先祖就在面前;祭神,也如神在。孔子又说:"如我不能亲自参加祭礼,由别人代祭,那就如不祭。"

[英译文]

He sacrificed to the dead, as if they were present. He sacrificed to the spirits, as if the spirits were present. The Master said, "I consider myself not being present at the sacrifice, as if I did not sacrifice."

3 - 13

王孫賈①問曰:"'與其媚於奧,寧媚於竈②',何謂也?"子曰:"不然。獲罪於天,無所禱也。"

[注释]

①王孙贾:卫国大夫,卫灵公的权臣。　②与其媚于奥,宁媚于灶:奥,人家堂屋西南角供奉的"家主神"。灶,指灶神,是地位最低的家神。"与其媚于奥,宁媚于灶。"这两句话可能是当时的俗语,以比喻要祈求什么事,向地位最高的烧香,不如向地位低而有实权的烧香来得有用。王孙贾说此语,乃暗示孔子与其争取卫君,不如巴结下面有权有势的人管用。

[白话文]

王孙贾向孔子说:"俗语'与其媚于奥,宁媚于灶。'这话是什么意思?"孔子说:"这话是不对的。如果得罪了天,那是没有地方可祷告祈求的呀!"

[英译文]

Wang Sun-jia asked, "What is the meaning of the saying—it is better to pay court to the furnace than to the south-west corner?" The Master said, "Not so. He who offends against Heaven has none to whom he can pray."

3-14

子曰："周監①於二代②，鬱鬱乎文③哉！吾從周。"

[注释]

①监：察看、比较的意思。　②二代：指夏、商。　③文：指礼乐典制。

[白话文]

孔子说："周朝的礼制，是根据夏、商两代的礼制，察其得失，较其长短，加以损益修订而成的，因而它的礼乐典制美盛极了。我是遵从周朝的礼制文物的。"

[英译文]

The Master said, "Zhou had the advantage of viewing the two past dynasties. How complete and elegant are its regulations! I follow zhou."

3-15

子入大廟①，每事問。或曰："孰謂鄹人之子②知禮乎？入大廟，每事問。"子聞之曰："是禮也。"

[注释]

①大庙：大，古同"太"，故有的版本写作"太"，现仍从《集注》。大庙，鲁开国君之庙，即鲁初受封的周公旦之庙。　②鄹人之子：鄹，读 zōu，春秋时鲁国的邑名，在今山东曲阜东南。孔子父叔梁纥曾为其邑大夫。鄹人之子，即指孔子。

[白话文]

孔子初次到周公庙助祭，对每件事都要问一问，有人讥孔子说："谁说叔梁纥的儿子知道礼呢？他到大庙，遇见什么事都要问。"孔子听后便说："遇事皆问，敬也。敬就是礼。"

[英译文]

The Master, when he entered the grand temple, asked about everything. Some one said, "Who will say that the son of the man of Zou knows the rules of propriety! He has entered the grand temple and asks about everything." The Master heard the remark, and said, "This is a rule of propriety."

3 - 16

子曰："射不主皮①,爲力不同科②,古之道也。"

[注释]

①射不主皮:射,古代六艺(礼、乐、射、御、书、数)之一。皮,古代射箭比赛用的靶子,用布或皮革做成,中心称"鹄"。射不主皮,乃指习艺或比赛射箭以中靶为主,不要求射穿靶。所谓"以射观德",射中即可。 ②为力不同科:为,因为。科,等。

[白话文]

孔子说:"比赛射箭,不一定要射穿靶子,中靶即可。因为各人的力气大小不等。这是古代射艺之道。"

[英译文]

The Master said, "In archery it is not going through the leather which is the principal thing; because people's strength is not equal. This was the old way."

3 - 17

子貢欲去告朔①之餼羊②。子曰："賜也！爾愛其羊,我愛其禮。"

[注释]

①告朔:农历每月初一谓"朔"。告朔,每年冬季由天子将来年十二月之朔颁发诸侯,以便安排农事等活动。诸侯接受农书,藏于祖庙。每月朔,进行一次"月祭",此谓告朔。但自鲁文公开始,无视于月祭,子贡愤王政之不行。 ②餼羊:餼,读 xì,活的牲口。餼羊,即活羊。

[白话文]

子贡要把鲁国每月告朔之祭要杀一只活羊来供奉的形式取消掉。孔子说:"赐(子贡)啊！你爱惜那只羊,我却爱惜这种礼。"

[英译文]

Zi-gong wished to do away with the offering of a sheep connected with the in-auguration of the first day of each month. The Master said, "Ci! You love the sheep; I love the ceremony."

3 - 18

子曰："事君盡禮,人以爲諂也①。"

[注释]

①事君尽礼,人以为谄也:当时君弱臣强,事君多简傲无理,反而以事君尽礼为谄媚。故《集注》引程子曰:"若他人言之,必曰……小人以为谄。"孔子非因人以为谄而愤慨,乃叹时人不知事君应有之礼。

[白话文]

孔子说:"事奉君上,完全按照为臣的礼节,别人反以为这是对君上的谄媚。"

[英译文]

The Master said, "The Full observance of the rules of propriety in serving one's prince is accounted by people to be flattery."

3 – 19

定公①問:"君使臣,臣事君,如之何?"孔子對曰:"君使臣以禮,臣事君以忠。"

[注释]

①定公:鲁国君,姓姬,名宋,定是谥号。鲁昭公之弟,在位十四年(公元前509年至公元前495年)。

[白话文]

鲁定公问:"君如何使用臣? 臣如何事奉君?"孔子回答说:"君要以礼来对待臣属,臣要以忠来对待君主。"

[英译文]

The duke Ding asked how a prince should employ his ministers, and how ministers should serve their prince. Confucius replied, "A prince should employ his ministers according to the rules of propriety; ministers should serve their prince with faithfulness."

3 – 20

子曰:"《關雎》①,樂而不淫,哀而不傷。"

[注释]

①《关雎》:雎,读 jū。关雎,诗篇名,见《诗经·风·周南》。诗的主题是君子追求淑女,是一首恋歌。

[白话文]

孔子说:"《关雎》这首诗,说到快乐处,不流于放荡;说到悲哀处,也不至于过分伤感。"

[英译文]

The Master said, "The Guan Ju is expressive of enjoyment without being licentious, and of grief without being hurtfully excessive."

3 – 21

哀公①問社②於宰我③。宰我對曰:"夏后氏以松,殷人以柏,周人以栗,曰,使民戰栗④。"子聞之曰:"成事不說,遂事不諫,既往不咎。"

[注释]

①哀公:鲁哀公〔参阅为政篇第十九章(2-19)注〕。　②问社:社,祭后土的地方。古有皇天后土之说,乃指天和地是最公道的万物之主宰。祭后土,即祭土地。有人又把它说成祭土地神。问社,一说是用何种木头来做社主牌位;一说是立社处当种何种树木。哀公问的社树的用意,似当从后。　③宰我:孔子弟子,姓宰,名予,字子我,鲁国人。比孔子小二十九岁,善言语。　④使民战栗:栗,树名,又作"恐惧"解。宰我鉴于鲁君在臣民中无威严,提出"周人以栗",以期君主能有威严,人民见之战战栗栗。但孔子却大不以为然。盖儒家政治是以德化民,不以威力来使民惶恐战栗。

[白话文]

哀公向宰我提出植木建社的问题。宰我答道:"夏后氏建社时种松树,殷人建社种柏树,周人建社时种栗树,意思是要使老百姓敬畏、战栗。"孔子听到便告诉宰我说:"已经做过了的事,就不必再解释了;事虽未完成而势不能已者,也不必再劝谏了;已经过去的事,就不必再追究了。"

[英译文]

The duke Ai asked Zai-wo about the altars of the spirits of the land. Zai-wo replied, "The Xia sovereign planted the pine tree about them; the men of the Yin planted the cypress; and the men of the Zhou planted the chestnut tree, meaning thereby to cause the people to be in awe." When the Master heard it, he said, "Things that are done, it is needless to speak about; things that have had their course, it is needless to remonstrate about; things that are past, it is needless to blame."

3－22

子曰:"管仲①之器小哉。"或曰:"管仲俭乎?"曰:"管氏有三归②,官事不摄,焉得俭?""然则管仲知礼乎?"曰:"邦君树塞门,管氏亦树塞门③。邦君为两君之好,有反坫④,管氏亦有反坫。管氏而知礼,孰不知礼?"

[注释]

①管仲:姓管,名夷吾,齐国人。齐桓公时的上卿,辅助桓公政绩显著,使齐国成为五霸之首〔参阅宪问篇第十七、十八章(14-17、14-18)〕。孔子评管仲器量小、不俭、不知礼,是以"如其仁"(肯定其如仁的功劳)为前提的。　②三归:妇人谓嫁曰归,这里指管仲娶三姓之女。　③树塞门:树,作动词,树立。塞门,用于间隔内外视线的照壁。　④坫:读 diàn,厅堂前部两柱间用土筑成放置酒器、食物用的土台子。两国君相会饮酒后,反爵于其上,故称"反坫"

[白话文]

孔子说:"管仲的器量狭小啊!"有人就问:"是不是他太节俭了?"孔子说:"管仲娶了三姓之女,有三个公馆,各处的家臣都一人各管一事,不兼代。这样怎算得节俭?"又有人问道:"那么,管仲知礼吗?"孔子说:"国君在门外树立了照壁,管仲家也树立照壁;两国君相会设宴,正堂前两柱间筑有覆放酒爵用的坫,管仲家也有那样的坫。他是位大夫,竟与国君一样的设施,如果说管氏知礼,那么谁不知礼呀?"

[英译文]

The Master said, "Small indeed was the capacity of Guan-zhong!" Some one said, "Was Guan-zhong parsimonious?" "Guan, " was the reply, "had the three wives, and his officers performed no double duties; how can he be considered parsimonious?" "Then, did Guan-zhong know the rules of propriety?" The Master said, "The princes of States have a screen intercepting the view at their gates. Guan had likewise a screen at his gate. The princes of States on any friendly meeting between two of them, had a stand on which to place their inverted cups. Guan had also such a stand. If Guan knew the rules of propriety, who does not know them?"

3 – 23

子語魯大師樂①,曰:"樂,其可知也。始作,翕②如也;從③之,純④如也,皦⑤如也,繹⑥如也,以成。"

[注释]

①子语鲁大师乐:语,告诉。大师是乐官。乐,音乐之乐。其时,鲁音乐废缺,故孔子教之(据朱注)。 ②翕:合的意思,指合奏,音律和合。 ③从:读 zòng,放开,指乐声扬开。 ④纯:和谐的意思,指乐调和谐。 ⑤皦:明白的意思,指音节分明。 ⑥绎:相续不断,指所奏全套音乐一气呵成。

[白话文]

孔子告诉鲁国乐官关于音乐的感受,说:"演奏音乐的全过程我知道:乐之初奏,音律相合,扬开乐声,纯一协和,旋律分明,连续不断,然后完成。"

[英译文]

The Master instructing the Grand music-master of Lu said, "How to play music may be known. At the commencement of the piece, all the parts should sound together. As it proceeds, they should be in harmony, while severally distinct and flowing without break, and thus on to the conclusion."

3－24

儀封人^①請見，曰：“君子之至於斯也，吾未嘗不得見也。”從者見之。出曰：“二三子^②何患於喪^③乎？天下之無道也久矣，天將以夫子爲木鐸^④。”

［注释］

①仪封人：仪，卫国的一个邑名。封人，官名，掌握封疆之官。　②二三子：你们几位弟子。③丧：失去。　④木铎：木舌铜铃。古时向民众宣布政令时，摇木铎召集他们来听。

［白话文］

卫国仪邑的封疆官求见孔子，说：“凡是君子到我这个地方来，我没有不相见的。”随从孔子的弟子就引领他去见孔子。等到他告辞出来，他对孔子的弟子们说：“诸位！何必忧虑夫子丢了官职呢？天下无道的时日已经很久了，天将请夫子作警世的木铎，垂教世人。”

［英译文］

The border-warden at Yi requested to be introduced to the Master, saying, "When men of superior virtue have come to this, I have never been denied the privilege of seeing them." The followers of the sage introduced him, and when he came out from the interview, he said, "My friends, why are you distressed by your master's loss of office? The kingdom had long been without the principles of truth and right. Heaven is going, to use your master as a bell with its wooden tongue."

3－25

子謂《韶》^①，“盡美矣，又盡善也。”謂《武》^②，“盡美矣，未盡善也。”

［注释］

①《韶》：虞舜时的乐章。　②《武》：周武王时的乐章。古时帝王功成治定后常创作一种乐章以歌舞太平。孔子评价其美和善，以音调、舞蹈的完美谓“尽美”；以乐章所含的道德意义完善谓“尽善”。

［白话文］

孔子评论《韶》乐说：“音调、舞蹈表演美极了。乐曲的内容也很好。”评论《武》乐说：“音乐、舞蹈很美，但乐曲的内容尚欠尽美。”

［英译文］

The Master said of the Shao that it was perfectly beautiful and also perfectly good. He said of the Wu that it was perfectly beautiful but not perfectly good.

3 – 26

子曰：“居上不寬，爲禮不敬，臨喪不哀，吾何以觀之哉？”

[白话文]

孔子说：“居上位的人如果不宽宏大度，行礼时不恭敬，到有丧事的人家也不悲哀，我如何能看得下去？”

[英译文]

The Master said, "High station filled without indulgent generosity; ceremonies performed without reverence; mourning conducted without sorrow; wherewith should I contemplate such ways?"

里仁第四

本篇凡二十六章(4−1~4−26)。

4-1

子曰:"里仁爲美①。擇不處仁,焉得知?"

[注释]

①里仁为美:里,邻里。仁,仁厚。里仁为美,意谓:所居住处,邻里有仁厚的风尚为美好。

[白话文]

孔子说:"居住在有仁厚风尚的地方是美好的。选择住处,却不选择在讲仁德、风尚淳厚的地方,那怎么能说是智慧的呢?"

[英译文]

The Master said, "It is virtuous manners which constitute the excellence of a neighbourhood. If a man in selecting a residence, do not fix on one where such prevail, how can he be wise?"

4-2

子曰:"不仁者,不可以久處約①,不可以長處樂。仁者安仁。知者利仁②。"

[注释]

①约:俭约。因贫困而生活俭约。　②利仁:知道实行仁对人对己都有助(专门利人),所以行仁。

[白话文]

(本章承上章,说明为什么要利仁。)孔子说:"不仁的人,不能与其长久共处于俭约的生活环境之中,否则必然会生出为非的事端;也不能长久共处于安乐的环境之中,因其易为富贵所移。仁德的人,能安于贫而过俭约的生活。智者更知道仁者利人的道理而推行仁。"

[英译文]

The Master said, "Those who are without virtue cannot abide long either in a condition of poverty and hardship, or in a condition of enjoyment, The virtuous rest in virtue; the wise desire virtue."

4-3

子曰:"惟仁者,能好人,能惡①人。"

[注释]

①恶:厌恶、憎恶。仁者,心存公正,能好人之好,恶人之恶。不仁者,往往出于私心而好恶不分。

[白话文]

孔子说:"只有仁德的人,才能公正地喜爱某个人之善,憎恶某个人之不善。"

[英译文]

The Master said, "It is only the (truly) virtuous man, who can love or hate others."

4-4

子曰:"苟志①於仁矣,無惡也。"

[注释]

①苟志:苟,读 gǒu,如果。志,立志。

[白话文]

孔子说:"一个人如果立志于实行仁德,他就不会做坏事。"

[英译文]

The Master said, "If the will be set on virtue, there will be no practice of wickedness."

4-5

子曰:"富與貴,是人之所欲也,不以其道得之,不處①也;貧與賤,是人之所惡也,不以其道得之,不去也。君子去仁,惡乎成名?君子無終食之間違②仁,造次③必於是,顛沛④必於是。"

[注释]

①处:相处。 ②违:违背,离开。 ③造次:仓促,急促,苟且之时。 ④颠沛:穷困潦倒。

[白话文]

孔子说:"富与贵,是人人想要的。但若不用合乎正道的方法得到它,君子是不会安处于这样的富贵中的;贫与贱,是人人厌恶的,但若不依正道的方法以去之,君子宁愿不脱离贫贱。君子如果背离了仁道,又怎能称得上君子呢?君子就是吃一顿饭的时间,也不会离开仁道;就是在仓促匆忙之际,也必不会离开仁道;就是颠沛穷困的时候,也必定和仁道在一起。"

[英译文]

The Master said, "Riches and honours are what men desire. If it cannot be obtained in the proper way, they should not be held. Poverty and meanness are what men dislike. If it cannot be obtained in the proper way, they should not be avoided. If a superior man abandon virtue, how can he fulfil the requirements of that name? The superior man does not, even for the space of a single meal, act contrary to virtue. In moments of haste, he cleaves to it in seasons of danger, he cleaves to it."

4－6

子曰:"我未見好仁者、惡不仁者①。好仁者,無以尚②之;惡不仁者,其爲仁矣,不使不仁者加乎其身。有能一日用其力於仁矣乎? 我未見力不足者。蓋③有之矣,我未之見也。"

[注释]

①好仁者、惡不仁者:有的版本在"好仁者,惡不仁者"中间用的是逗点,似若两种人;也有的版本中间用顿号,或者都不用,并解释为好仁者不容有不仁之意同时存在,也就是孔子所说未见之者。似当从后者为宜。　②尚:超过。　③盖:大概。

[白话文]

孔子说:"我没有见到真正爱好仁德而憎恶不仁德的人。真正爱好仁德者会觉得世上没有比仁德更重要的了;真正憎恶不仁者就不会使不仁的东西(包括意念或行事)沾加在自己身上,在实践仁德时,至少不会心存不仁的念头。有谁能整天努力于实行仁德而感到力量不够的? 只是不肯用力于仁罢了。大概真有行仁而感力量不够的,但是我还没有见到过。"

[英译文]

The Master said, "I have not seen a person who loves virtue, or one who hated what was not virtuous. He who loved virtue, would esteem nothing above it. He who hated what is not virtuous, would practice virtue in such a way that he would not allow anything that is not virtuous to approach his person. Is any one able for one day to apply his strength to virtue? I have not seen the case in which his strength would be insufficient. Should there possibly be any such case, I have not seen it."

4－7

子曰:"人之過也,各於其黨①。觀過,斯知仁矣②。"

[注释]

①党:类别。　②观过,斯知仁矣:无论君子或小人,总会有过错的,友君子则其过也君子,友小人则其过也小人,所以有人说:"观其交游,则贤不肖可察。"说明人犯过失,每与他属于什么群类有关;看他的过失,可知他好仁或不好仁。

[白话文]

孔子说:"人们所犯的过错,跟他属于哪一群类的人有关。什么类别的人,犯的过错就是什么类别的。看一个人所犯的过错,就可以知道他有没有仁德。"

[英译文]

The Master said, "The faults of men are characteristic of the class to which they belong. By observing a man's faults, it may be known that he is virtuous."

4-8

子曰:"朝闻道,夕死可矣①。"

[注释]

①朝闻道,夕死可矣:《集注》曰:"道者,事物当然之理。苟得闻之,则生顺死安,无复遗恨矣。"《礼祀·檀弓上》又记述了曾子临死前获知所卧席垫是大夫档所用者,自己不是大夫,知非礼,即起而易之,易毕绝气的事例,说明其闻道理,行之而安心。

[白话文]

孔子说:"若是早上听到(获知)道理,就是当晚死了也无所遗憾。"

[英译文]

The Master said, "If a man in the morning hear the right way, he may die in the evening without regret."

4-9

子曰:"士志於道,而耻恶衣恶食者,未足與議也。"

[白话文]

孔子说:"一个读书人,若立志于学求事物之真理,却还耻于自己穿得不好,吃得不好。这样的人,就不值得和他讨论学问了。"

[英译文]

The Master said, "A scholar, whose mind is set on truth, and who is ashamed of bad clothes and bad food, is not fit to be discoursed with."

4-10

子曰:"君子之於天下也,無適也,無莫也①,義之與比。"

[注释]

①无适也,无莫也:不固执于一定可以、一定不可的成见。

[白话文]

孔子说:"君子对于天下事,不是认为一定要怎样做,或一定不可怎样做,而是怎样合于道义就怎样做。"

[英译文]

The Master said, "The superior man, in the world, does not set his mind either for anything, or against anything; what is right he will follow."

4-11

子曰:"君子懷德,小人懷土;君子懷刑,小人懷惠①。"

[注释]

①君子怀德,小人怀土;君子怀刑,小人怀惠:怀,心里所想的。德,道德。土,田宅。刑,法纪、刑罚。惠,财物赐惠。

[白话文]

孔子说:"君子讲求道德,小人关注田宅;君子重视守法,小人在意财物。"

[英译文]

The Master said, "The superior man thinks of virtue; the mean man thinks of comfort. The superior man thinks of the sanctions of law; the mean man thinks of favours which he may receive."

4-12

子曰:"放於利①而行,多怨。"

[注释]

①放于利:放,依也。放于利,依照利。

[白话文]

孔子说:"每事依照利益而行动,必招来很多怨恨。"

[英译文]

The Master said, "He who acts with a constant view to his own advantage will be much murmured against."

4-13

子曰:"能以禮讓爲國①乎,何有? 不能以禮讓爲國,如禮何②?"

[注释]

①为国:治国。 ②如礼何:如此之礼(礼之实已亡,只是形式而已),又有何用?

[白话文]

孔子说:"能够以礼让来治理国家,治国还有什么困难呢? 不能以礼让来治国,则礼之实已亡,徒具形式,礼又有什么用呢?"

［英译文］

The Master said, "If a prince is able to govern his kingdom with the complaisance proper to the rules of propriety, what difficulty will he have? If he cannot govern it with that complaisance, what has he to do with the rules of propriety?"

4-14

子曰："不患無位,患所以立。不患莫已知,求爲可知也。"

［白话文］

孔子说："不担心没有职位,只担心自己有何才德去立足于该职位;不愁别人不知道我,而要责求自己有哪些才德可以值得被人家知道。"

［英译文］

The Master said, "A man should say, I am not concerned that. I have no place, I am concerned how I may fit myself for one. I am not concerned that I am not known, I seek to be worthy to be known."

4-15

子曰："参乎! 吾道一以貫之①。"曾子曰:"唯。"子出,門人問曰:"何謂也?"曾子曰:"夫子之道,忠恕②而已矣!"

［注释］

①一以贯之:贯,同"也"。这里指孔子的学说,可用一个根本的道理贯通起来。　②忠恕:朱子云:"尽己之谓忠,推己之谓恕。"

［白话文］

孔子对曾子说:"参(曾参)呀! 我的学说可用一个根本的道理将它贯通起来!"曾子说:"是的。"孔子离去,其他同学问曾子:"那是什么意思?"曾子说:"老师的学说,就是忠恕二字而已。"

［英译文］

The Master said, "Can! My doctrine is that of an all-pervading unity." The disciple Zeng replied, "Yes." The Master went out, and the other disciples asked, "What do his words mean?" Zeng said, "The doctrine of our master is to be true to the principles of our nature and the benevolent exercise of them to others—this and nothing more."

4-16

子曰："君子喻①於義,小人喻於利。"

[注释]

①喻：知道，知晓。

[白话文]

孔子说："君子知道义，小人只晓得利。"

[英译文]

The Master said, "The mind of the superior man is conversant with righteousness; the mind of the mean man is conversant with gain."

4－17

子曰："見賢思齊①焉，見不賢而內自省也。"

[注释]

①思齐：希望和贤者一样。

[白话文]

孔子说："看到贤德的人，想和他看齐，做贤者所做的好事；看到不贤德的人，当自我反省，有没有像他那样不好的言行。"

[英译文]

The Master said, "When we see men of worth, we should think of equaling them; when we see men of a contrary character, we should turn inwards and examine ourselves."

4－18

子曰："事父母幾①諫，見志不從，又敬不違②，勞③而不怨。"

[注释]

①几：即微，轻微、婉转。　②不违：不放弃（目的）。　③劳：忧心。

[白话文]

孔子说："侍奉父母，如果父母有过错，要委婉劝告。他们如果不接受，做子女的仍应态度恭敬，不放弃劝告，虽然心里担忧，也不抱怨。"

[英译文]

The Master said, "In serving his parents, a son may remonstrate with them, but gently; when he sees that they do not incline to follow his advice, he shows an increased degree of reverence, but does not abandon his purpose; and should they punish him, he does not allow himself to murmur."

4 – 19

子曰："父母在,不遠遊,遊必有方。"

[白话文]

孔子说："父母在世时,做子女的不要出远门。如果不得已要出远门,也必定要将去向告知父母,以免父母担心。"

[英译文]

The Master said, "While his parents are alive, the son may not go abroad to a distance. If he does go abroad, he must have a fixed place to which be goes."

4 – 20

子曰："三年無改於父之道,可謂孝矣。"

[注释]

此章重出,参阅学而篇第十一章(1-11)。

4 – 21

子曰："父母之年,不可不知也。一則以喜,一則以懼。"

[白话文]

孔子说："父母的年纪,不可以不记在心里。一方面为父母高寿而感到欣喜,一方面又担忧父母逐年衰老。"

[英译文]

The Master said, "The years of parents may by no means not be kept in the memory, as an occasion at once for joy and for fear."

4 – 22

子曰："古者言之不出,恥躬之不逮①也。"

[注释]

①恥躬之不逮:躬,躬行,亲身去实行。逮,读 dài,到、及。恥躬之不逮,指亲身去实行而做不到,由此而感到可耻。

[白话文]

孔子说："古人不肯轻易出言,怕说的话自己去做而做不到,由此而感到可耻。"

[英译文]

The Master said, "The reason why the ancients did not readily give utterance to their words, was that they feared lest their actions should not come up to them."

4 - 23

子曰:"以約失之者,鮮矣。"

[白话文]

孔子说:"因严于律己而还有过失的人,那是很少的了。"

[英译文]

The Master said, "The cautious seldom err."

4 - 24

子曰:"君子欲訥於言而敏於行。"

[白话文]

孔子说:"君子要慎重说话,敏捷做事。"

[英译文]

The Master said, "The superior man wishes to be slow in his speech and earnest in his conduct."

4 - 25

子曰:"德不孤,必有鄰。"

[白话文]

孔子说:"有道德的人不会孤单,必有志向相同的人亲近他。"

[英译文]

The Master said, "Virtue is not left to stand alone. He who practices it will have neighbours."

4 - 26

子游曰:"事君數①,斯辱矣;朋友數,斯疏矣。"

[注释]

①数:次数频繁。这里是指侍君交友的来往、劝谏过密过繁或过于亲近。

[白话文]

子游说:"侍奉君主或进谏过于频繁,会招致侮辱;对朋友来往过狎过繁,规劝太过啰嗦,反而会招致疏远。"

[英译文]

Zi-you said, "In serving a prince, frequent remonstrances lead to disgrace; between friends frequent reproofs make the friendship distant."

公冶长第五

本篇凡二十七章(5—1～5—27)。

5-1

子謂公冶長①："可妻也。雖在縲絏之中②，非其罪也。"以其子③妻之。子謂南容④："邦有道，不廢。邦無道，免於刑戮。"以其兄之子妻之。

[注释]

①公冶长：孔子弟子，复姓公冶，字子长。他蹲过监狱，孔子认为他是无辜的，于是将女儿嫁给他。 ②縲絏之中：縲，读 léi，捆绑犯人的绳索。絏，读 xiè，捆的意思。縲絏之中，即被拘狱中。 ③子：指女儿。 ④南容：孔子弟子，也是孔子侄婿。氏南宫，名适（读 kuò，不是"適"的简化字），字子容。

[白话文]

孔子谈到公冶长说："可以把女儿嫁给他。虽然他曾经坐过牢，但是被冤枉的，并不是他的罪。"于是就把自己的女儿嫁给了他。孔子说到南容："国家政治清明，他的才能不会被埋没，一定会被重用。国家政治混乱黑暗，也不至陷于刑戮。"所以把侄女嫁给了他（其时，孔子兄孟皮已卒）。

[英译文]

The Master said of Gong Ye-zhang that he might be wived; although he was put in bonds, he had not been guilty of any crime. Accordingly, he gave him his own daughter to wife.

Of Nan-rong he said that if the country were well governed, he would not be out of office, and if it were in-governed, he would escape punishment and disgrace. He gave him the daughter of his own elder brother to wife.

5-2

子謂子賤①："君子哉若人！ 魯無君子者，斯焉取斯②？"

[注释]

①子贱：孔子弟子，姓宓，名不齐，子贱（读 jiǎn）是他的号，鲁国人，比孔子小三十岁。 ②斯焉取斯：前一个"斯"字指此人；后一个"斯"指这样（如此）的品德。

[白话文]

孔子谈到子贱："像这样的人，真是一个君子啊！如果不是鲁国有许多君子，他从哪里能学到如此的品德呢？"

[英译文]

The Master said of Zi-jian, "Of superior virtue indeed is such a man! If there were not virtuous men in Lu, how could this man have acquired this character?"

5－3

子貢問曰:"賜①也何如?"子曰:"女②器③也。"曰:"何器也?"曰:"瑚璉④也。"

[注释]

①赐:即端木赐,字子贡,是一个善于外交和贸易的人才。其在《论语》中出现次数仅次于子路。 ②女:同"汝",你的意思。 ③器:器具、器材。 ④瑚琏:宗庙中盛黍稷的贵重祭具。

[白话文]

子贡问道:"我如何呢?"孔子说:"你是一个能成为有用器材的人。"子贡问:"什么器材呢?"孔子说:"像那宗庙里的贵重祭具瑚琏。"

[英译文]

Zi-gong asked, "What do you say of me?" The Master said, "You are a utensil." "What utensil?" "A gemmed sacrificial utensil."

5－4

或曰:"雍①也,仁而不佞②。"子曰:"焉用佞?禦人以口給③,屢憎於人。不知其仁,焉用佞?"

[注释]

①雍:孔子的弟子,姓冉(读 rǎn),名雍,字仲弓。鲁国人,比孔子小二十九岁,为人忠厚。②佞:口才。 ③御人以口给:御,抵挡,这里指口头答应。口给,指言辞敏捷。

[白话文]

有人说:"雍,虽仁德,但口才不好。"孔子说:"何必要口才好?用犀利的口才来对付人,反而遭人讨厌。我不知道冉雍算不算仁人,但为什么要有口才呢?"

[英译文]

Some one said, "Yong is truly virtuous, but he is not ready with his tongue." The Master said, "What is the good of being ready with the tongue? They who encounter men with smartness of speech for the most part procure themselves hatred. I know not whether he be truly virtuous, but why should he show readiness of the tongue?"

5－5

子使漆雕開①仕。對曰:"吾斯之未能信。"子説。

[注释]

①漆雕开:漆雕是复姓,名开,孔子弟子,鲁国人,比孔子小十一岁。

[白话文]

孔子想叫漆雕开去做官。漆雕开回答说:"我对做官这种事还没有信心。"孔子听了很喜悦(赞许他谦虚不矜)。

[英译文]

The Master was wishing Qi Diao-kai to enter on official employment. He replied, "I am not yet able to rest in the assurance of this." The Master was pleased.

5-6

子曰:"道不行,乘桴①浮於海。從我者,其由與?"子路聞之喜。子曰:"由也,好勇過我,無所取材②。"

[注释]

①桴:读fú,竹筏。 ②无所取材:朱子曰:"材,与裁通,古字借用。"无所取材,指不能裁度事理。

[白话文]

孔子说:"我的道不能行于世,我想乘竹筏去海外。随我去的,大概只有仲由(子路)吧!"子路听到后好高兴。孔子说:"仲由啊!你真比我还勇敢,可惜不能够裁度事理。"

[英译文]

The Master said, "My doctrines make no way. I will get upon a raft, and float about on the sea. He that will accompany me will be You, I dare to say." Zi-lu hearing this was glad. Upon which the Master said, "You is fonder of daring than I am. He does not exercise his judgment upon matters."

5-7

孟武伯①問:"子路仁乎?"子曰:"不知也。"又問。子曰:"由也,千乘之國,可使治其賦②也;不知其仁也。""求也何如?"子曰:"求也,千室之邑③,百乘之家④,可使爲之宰⑤也;不知其仁⑥也。""赤也何如?"子曰:"赤也,束帶立於朝,可使與賓客言也;不知其仁也。"

[注释]

①孟武伯:参阅为政篇第六章(2-6)注。 ②赋:兵赋。治其赋,指治其军。 ③千室之邑:有一千户的县邑。 ④百乘之家:一车四马叫乘,诸侯千乘,卿大夫百乘。 ⑤宰:卿大夫的家臣,也叫家宰。 ⑥不知其仁:仁是道德学问的最高理想。本章多次提到"不知其仁",说明孔子

不轻易称许人为仁者。

[白话文]

　　孟武伯问孔子说："子路是仁者吗？"孔子说："不知道。"孟武伯接着又问。孔子说："仲由啊，如果拥有千辆兵车的国家，可以派他去治理军队，但我不知他是不是仁者。""那么，冉求如何呢？"孔子说："冉求啊，千户人口的大县，有百辆兵车的大夫家，可以让他去当家宰。但我不知他是不是仁者。""那么，公西赤（子华）如何呢？"孔子说："赤啊！穿着礼服束着带，立于朝廷，可以去和外宾会谈，但我不知道他是不是仁者。"

[英译文]

　　Meng Wu-bo asked about Zi-lu, whether he was perfectly virtuous. The Master said, "I do not know."

　　He asked again, when the Master replied, "In a kingdom of a thousand chariots. You might be employed to manage the military levies, but I do not know whether he be perfectly virtuous."

　　"And what do you say of Qiu?" The Master replied, "In a city of a thousand families, or a clan of a hundred chariots, Qiu might be employed as governor, but I do not know whether he is perfectly virtuous."

　　"What do you say of Chi?" The Master replied, "With his sash girt and standing in a court, Chi might be employed to converse with the visitors and guests, but I do not know whether he is perfectly virtuous."

5-8

　　子謂子貢曰："女與回也孰愈[①]？"對曰："賜也何敢望回。回也聞一以知十，賜也聞一以知二。"子曰："弗如也。吾與女弗如也。"

[注释]

　　①愈：同"胜"。

[白话文]

　　孔子对子贡说："你和颜回两人，谁比较优胜？"子贡回答说："我哪里敢望颜回呢？他啊！听到一分道理，就能够推知十分。我听到一分，只能推知二分。"孔子说："你的确不如他。我和你都不如他。"

[英译文]

　　The Master said to Zi-gong, "Which do you consider superior, yourself of Hui?" Zi-gong replied, "How dare I compare myself with Hui? Hui heard one point and knows all about a subject; I hear one point and know a second." The Master said, "You are not equal to him. I grant you, you are not equal to him."

5-9

宰予①畫寝。子曰:"朽木不可雕也,糞土之牆不可杇②也! 於予與何誅③?"子曰:"始吾於人也,聽其言而信其行;今吾於人也,聽其言而觀其行。於予與改是。"

[注释]

①宰予:即宰我。参阅八佾篇第二十一章(3-21)注。 ②杇:即圬,读 wū,涂墙的泥镘(抹子)。在这里作动词,指涂抹墙面。 ③诛:责备。

[白话文]

宰予在大白天睡觉。孔子说:"腐朽的木头没办法拿来雕刻,垃圾粪土垒的墙,不能够涂抹粉面。宰予这种人,还有什么可以苛责的?"孔子又说:"过去我对人的看法是:听他说的就相信他做得到。现在我对人的看法是:听他所言,还要看他的所行。从宰予身上,我改变了看待人的方法。"

[英译文]

Zai-yu being asleep during the daytime. The Master said, "Rotten wood cannot be carved; a wall of dirty earth will not receive the trowel. This Yu! What is the use of my reproving him?" The Master said, "At first, my way with men was to hear their words, and give them credit for their conduct. Now my way is to hear their words, and look at their conduct. It is from Yu that I have learned to make this change."

5-10

子曰:"吾未見剛者。"或對曰:"申棖①。"子曰:"棖也慾,焉得剛?"

[注释]

①申棖:即申党(也有写为申棠、申堂者。棠、堂、棖均为"党"的借字),字子周,鲁人,孔子弟子。

[白话文]

孔子说:"我没有见过刚毅的人。"有人说:"申棖可不就是吗?"孔子说:"申棖啊! 他欲望过多,怎么谈得上刚毅呢?"

[英译文]

The Master said, "I have not seen a firm and unbending man." Some one replied, "There is Shen cheng." "Cheng." said the Master, "Is under the influence of his passions; how can he be pronounced firm and unbending?"

5－11

子貢曰："我不欲人之加諸我也，吾亦欲無加諸人。"子曰："賜也，非爾所及也。"

[白话文]

子贡说："我不想要人家加到我身上的那些事，我也不想有同样的情形加到别人身上。"孔子听了便说："子贡啊，这不是你所能做得到的。"

[英译文]

Zi-gong said, "What I do not wish men to do to me, I also wish not to do to men." The Master said, "Ci! You have not attained to that."

5－12

子貢曰："夫子之文章①可得而聞也；夫子之言性與天道②，不可得而聞也。"

[注释]

①夫子之文章：指诗、书、礼、乐。　②性与天道：性，人的本性。天道，指自然与人类社会凶吉祸福的关系。

[白话文]

子贡说："夫子的诗、书、礼、乐，是可以听得到的；夫子讲人性和天道，就不容易听到了。"

[英译文]

Zi-gong said, "The master's personal displays of his principles and ordinary descriptions of them may be heard. His discourses about man's nature, and the way of Heaven, cannot be heard."

5－13

子路有聞，未之能行，唯恐有聞①。

[注释]

①有闻：一说"复有"所闻（另一道理）。

[白话文]

子路听到某个道理，还没有去做到，就恐听到另一个道理。

[英译文]

When Zi-lu heard anything, if he had not yet succeeded in carrying it into practice, he was only afraid lest he should hear something else.

5 – 14

子貢問曰:"孔文子①何以謂之'文'也?"子曰:"敏而好學,不恥下問,是以謂之'文'也。"

[注释]

①孔文子:即卫国卿大夫仲叔圉,文是谥号。

[白话文]

子贡问孔子说:"孔文子这个人,为什么称他为'文'呢?"孔子说:"他聪颖而好学,谦虚而不耻下问,所以称他为'文'。"

[英译文]

Zi-gong asked, "On what ground did Kong Wen-zi get that title of 'Wen'?" The Master said, "He was of an active nature and yet fond of learning, and he was not ashamed to ask and learn of his inferiors! On these grounds he has been styled 'Wen'."

5 – 15

子謂子産①:"有君子之道四焉:其行已也恭,其事上也敬,其養民也惠,其使民也義。"

[注释]

①子产:姓公孙,名侨,字子产,又字子美,是郑国有名的执政大臣,《春秋左氏传·襄公二十九年至襄公三十一年》等多有他的政绩和治国思想记载。孔子也说:"……人谓子产不仁,我不信也。"

[白话文]

孔子说:"子产有四种行为合乎君子之道:他的行事很谦恭;对在上位的人,办事认真负责;教养百姓,广施恩惠;使用民力,合理得宜。"

[英译文]

The Master said, "Of Zi-chan that he had four of the characteristics of a superior man: in his conduct of himself, he was humble; in serving his superiors, he was respectful; in nourishing the people, he was kind; in ordering the people, he was just."

5－16

子曰:"晏平仲①善與人交,久而敬之。"

[注释]

①晏平仲:即晏子,名婴,平仲是字,为晏桓子之子,齐国最著名的执政大臣。《晏子春秋》收集编辑了他的言行。

[白话文]

孔子说:"晏平仲善于和人交往,相处久了,人们越加尊敬他。"

[英译文]

The Master said, "Yan Ping-zhong knew well how to maintain friendly intercourse. The acquaintance might be long, but he showed the same respect as at first."

5－17

子曰:"臧文仲①居蔡②,山節藻梲③,何如其知也?"

[注释]

①臧文仲:鲁国大夫臧孙辰,仲是字,文是谥号。历仕鲁庄公、闵公、僖公、文公四国君。曾为推动商业往来,废除关卡。 ②居蔡:蔡,大乌龟。居蔡,使大乌龟住在室内。 ③山节藻梲:节,柱上的斗拱,梲,梁的短柱,斗拱雕刻着山,梲画着水藻。

[白话文]

孔子说:"臧文仲把问卜用的大乌龟养在房子内,房子柱的斗拱雕刻着山,梁的短柱上画着藻草,这种人能算得上聪明吗?"

[英译文]

The Master said, "Zang Wen-zhong kept a large tortoise in a house, on the capitals of the pillars of which he had hills made, and with representations of duckweed on the small pillars above the beams supporting the rafters. Of what sort was his wisdom?"

5－18

子張問曰:"令尹子文①,三仕爲令尹,無喜色;三已之,無慍色。舊令尹之政,必以告新令尹。何如?"子曰:"忠矣。"曰:"仁矣乎?"曰:"未知,焉得仁?""崔子弑齊君②,陳文子③有馬十乘,棄而違之,至於他邦,則曰:'猶吾大夫崔子也。'違之。之一邦,則又曰:'猶吾大夫崔子也。'違之。何如?"子曰:"清矣。"曰:"仁矣乎?"曰:"未知,焉得仁?"

［注释］

①令尹子文:令尹,楚国的官名,相当于宰相之职。令尹子文,姓斗,名穀於菟,子文是他的字。　②崔子弑齐君:崔子,即齐国大夫崔杼。齐君,即齐庄公。襄公二十五年夏,崔杼在家中由甲士们弑了齐庄公。参阅《春秋左氏传·襄公二十五年》。　③陈文子:齐大夫,名须无。见崔杼弑君,齐国乱,避往别国。

［白话文］

　　子张(颛孙师)问孔子说:"楚国的令尹子文,三次出任令尹,没有一点得意高兴的样子;三次被免职,也没有懊恼的脸色;移交工作时,总是将自己在职时的一切施政情况,详细告诉接任的令尹。像这样的人,你以为如何?"孔子说:"可以算得是尽心尽力于自己的职责,够忠诚的。"子张说:"可以算是仁者吗?"孔子说:"我不知道。这怎么可算仁者呢?"子张又问:"齐国崔杼弑国君庄公,齐国的大夫陈子文有四十匹马也不要了,离开齐国。到了别国一看,说:'这里的执政者还不是跟崔杼一样。'于是又离去。到了另一个国家,又说:'这里的也和崔杼一样。'于是又离开。像他这样的人,你以为如何?"孔子说:"洁身去乱,可谓清白。"子张说:"可算为仁者吗?"孔子说:"那我就不知道了,这怎么算得上是仁者呢?"

［英译文］

　　Zi-zhang asked, "The minister Zi-wen thrice took office, and manifested no joy in his countenance. Thrice he retired from office, and manifested no displeasure. He made it a point to inform the new minister of the way in which he had conducted the government; what do you say of him?" The Master replied, "He was loyal." "Was he perfectly virtuous?" "I do not know. How can he be pronounced perfectly virtuous?" Zi-zhang proceeded, "When the officer Cui-zhu killed the prince of Qi, Chen Zi-wen, though he was the owner of forty horses, abandoned them and left the country. Coming to another state, he said, 'They are here like our great officer, Cui,' and left it. He came to a second state, and with the same observation left it also; what do you say of him?" The Master replied, "He was pure." "Was he perfectly virtuous?" "I do not know. How can he be pronounced perfectly virtuous?"

5-19

　　季文子①三思而後行。子聞之曰:"再,斯可矣。"

［注释］

①季文子:鲁国三桓之一,季孙氏的第一代。名意如,字行父,文是谥号。

[白话文]

季文子做事，都经再三的思考后才行动。孔子听到后就说："考虑两次就够了。"

[英译文]

Ji Wen-zi thought thrice, and then acted. When the Master was informed of it, he said, "Twice may do."

5 - 20

子曰："甯武子①，邦有道则知，邦无道则愚。其知可及也，其愚不可及也。"

[注释]

①甯武子：卫国世卿，姓甯名俞（读 shù），武是谥号。他出世比孔子早约一百年。

[白话文]

孔子说："甯武子，在国家政治清明，社会安定的时候，显得很有聪明才智；国家政治混乱的时候，他就变得愚拙。他的那种聪明才智，别人还赶得上，他那种装愚作呆的劲儿，别人就望尘莫及了。"

[英译文]

The Master said, "When good order prevailed in his country, Ning Wu-zi acted the pert of a wise man. When his country was in disorder, he acted the part of a stupid man. Others may equal his wisdom, but they cannot equal his stupidity."

5 - 21

子在陈①曰："归与！归与！吾党②之小子狂简③，斐然成章④，不知所以裁之。"

[注释]

①陈：陈国。在今河南开封以东，安徽亳县以北。司马迁记载孔子在公元前 491 年至公元前 489 年仕陈潜公时讲的此话。　②党：乡党。　③狂简：志趣大而疏略实事。　④斐然成章：朱子曰："斐，文貌。成章，言其文理成就，有可观者。"

[白话文]

孔子在陈国说："回去吧！回去吧！我家乡的那些学生，志趣远大，文理成就也可观，我不知道怎样去裁正他们。"

[英译文]

When the Master was in Chen, he said, "Let me return! Let me return! The little children of my school are ambitious and too hasty. They are accomplished and complete so far, but they do not know how to restrict and shape themselves."

5－22

子曰："伯夷、叔齐①，不念旧恶，怨是用希②。"

[注释]

①伯夷、叔齐：殷末年竹君国因让位出走的俩兄弟，当时不满纣王无道而奔投周文王，后又不满周的革命，不食周粟，最后饿死在首阳山。《论语》中几次提到他们，并为孔子所推崇者。〔参阅述而篇第十四章(7-14)、微子篇第八章(18-8)〕　②怨是用希：指别人对他们没什么怨恨。

[白话文]

孔子说："伯夷、叔齐不记过去别人对他们的不好，所以别人对他们也没什么怨恨。"

[英译文]

The Master said, "Bo-yi and Shu-qi did not keep the former wickednesses of men in mind, and hence the resentments directed towards them were few."

5－23

子曰："孰谓微生高①直？或乞醯②焉，乞诸其邻而与之。"

[注释]

①微生高：微生是姓，高是名，鲁国人。素有直名，但孔子却不以为然。　②醯：读 xī，同"醋"。

[白话文]

孔子说："谁说微生高正直？有人向他要些醋，却不说自己没有，而是向邻居要来再给他。"

[英译文]

The Master said, "Who says of Wei Sheng-gao that he is upright? One begged some vinegar of him, and he begged it of a neighbor and gave it to the man."

5－24

子曰："巧言、令色、足恭①，左丘明②耻之，丘亦耻之。匿怨③而友其人，左丘明耻之，丘亦耻之。"

[注释]

①足恭:足,过度。足恭,过度卑躬。　②左丘明:《春秋左氏传》作者。一说姓左丘,名明;一说姓左,名丘明。孔子称道的前贤。　③匿怨:匿,隐藏。匿怨,有怨恨,却把它隐藏在心里。

[白话文]

孔子说:"说阿谀好听的话、装谄媚讨人喜欢的脸色、过度的谦卑,左丘明耻之,我也感到可耻。心里怨恨那个人,表面上却装得很友好,左丘明耻之,我也感到可耻。"

[英译文]

The Master said, "Fine words, an insinuating appearance, and excessive respect; Zuo Qiu-ming was ashamed of them. I am also ashamed of them. To conceal resentment against a person, and appear friendly with him; Zuo Qiu-ming was ashamed of such conduct. I am also ashamed of it."

5-25

颜渊、季路侍。子曰:"盍①各言尔志。"子路曰:"愿车马、衣轻裘,与朋友共,敝②之而无憾。"颜渊曰:"愿无伐③善,无施劳④。"子路曰:"愿闻子之志。"子曰:"老者安之,朋友信之,少者怀之。"

[注释]

①盍:何不。　②敝:坏。　③伐:夸耀。　④施劳:施,张大、宣扬。劳,功劳。

[白话文]

颜渊、季路(子路)侍立于孔子身边。孔子说:"何不各人说说自己的志愿?"子路说:"我愿意把自己的车马、衣服都拿来和朋友共同使用,就是用坏了也没有遗憾。"颜渊说:"我愿不夸耀自己的优点,不宣扬自己的功劳。"子路又说:"我们也想听听老师的志愿!"孔子说:"我的志愿是:老年人养之以安,朋友间相互信任,让少小都得到关怀。"

[英译文]

Yan-yuan and Ji-lu being by his side, the Master said to them, "Come, let each of you tell his wishes." Zi-lu said, "I should like, having chariots and horses, and light fur dresses, to share them with my friends, and though they should spoil them, I would not be displeased." Yan-yuan said, "I should like not to boast of my excellence, nor to make a display of my meritorious deeds." Zi-lu then said, "I should like, sir, to hear your wishes." The Master said, "They are, in regard to the aged, to give them rest; in regard to friends, to show them sincerity; in regard to the young, to treat them tenderly."

5 - 26

子曰:"已矣乎①! 吾未見能見其過,而内自訟②者也。"

[注释]

①已矣乎:算了吧! ②自讼:讼,责备。自讼,自责,自我批评。

[白话文]

孔子说:"算了吧! 我未见过发现自己有过错而自我批评的人。"

[英译文]

The Master said, "It is all over! I have not yet seen one who could perceive his faults, and inwardly accuse himself."

5 - 27

子曰:"十室之邑①,必有忠信如丘者焉,不如丘之好學也。"

[注释]

①邑:县、国都、封地都叫邑。人聚居的地方也可称邑。

[白话文]

孔子说:"就是只有十户人家的小村子,也总会有像我这样忠实和守信用的人,但没有像我这样好学的。"

[英译文]

The Master said, "In a hamlet of ten families, there may be found one honourable and sincere as I am, but not so fond of learning."

雍也第六

本篇凡二十八章(6—1～6—28)。

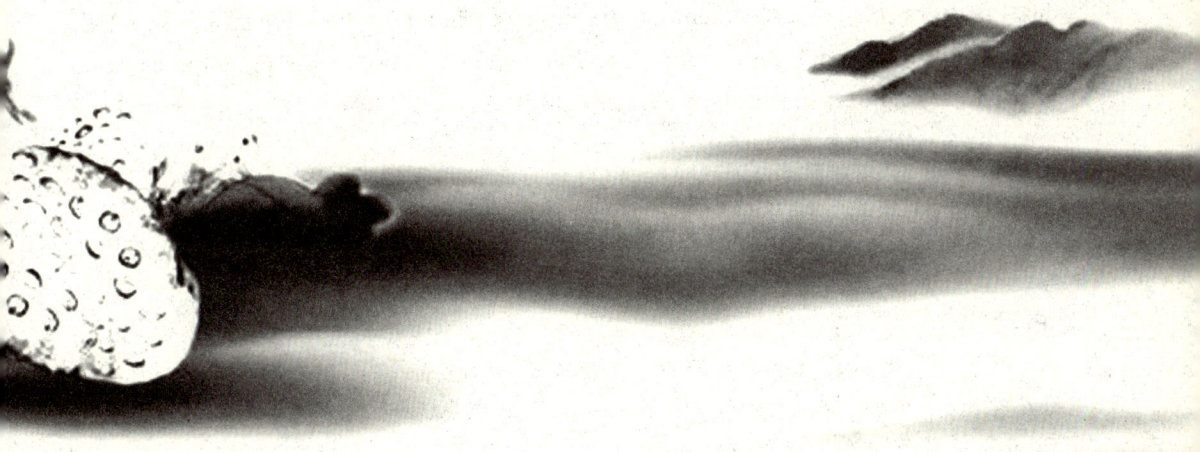

6-1

子曰："雍①也,可使南面②。"仲弓問子桑伯子③。子曰:"可也,簡④。"仲弓曰:"居敬而行簡⑤,以臨其民,不亦可乎? 居簡而行簡,無乃大簡乎⑥?"子曰:"雍之言然。"

[注释]

①雍:即冉雍,字仲弓,孔子弟子。参阅公冶长篇第四章(5-4)注。　②可使南面:南面,人君之位。故一说孔子称赞冉雍有人君之度;另一说谓"可使南面"即可以出使大国,朝见人君;又一说是古代以坐北朝南位者最尊重,所以说他可以做大官。《集注》曰:"言仲弓宽洪简重,有人君之度也。"　③子桑伯子:子桑,复姓,名伯,鲁国贤人。也有疑为是庄子所称的子桑户。　④简:简约。这里指子桑伯子处事简约。　⑤居敬而行简:居心恭敬,处事严肃认真而不烦琐。　⑥无乃大简乎:大简即太简。无乃,不是的意思,作反问句用。无乃太简乎,不是太过简约了吗?

[白话文]

孔子说:"冉雍宽宏简重,有人君之度。"仲弓问子桑伯子其人如何? 孔子说:"还可以,做事还算简约。"仲弓说:"居心敬肃而行事简约,这样来治理人民,不就可以了吗? 如果一心图简便,又简便行事,那未免太过简约了!"孔子说:"你的话很对。"

[英译文]

The Master said, "There is Yong! He might occupy the place of a prince."

Zhong-gong asked about Zi-sang Bo-zi. The Master said, "He may pass. He does not mind small matters." Zhong-gong said, "If a man cherish in himself a reverential feeling of the necessity of attention to business, though he may be easy in small matters in his government of the people, that may be allowed. But if he cherish in himself that easy feeling, and also carry it out in his practice, is not such an easy mode of procedure excessive?" The Master said, "Yong is right."

6-2

哀公問:"弟子執爲好學?"孔子對曰:"有顏回者好學,不遷怒,不貳過。不幸短命死矣。今也則亡,未聞好者學也。"

[白话文]

鲁哀公问孔子:"你的弟子中谁最好学?"孔子回答说:"只有颜回最好学。他不乱发脾气,不迁怒于人;有过错,绝不重犯。不幸他短命死了。如今没有这样的人了,没有听说哪一个真正好学的人了。"

[英译文]

The duke Ai asked which of the disciples loved to learn. Confucius replied to him, "There was Yan-hui; he loved to learn. He did not transfer his anger; he did not repeat a fault. Unfortunately, his appointed time was short and he died; and now there is not such another. I have not yet heard of any one who loves to learn as he did."

6 – 3

子華①使於齊，冉子②爲其母請粟。子曰：“與之釜③。”請益。曰：“與之庾④。”冉子與之粟五秉⑤。子曰：“赤之適齊也，乘肥馬⑥，衣輕裘。吾聞之也，君子周急不繼⑦富。”原思⑧爲之宰，與之粟九百⑨，辭。子曰：“毋！以與爾鄰里鄉黨⑩乎！”

[注释]

①子华：孔子弟子。姓公西，名赤，字子华。比孔子小四十二岁。　②冉子：即冉求。参阅上篇第七章(5-7)注。　③釜：古容量单位，六斗四升为一釜。　④庾：读 yǔ，古容量单位，一庾等于十六斗。　⑤秉：古容量单位，一秉为十六斛，一斛为十斗。　⑥乘肥马：马拉的车叫“乘”。乘坐着肥马拉的车子。　⑦继：接济、增益。　⑧原思：孔子弟子。姓原，名宪，字子思。此时，孔子为鲁马寇，原思为家宰。　⑨九百：原文缺计量单位名称，不可考。　⑩邻里乡党：古时以五户为邻，二十五户为党。

[白话文]

孔子派子华到齐国去。冉求替子华的母亲向孔子请求发给米粮。孔子说：“给她一釜吧。”冉求请增加数量。孔子说：“就给一庾吧。”冉求却给了她五秉小米。孔子说：“公西赤这次去齐国，乘驾肥马拉的车子，穿的是轻裘。我听说过，君子只周济贫困的人，不是给富有的人继增财富。”

原思为孔子的家宰，孔子给他九百的小米作为俸禄。原思觉得太多，不肯接受。孔子说：“不要推辞了。如果你觉得多，可以给你贫困的乡邻啊！”

[英译文]

Zi-hua being employed on a mission to Qi, the disciple Ran requested grain for his mother. The Master said, "Give her a Fu." Ran requested more. "Give her a Yu," said the Master. Ran gave her five Bing. The Master said, "When Chi was proceeding to Qi, he had fat horses to his carriage, and wore light furs. I have heard that a superior man helps the distressed, but does not add to the wealth of the rich." Yuan-si being made governor of his town by the Master, he gave him nine hundred measures of grain, but Si declined them. The Master said,

"Do not decline them May you not give them away in the neighbourhoods, hamlets, towns, and villages."

6 – 4

子謂仲弓曰:"犁牛①之子骍且角②,雖欲勿用,山川其舍諸③?"

[注释]

①犁牛:杂色的耕牛。 ②骍且角:骍,赤色。角,两角长的端正。古代崇尚赤色,祭祀时要用赤色而两角端正的牛作祭牲。 ③山川其舍诸:山川,指山川之神。舍,舍弃的意思。诸,"之乎"的合音,疑问语气词,相当于现代汉语的"吗"。本章乃孔子意喻冉雍(仲弓)之父虽出身低下而行恶,但他的儿子却是位可以南面的人才。

[白话文]

孔子评论仲弓说:"杂色的犁牛所生的小牛,毛色纯赤,头角端正。人们即使不想用它来作祭品,山川之神又怎么肯舍弃它呢?"

[英译文]

The Master, speaking of Zhong-gong, said, "If the calf of a brindled cow be red and horned, although men may not wish to use it, would the spirits of the mountains and rivers put it aside?"

6 – 5

子曰:"回也,其心三月①不違仁,其餘則日月②至焉而已矣。"

[注释]

①三月:朱注:"三月,言其久也。"如今人所说的"一年到头"。 ②日月:一日或一月,短时间的偶然而已。

[白话文]

孔子说:"颜回呀!他心里能够长时间不离仁,无时无刻不以仁存心。其他的弟子则做不到,只是偶然存心于仁而已。"

[英译文]

The Master said, "Such was Hui that for three months there would be nothing in his mind contrary to perfect virtue. The others may attain to this on some days or in some months, but noting more."

6 – 6

季康子①問:"仲由②可使從政也與?"子曰:"由也果,於從政乎何有?"曰:"賜③也,可使從政也與?"曰:"賜也達,於從政乎何有?"曰:"求也,可使從政也與?"曰:"求也藝④,於從政乎何有?"

[注释]

①季康子:即本书以后多次提到的季孙氏,鲁国的执政大夫,他任用了较多的孔子弟子。参阅为政篇第二十章(2-20)。 ②仲由:即子路。 ③赐:即子贡(端木赐)。参阅学而篇第十章(1-10)注。 ④艺:指才能。

[白话文]

季康子问孔子说:"仲由这个人,可以让他从事政治吗?"孔子说:"由,这人有决断,从事政治有什么难呢?"季康子又问:"端木赐这个人,可以让他从事政治吗?"孔子说:"赐,这人通达事理,从政有什么难呢?"季康子又说:"冉求,可以使他从政吗?"孔子说:"求,多才多艺,从政有什么难呢?"

[英译文]

Ji Kang-zi asked about Zhong-you, whether he was fit to be employed as an officer of government. The Master said, "You is a man of decision. What difficulty would he find in being an officer of government?" Kang asked, "Is Ci fit to be employed as an officer of government?" and was answered, "Ci is a man of intelligence; what difficulty would he find in being an officer of government?" And to the same question about Qiu, the Master gave the same reply, saying, "Qiu is a man of various ability."

6-7

季氏①使闵子骞②爲費宰③。閔子騫曰:"善爲我辭焉。如有復我者,則吾必在汶上④矣。"

[注释]

①季氏:即季孙氏。 ②闵子骞:孔子弟子。姓闵,名损,字子骞。一个有名的孝子。 ③费宰:费,旧读bì,地名,在今山东费县西北,当时为季氏邑。费宰,即邑宰,费邑的地方长官。 ④吾必在汶上:汶,水名,即今山东汶河。汶上,指汶水北,也是鲁北,已近齐。闵子骞此语,表示他不愿为费邑宰,否则将离鲁去齐。

[白话文]

季孙氏派使者来请闵子骞做费邑宰。闵子骞对来者说:"请替我婉言辞掉吧!如果再来要我去,那我必上汶水之北了。"

[英译文]

The chief of the Ji family sent to ask Min Zi-qian to be governor of Bi. Min Zi-qian said, "Decline the offer for me politely. If any one comes again to me with a second invitation, I shall be obliged to go and live on the banks of the Wen."

6-8

伯牛有疾①,子问之,自牖执其手,曰:"亡之,命矣夫! 斯人也,而有斯疾也! 斯人也,而有斯疾也!"

[注释]

①伯牛有疾:伯牛,孔子弟子,姓冉,名耕,伯牛是字。疾,朱注曰:"先儒以为癞。"即今称之麻风病。

[白话文]

伯牛患了恶疾,将死,孔子去看望他,从窗户伸手进去握着他的手,说:"不行了,真是命呀! 这样好的人,怎么会生这种恶病? 这样好的人,怎么会生这种恶病?"

[英译文]

Bo-niu being ill, the Master went to ask for him. He took hold of his hand through the window, and said, "It is killing him. It is the appointment of Heaven, alas! That such a man should have such a sickness! That such a man should have such a sickness!"

6-9

子曰:"贤哉,回①也! 一箪食②,一瓢③饮,在陋巷。人不堪其忧,回也不改其乐。贤哉,回也!"

[注释]

①回:即颜渊。参阅为政篇第九章(2-9)。　②一箪食:箪,盛饭用的竹器。食,饭。　③瓢:今称的葫芦,舀水用。

[白话文]

孔子说:"颜回真是贤德! 一小筐的饭,一葫芦瓢的水,住在简陋的巷子里。别人都因受不了这样的贫苦而忧愁,可是颜回却不改变他自得的乐趣。颜回真是贤德呀!"

[英译文]

The Master said, "Admirable indeed was the virtue of Hui! With a single bamboo dish of rice, a single gourd dish of drink, and living in his mean narrow lane. While others could not have endured the distress, he did not allow his joy to be affected by it. Admirable indeed was the virtue of Hui!"

6 – 10

冉求曰:"非不说①子之道,力不足也。"子曰:"力不足者,中道而廢。今女畫②。"

[注释]

①说:同"悦"。　②今女画:今,现在。女,汝,你。画,画地自限,不愿前进。

[白话文]

冉求说:"不是我不喜欢老师的学说,实在是我的力量不够。"孔子说:"如果是力量不够的话,会在走到半路时走不动而停下来。可你现在不是走不动,而是画地自限,根本没有迈步。"

[英译文]

Ran-qiu said, "It is not that I do not delight in your doctrines, but my strength is insufficient." The Master said, "Those whose strength is insufficient give over in the middle of the way, but now you limit yourself."

6 – 11

子謂子夏曰:"女爲君子儒①,無爲小人儒。"

[注释]

①君子儒:"君子"一词,在《论语》中提到一百多次,大多指有道德学问的人,少数指上位者。儒,读书人。

[白话文]

孔子对子夏说:"你要做君子一类的读书人,不要做小人般的读书人。"

[英译文]

The Master said to Zi-xia, "Do you be a scholar after the style of the superior man, and not after that of the mean man."

6 – 12

子游爲武城①宰。子曰:"女得人焉耳②乎?"曰:"有澹臺滅明③者,行不由徑④;非公事,未嘗至於偃⑤之室也。"

[注释]

①武城:鲁国城邑,在今山东费县。　②耳:在这里作助词。　③澹台灭明:人名,姓澹台,名灭明,字子羽。比孔子小三十九岁,貌难看。曾来孔子处愿做孔子的学生,未引起孔子看重,不久离去。为人有才德。据史载,他在南方和他的弟子们"名动诸侯",受各国欢迎。所以古有"以貌取人,失之子羽"句,说的就是他。　④径:朱熹曰:"径,路之小而捷者。"　⑤偃:子游之名。参阅为政篇第七章(2-7)。

[白话文]

　　子游做了武城的邑宰。孔子问他："你在那里得到了什么人才了吗?"子游说:"有个叫澹台灭明的人,他走路从不抄小路捷径;不是公事,他也从不到我的住处来。"

[英译文]

　　Zi-you being governor of Wu-cheng, the Master said to him, "Have you got good men there?" He answered, "There is Tan-tai Mie-ming, who never in walking takes a short cut, and never comes to my office, excepting on public business."

6－13

　　子曰:"孟之反①不伐②,奔而殿③,將入門,策④其馬,曰:'非敢後也,馬不進也。'"

[注释]

　　①孟之反:鲁国大夫。姓孟,名侧,字之反。　　②不伐:伐,矜己夸人。不伐,即不自夸。③奔而殿:奔,战败逃跑。殿,殿后,在后面拒敌。这里是指鲁哀公十一年齐鲁之战,鲁军败退,孟之反殿后事。　　④策:鞭策。《春秋左氏传·哀公十一年》载:"孟子侧……抽矢策其马,曰'马不进也'。"

[白话文]

　　孔子说:"孟之反这个人不自夸功劳。当军队败退时,他殿后。快要进国门时,他鞭策着坐骑,说:'不是我敢留在后面,是马不肯快跑往前。'"

[英译文]

　　The Master said, "Meng Zhi-fan does not boast of his merit. Being in the rear on an occasion of flight, when they were about to enter the gate, he whipped up his horse, saying, 'It is not that I dare to be last. My horse would not advance.'"

6－14

　　子曰:"不有祝鮀之佞①而有宋朝之美②,難乎免於今之世矣③!"

[注释]

　　①祝鮀之佞:祝,管理宗庙、国家祭祀之官职。鮀,人名,卫国大夫,字子鱼。不但"长卫于祭"(懂得卫国的祭祀),且善辞令,以口才著称。　　②宋朝之美:宋国的公子,名朝,以貌美闻于当时。　　③难乎免于今之世矣:孔子慨叹当今之世不尚德而好谀悦色,喻君子才美而不能以颜色辞令事人,难于有为。

［白话文］

　　孔子说："没有祝鮀那样的口才、宋朝那样的貌美,在当今社会里直道事人,难免遇到沮遏(吃不开,行不通)。"

［英译文］

　　The Master said, "Without the specious speech of the litanist Tuo, and the beauty of the prince Chao of Song, it is difficult to escape in the present age."

6－15

　　子曰:"誰能出不由户? 何莫由斯道也?"

［白话文］

　　孔子说:"谁能不由门户进出呢? 为什么不知道立身处世必由之道?"

［英译文］

　　The Master said, "Who can go out but by the door? How is it that men will not walk according to these ways?"

6－16

　　子曰:"質勝文則野①,文勝質則史②。文質彬彬③,然後君子。"

［注释］

　　①质胜文则野:质,本的意思。质朴,即本质朴实,犹言德。文,文采,犹言礼仪、文饰。野,粗野。　②史:古时掌文书之书吏,辞多浮华。　③文质彬彬:指文和质相均衡。

［白话文］

　　孔子说:"一个人如质朴胜过文采,就会显得粗野;如礼仪文采胜过朴实,就会像掌管文书之吏官,辞多浮华。必须朴实和文采相均衡,然后才可说是个君子。"

［英译文］

　　The Master said, "Where the solid qualities are in excess of accomplishments, we have rusticity; where the accomplishments are in excess of the solid qualities, we have the manners of a clerk. When the accomplishments and solid qualities are equally blended, we them have the man of virtue."

6－17

　　子曰:"人之生也直①,罔之生也幸而免②。"

［注释］

　　①直:正直。　②罔之生也幸而免:罔,邪曲诬罔,指不正直者。本句两个"生"字,朱熹曰:"上生字为始生之生;下生字为生存之生。"

[白话文]

孔子说:"人生本来就是正直的,至于受染了坏的习气而邪曲诬罔,失去了正直,难免遭受祸害;如果仍然得以生活着,那只是侥幸而已。"

[英译文]

The Master said, "Man is born for uprightness. If a man lose his uprightness, and yet live, his escape from death is the effect of mere good fortune."

6-18

子曰:"知之者不如好之者,好之者不如樂之者。"

[白话文]

孔子说:"一切学问道德,知道它的人,不如爱好它的人;爱好它的人,不如以从事它而感到快乐的人。"

[英译文]

The Master said, "They who know the truth are not equal to those who love it, and they who love it are not equal to those who delight in it."

6-19

子曰:"中人以上,可以語上也;中人以下,不可以語上也。"

[白话文]

孔子说:"资质中等以上的人,可以和他谈高深的道理;资质中等以下的人,无法和他谈高深的道理。"

[英译文]

The Master said, "To those whose talents are above mediocrity, the highest subjects may be announced. To those who are below mediocrity, the highest subjects may not be announced."

6-20

樊遲問知①。子曰:"務民之義②,敬鬼神而遠之③,可謂知矣。"問仁。曰:"仁者先難而後獲④,可謂仁矣。"

[注释]

①知:同"智"。　②务民之义:务,专力。义,当做之事。务民之义,专心致力于为人当做的事情上。　③敬鬼神而远之:本句是紧接上句专心于为人的事,而对鬼神则敬而远之,不惑于不可知者。　④先难而后获:《集注》引程子曰:"先难,克己也。以所难为先而不计所获,仁也。"

[白话文]

樊迟问什么是智。孔子说:"专心致力于为人所应当做的事情上,而对鬼神敬重却不惑不可知的事情上,这样就称得上智。"又问什么是仁。孔子说:"先身为其难的事——克己,把获得放在后面,这就是仁。"

[英译文]

Fan-chi asked what constituted wisdom. The Master said, "To give one's self earnestly to the duties due to men, and while respecting spiritual beings, to keep aloof from them, may be called wisdom." He asked about perfect virtue. The Master said, "The man of virtue makes the difficulty to be overcome his first business, and success only a subsequent consideration; this may be called perfect virtue."

6 - 21

子曰:"知者樂水,仁者樂山;知者動,仁者静;知者樂,仁者壽。"

[白话文]

孔子说:"聪明的人容易知晓事理而流动无滞,所以多半爱好水;仁慈的人多半宁静深厚,安于义理,所以喜好山。聪明的人,活泼好动;仁慈的人,心情好静。聪明的人,兴趣广泛,自得其乐;仁慈的人,淡泊寡欲,所以长寿者多。"

[英译文]

The Master said, "The wise find pleasure in water; the virtuous find pleasure in hills. The wise are active; the virtuous are tranquil. The wise are joyful; the virtuous are long-lived."

6 - 22

子曰:"齊一變,至於魯;魯一變,至於道①。"

[注释]

①齐一变,至于鲁;鲁一变,至于道:周武王灭纣,统一天下后,周公的后代封于鲁,太公的后代封于齐。而后,在文化和经济发展上,逐渐产生了差异,齐强而鲁弱。齐成为霸王,鲁实行王化,保留了周文化的一线命脉,重礼教,遵信义。所以孔子说,如果齐一旦变革,至于鲁,鲁国的政教再变革进化,就可达到先王之道。

[白话文]

孔子说:"如果把齐国的霸道改变一下,便能像鲁国一样;如果把鲁国的政治再变革进化,便可达到先王之道了。"

[英译文]

The Master said, "Qi, by one change, would come to the state of Lu. Lu, by one change, would come to a state where true principles predominated."

6－23

子曰:"觚不觚①,觚哉! 觚哉!"

[注释]

①觚不觚:觚,读 gū,古代一种盛酒的器具,方形而有四条棱角。但其时孔子看到的形状已改变了,失去了棱角,觚不像个觚。孔子以此比喻当时君不君、臣不臣、父不父、子不子的现象。

[白话文]

孔子说:"觚不像个觚,这还是觚吗? 这还是觚吗?"

[英译文]

The Master said, "A cornered vessel without corners. A strange cornered vessel! A strange cornered vessel!"

6－24

宰我問曰:"仁者,雖告之曰,'井有仁①焉',其從之也②?"子曰:"何爲其然③也? 君子可逝④也,不可陷也;可欺⑤也,不可罔⑥也。"

[注释]

①仁:作"人"字解。 ②也:作疑问词,相当于"欤"、"吗"。 ③然:如此、这样的意思。 ④逝:去。 ⑤欺:诳骗。 ⑥罔:昧于事理。

[白话文]

宰我(宰予)问孔子说:"有仁德的人,如有人对他说:'井里掉下一个人。'他会跟从跳下去救吗?"孔子说:"为什么要这样呢? 君子可以去,但不会陷之入井。君子有不惜舍己救人之心而受诳骗,但不会昧于事理而被蒙蔽受陷。"

[英译文]

Zai-wo asked, "A benevolent man, though it be told him, 'there is a man in well', will go in after him, I suppose." The Master said, "Why should he do so? A superior man may be made to go to the well, but he cannot be made to go down into it. He may be imposed upon, but he cannot be fooled."

6－25

子曰:"君子博學於文①,約之以禮,亦可以弗畔②矣夫!"

[注释]

①博学于文：学识要渊博，博而后精。文，不仅是文学，而是各种学术文化。　②畔：同"叛"。

[白话文]

孔子说："君子要广泛学习各方面的文化知识，循守礼法，也就不会离经叛道了。"

[英译文]

The Master said, "The superior man, extensively studying all learning, and keeping himself under the restraint of the rules of propriety, may thus likewise not overstep what is right."

6－26

子見南子①，子路不説。夫子矢之②曰："予所否③者，天厭之！天厭之！"

[注释]

①南子：卫灵公的夫人，是个对国政有影响的人物，但在当时女性干政不被社会接受，且多流言。南子召请孔子去，故子路不悦。　②矢之：一说是"发誓"，似与情理欠合。一说是"直陈"，即直言，从之。　③所否：所，假若。否，不当。

[白话文]

孔子应请去见南子，子路不高兴。孔子对他直言："我假若有不当的地方，老天必厌弃之！老天必厌弃之！"

[英译文]

The Master having visited Nan-zi, Zi-lu was displeased on it. The Master swore, saying, "Wherein I have done improperly, may Heaven reject me! May Heaven reject me!"

6－27

子曰："中庸之爲德①也，其至矣乎！民鮮②久矣。"

[注释]

①中庸之为德：中庸，中是不偏不倚，不太过和不及，是综合各种对立的原则和方法；庸是用的意思。中庸之道也就是尧让位给舜时所说的"执其中"（参阅尧曰篇。用今天的话来说，就是不左不右的正确路线。大到治国安邦的政治方针、路线，小到待人接物、处事为人，都需要用到它的至德。　②鲜：少的意思。

[白话文]

孔子说："中庸之道是天下事无所不用的至德，可惜人民缺乏认识和应用它已经少而久了。"

[英译文]

The Master said, "Perfect is the virtue which is according to the Constant Mean! Rare for a long time has been its practice among the people."

6-28

子貢曰："如有博施於民而能濟衆，何如？可謂仁乎？"子曰："何事於仁，必也聖乎！堯、舜其猶病諸！夫仁者，己欲立而立人，己欲達而達人。能近取譬，可謂仁之方也已。"

[白话文]

子贡说："如果有人广泛施惠于人民，又能济助大众，怎么样？可以算仁人吗？"孔子说："这何止于仁人？一定是圣人了！恐怕连尧舜还愁做不到呢！"接着又说："所谓仁者，是推己及人。自己能建立的，也要使人家能建立；自己能达到的，也要使人家能达到。能够以就近（眼前）自己所欲的事来譬之他人，从一点一滴做起，不必说得太高太远，这就是实行仁德的方法。"

[英译文]

Zi-gong said, "Suppose the case of a man extensively conferring benefits on the people, and able to assist all, what would you say of him? Might he be called perfectly virtuous?" The Master said, "Why speak only of virtue in connection with him? Must he not have the qualities of a sage? Even Yao and Shun were still solicitous about this. Now the man of perfect virtue, wishing to be established himself, seeks also to establish others; wishing to be enlarged himself, he seeks also to enlarged others. To be able to judge of others by what is nigh in ourselves; this may be called the art of virtue."

述而第七

本篇凡三十七章(7-1～7-37)。

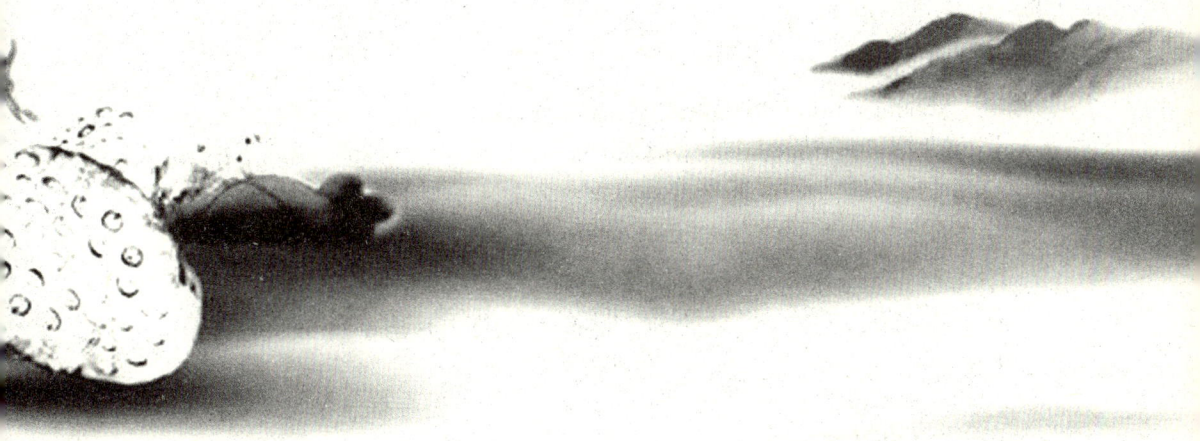

7-1

子曰："述而不作①,信而好古,窃比於我老彭②。"

[注释]

①述而不作：《集注》曰："述,傅旧而已……孔子删《诗》、《书》,定礼乐,赞《周易》,修《春秋》,皆傅先王之旧,而未尝有所作也,故其自言如此。""不作"就是没有自己的创作,"自附于古之贤人"。　②老彭：一说指老子、彭祖二人。朱注："老彭,商贤大夫。"从朱注。

[白话文]

孔子说："傅述旧有的文化典籍而不创作,笃信并喜好古代的文化,我是在私下效法商初的贤大夫老彭。"

[英译文]

The Master said, "A transmitter and not a maker, believing in and loving the ancients, I venture to compare myself with our old Peng."

7-2

子曰："默而识①之,学而不厌,诲人不倦,何有於我②哉?"

[注释]

①识：读 zhì,记的意思,如"博闻强识"。默识,就是不在口头,而在心里默默记住。　②何有于我：有的版本解释为默识、学不厌、诲人不倦这三件事,我做到了哪一件呢? 可能是据朱注"言何者能有于我"而作此解释。但据《孟子·公孙丑章句上》,引孔子答子贡问,解释为"圣则吾不能。我学不厌而教不倦也"。这些,对我有何困难呢? 从《孟子》。

[白话文]

孔子说："把所学到的默默地记在心里,坚持学习而不厌烦,教诲人而不厌倦,如是而已,我还有什么呢?"

[英译文]

The Master said, "The silent treasuring up of knowledge; learning without satiety; and instructing others without being wearied—which one of there things belongs to me?"

7-3

子曰："德之不脩,学之不讲,闻义不能徙,不善不能改,是吾忧也。"

[白话文]

孔子说："不好好地修养道德,不认真地讲习学问,听到正当的道义不能徙从,有过错不能改过向善,这是我所担忧的。"

[英译文]

The Master said, "The leaving virtue without proper cultivation; the not thoroughly discussing what is learned; not being able to move towards righteousness of which a knowledge is gained; and not being able to change what is not good—there are the things which occasion me solicitude."

7-4

子之燕居①，申申如也，夭夭如也②。

[注释]

①燕居：燕，宴、安的意思。燕居，即闲居。　②申申如也，夭夭如也：申申，其容舒也。夭夭，其色愉也。

[白话文]

孔子闲居在家的时候，容态舒展自如，神色和悦。

[英译文]

When the Master was unoccupied with business, his manner was easy, and he looked pleased.

7-5

子曰："甚矣，吾衰也！久矣，吾不復夢見周公①！"

[注释]

①周公：姓姬，名旦，周文王之子，周武王之弟，鲁国的始祖。他是奠定周王朝基础的大政治家，辅助周成王而有德政，并创造了周礼，是孔子崇仰的古代圣人。

[白话文]

孔子说："我衰老得多厉害呀！有很长时间，我不再梦见周公了。"

[英译文]

The Master said, "Extreme is my decay. For a long time, I have not dreamed, as I was wont to do that I saw the duke of Zhou."

7-6

子曰："志於道，據於德，依於仁，游於藝。"

[白话文]

孔子说："立志于道，执守于德，不违背仁，游习于六艺（礼、乐、射、御、书、数）之中。"

[英译文]

The Master said, "Let the will be set on the path of duty. Let every attainment in what is good be firmly grasped. Let perfect virtue be accorded with. Let relaxation and enjoyment be found in the polite arts."

7－7

子曰："自行束脩^①以上,吾未尝無誨焉。"

[注释]

①束脩:送给老师的报酬称束脩。初次拜老师时送上的礼品(金钱)称贽礼(或贽金),也有的称束脩。此"脩"不作"修",是肉干的意思。一长条的肉干称一脡,十脡称一束。一说"束脩"指古代男子入学行"束脩之礼"之年龄(一般十五岁入学),所备之礼物称束脩。束脩也同时代表入学年龄(十五岁)之称。倘从此,则"束脩以上"应解释为十五岁以上。现仍从前说。

[白话文]

孔子说:"只要自愿送上一束肉干而来求学的人,我没有不收他做学生而教诲他的。"

[英译文]

The Master said, "From the man bringing his bundle of dried flesh for my teaching upwards, I have never refused instruction to any one."

7－8

子曰："不憤不啟^①;不悱不發^②。舉一隅不以三隅反^③,則不復也。"

[注释]

①不愤不启:"愤者,心求通而未得之意。"不愤不启,乃指在学问上不到心想求通而未通之际,是不去开启他的。　②不悱不发:"口欲言而未能之貌。"不悱不发是指,不到想要说而说不出来的时候是不去启发他的。　③一隅不以三隅反:隅,读 yú,角落,如物有四隅者(例如屋有东南西北四个隅向)。一隅不以三隅反,乃指举一隅不能推知其他三隅者,即通常所说不能举一反三、不动脑的人,就不必再说教他。以上都是孔子的启发教育方法。

[白话文]

孔子说:"不是到心里想通未通的时候,我不去开启他;不是到想要说而说不出来的时候,我也不去启发他。如果举一个事物的隅角给他,他不能推知其他三个隅角,我也就不必再教他了。"

[英译文]

The Master said, "I do not open up the truth to one who is not eager to get knowledge, nor help out any one who is not anxious to explain himself. When I have presented one corner of a subject to any one, and he cannot from it learn the other three, I do not repeat my lesson."

7-9

子食於有喪者之側，未嘗飽也。子於是日哭，則不歌。

[白话文]

孔子在有丧事的人旁边吃饭，从来没有吃饱过。孔子在参加丧礼的这天哭过，就不再唱歌了。

[英译文]

When the Master was eating by the side of a mourner, he never ate to the full. He did not sing on the same day in which he had been weeping.

7-10

子謂顏淵曰："用之則行，舍之則藏①，惟我與爾有是夫！"子路曰："子行三軍則誰與②？"子曰："暴虎馮河③，死而無悔者，吾不與也。必也臨事而懼，好謀而成者也。"

[注释]

①用之则行，舍之则藏：即孟子所说的"可以仕则仕，可以止则止"（参阅《孟子·公孙丑章句上》）。出仕，则推行大道。舍而不用则隐。 ②行三军则谁与：行三军，统率军队。谁与，同谁在一起。 ③暴虎冯河：暴虎，空手打虎。冯河，徒步过河，喻指有勇无谋、冒险蛮干。

[白话文]

孔子对颜渊说："如果对我见用于世，则推行圣贤的治国平天下的大道；如果舍弃不用我，则退藏自守。这只有我和你能够做到的。"子路在旁插嘴问："要是让老师统率三军出征，愿和谁同去？"孔子说："空手打虎、徒步过河，到死还不知悔悟的人，我是不会要他同去的。一定要临事谨慎严肃，善用谋略，必能完成任务的人同去。"

[英译文]

The Master said to Yan-yuan, "When called to office, to undertake its duties; when not so called, to lie retired; it is only I and you who have attained to this."

Zi-lu said, "If you had the conduct of the armies of a great state, whom would you have to act with you?" The Master said, "I would not have him to act with me, who will unarmed attack a tiger, or cross a river without a boat, dying without any regret. My associate must be the man who proceeds to action full of solicitude, who is fond of adjusting his plans, and then carries them into execution."

7 - 11

子曰:"富而可求也,雖執鞭之士^①,吾亦爲之;如不可求,從吾所好。"

[注释]

①执鞭之士:拿着鞭子赶车的人。一说手拿皮鞭守市场门口的人。

[白话文]

孔子说:"富,如果可以求得,就是拿着皮鞭赶车的这种行业,我也愿意干。如果富求不到,还是去做我所喜欢的事吧!"

[英译文]

The Master said, "If the search for riches is sure to be successful. Though I should become a groom with whip in hand to get them, I will do so. As the search may not be successful, I will follow after that which I love."

7 - 12

子之所慎:齊^①、戰、疾。

[注释]

①齐:同"斋"。斋,即斋戒,指沐浴、吃素。祭祀期间以斋戒表示虔敬。

[白话文]

孔子所慎重对待的三件事:斋戒、战争、疾病。

[英译文]

The things in reference to which the Master exercised the greatest caution were:fasting, war, and sickness.

7 - 13

子在齊聞《韶》^①,三月^②不知肉味。曰:"不圖^③爲樂之至於斯也!"

[注释]

①《韶》:虞舜时升平之乐。　②三月:泛指许多时日。　③图:料想。

[白话文]

孔子在齐听到《韶》乐,三个月之久连吃肉都不觉得有味。他感叹说:"真没有料到舜时的音乐竟达到了如此美妙的境界。"

[英译文]

When the Master was in Qi, he heard the Shao and for three months did not know the taste of flesh. "I did not think," he said, "that music could have been made so excellent as this."

7-14

冉有曰:"夫子為①衞君②乎?"子貢曰:"諾,吾將問之。"入,曰:"伯夷、叔齊③何人也?"曰:"古之賢人也。"曰:"怨乎?"曰:"求仁而得仁,又何怨?"出,曰:"夫子不為也。"

[注释]

①为:帮助。 ②卫君:指当时卫国的国君卫出公,名辄(读 zhé),卫灵公的孙子,蒯(读 kuǎi)聩(读 kuì)的儿子。蒯聩因得罪了卫灵公的夫人南子,出亡于宋。卫灵公死后,立辄为国君,蒯聩又回来与辄争帝位,发生了父子之争。 ③伯夷、叔齐:商朝末年,孤竹君的两个儿子,因谁都不愿嗣位当国君,兄弟让位,都逃到别处去。后闻周文王善养老而投奔文王。文王崩,武王秘不发丧,载其木主伐商。伯夷、叔齐叩马谏,不听。商灭后,二人耻食周粟,最后饿死在首阳山〔参阅公冶长篇第二十二章(5-22)、季氏篇第十二章(16-12)〕。孔子用他俩和卫国的父子争帝位作对比,并赞扬伯夷、叔齐,所以子贡悟出孔子是必不会去帮助争位的人。

[白话文]

冉有问子贡说:"老师会不会去辅助卫君?"子贡说:"好! 我去问问看。"就进去问孔子说:"伯夷、叔齐是怎么样的人?"孔子告知说:"古时的贤人。"子贡又问:"他们让位逊国有悔恨吗?"孔子说:"他们想求仁,终于得到仁。有什么悔恨呢?"子贡出来说:"老师是不会去帮助卫君的。"

[英译文]

Ran-you said, "Is our master for the ruler of Wei?" Zi-gong said, "Oh! I will ask him." He went in accordingly, and said, "What sort of men were Bo-yi and Shu-qi?" "They were ancient worthies," said the Master. "Did they have any re-pining, because of their course?" The Master again replied, "They sought to act virtuously, and they did so; what was there for them to repine about?" On this, Zi-gong went out and said, "Our master is not for him."

7-15

子曰:"飯疏食①,飲水,曲肱②而枕之,樂在其中矣。不義而富且貴,於我如浮雲。"

[注释]

①饭疏食:饭,吃的意思。疏食,朱子注:"疏食,粗食也。" ②曲肱:曲臂。

[白话文]

孔子说:"吃粗粮,喝淡水,曲臂当枕而睡,其中也有乐趣。用不正当的方法得到的财富和尊贵,在我看来如同浮云一般。"

[英译文]

The Master said, "With coarse rice to eat, with water to drink, and my bended arm for a pillow—I have still joy in the midst of these things. Riches and honours acquired be unrighteousness, are to me as a floating cloud."

7－16

子曰:"加我數年,五十以學《易》①,可以無大過矣。"

[注释]

①易:指《易经》,或称《周易》。

[白话文]

孔子说:"如果能让我多活几年,到五十岁来研读《易经》,就可以没有什么大的过错了。"

[英译文]

The Master said, "If some years were added to my life, I would give fifty to the study of the Yi, and then I might come to be without great faults."

7－17

子所雅言:《詩》、《書》,執禮,皆雅言①也。

[注释]

①雅言:即正言之音,陕西人的口音。其意义相当于现代所称的普通话。周朝旧都在今之陕西,故以陕西语音为正音。

[白话文]

孔子有时说周朝的正音,如诵《诗》、读《书》和行礼时,都用正音。

[英译文]

The Master's frequent themes of discourse were: the Odes, the History, and the maintenance of the Rules of propriety. On all these he frequently discoursed.

7－18

葉公①問孔子於子路,子路不對。子曰:"女奚不曰②:'其爲人也,發愤忘食,樂以忘憂,不知老之將至云爾。'"

[注释]

①叶公:叶,读 xié。叶公,楚大夫,姓沈,名诸梁,字子高,叶是他的食邑,公是他的借称。②女奚不曰:女,即汝(你)。奚,何也。曰,说。女奚不曰,你何不这样说?

[白话文]

叶公问子路,孔子为人如何?子路不回答他。孔子知道后对子路说:"你为什么不这样说:'他的为人,用功时会忘记吃饭,心里快乐时会忘记所有的忧愁,甚至不知道自己将要老了,如此而已。'"

[英译文]

The duke of Xie asked Zi-lu about Confucius, and Zi-lu did not answer him. The Master said, "Why did you not say to him—he is simply a man, who in his eager pursuit of know ledge, forgets his food, who in the joy of its attainment forgets his sorrows, and who does not perceive that old age is coming on?"

7-19

子曰:"我非生而知之者,好古,敏以求之者也。"

[白话文]

孔子说:"我不是生下来就知道一切道理的,而是爱好古代文化,敏捷勤奋地求得的。"

[英译文]

The Master said, "I am not one who was born in the possession of knowledge; I am one who is fond of antiquity, and earnest in seeking it there."

7-20

子不語:怪、力、亂、神。

[白话文]

孔子不谈怪异、暴力、悖乱和鬼神的事情。

[英译文]

The subjects on which the Master did not talk were: extraordinary things, feats of violence, disorder, and spiritual beings.

7-21

子曰:"三人行,必有我師^①焉。擇其善者而從之,其不善者而改之。"

[注释]

①三人行,必有我师:孔子主张学无常师,而且学习不仅是啃书本。三人行者,除了自己还有二人,都可以作为我的老师,善者与不善者皆可供我借鉴。

[白话文]

孔子说:"三个人同行在一起,一定有可以作为我的老师的。选择他们的长处加以学习,他们的短处也可以作为我的反面老师。"

[英译文]

The Master said, "When I walk along with two others, they may serve me as my teachers. I will select their good qualities and follow them, their bad qualities and avoid them."

7－22

子曰:"天生德於予,桓魋①其如予何!"

[注释]

①桓魋:读 Huán Tuí,宋国的大司马,又叫向魋。因是宋桓公的后代,故又称桓魋。孔子经宋,桓魋想谋杀孔子。弟子们劝孔子早点离开,孔子自信地说这话。结果证明了桓魋虽然把孔子带弟子习礼处的大树砍掉,却无法把孔子怎么样。

[白话文]

孔子说:"天既然赋予我这样的道德和使命,桓魋又能把我怎么样呢?"

[英译文]

The Master said, "Heaven produced the virtue that is in me. Huan Tui—what can he do to me?"

7－23

子曰:"二三子①以我爲隱乎？吾無隱乎爾。吾無行而不與二三子者,是丘也。"

[注释]

①二三子:称诸弟子。

[白话文]

孔子说:"诸弟子,你们以为我有什么隐匿而没有告诉你们的吗？我实在没有什么隐匿的喽！我做的事没有一件是你们不知道的。我就是这样一个人。"

[英译文]

The Master said, "Do you think, my disciples, that I have any conceal-ments? I conceal nothing from you. There is nothing which I do that is not shown to you, my disciples—that is my way."

7－24

子以四教：文、行、忠、信①。

[注释]

①文、行、忠、信：文，指诗、书、礼、乐等典籍文献。行，德行。忠与信，人的品质。孔子以此四者教人，文化知识、行为品质并重。

[白话文]

孔子教育的四个方面：典籍文献、德行修养、为人忠诚、待人信实。

[英译文]

There were four things which the Master taught：letters, ethics, devotion of soul, and truthfulness.

7－25

子曰："聖人，吾不得而見之矣！得見君子者，斯可矣。"子曰："善人，吾不得而見之矣！得見有恒者①，斯可矣。亡②而爲有，虚而爲盈，約而爲泰，難乎有恒矣！"

[注释]

①有恒者：有操守，不二心，不因环境改变而影响学问道德的人。 ②亡：同"无"。

[白话文]

孔子说："圣人，我是看不到了，能见到（才德出众的）君子，也就可以了。"孔子又说："（志于仁而无恶的）善人，我是看不到了，能见到有恒的人，也就可以了。如果把没有的假装有，空虚的作为充实，穷约的冒充奢泰，这样的人是难以有守恒不变之心的。"

[英译文]

The Master said, "A sage it is not mine to see; could I see a man of real talent and virtue, that would satisfy me." The Master said, "A good man it is not mine to see; could I see a man possessed of constancy, that would satisfy me. Having not and yet affecting to have, empty and yet affecting to be full, straitened and yet affecting to be at ease—it is difficult with such characteristics to have constancy."

7－26

子釣而不網，弋①不射宿。

[注释]

①弋：读 yì，用带有生丝线的箭射鸟。

[白话文]

孔子用钓竿钓鱼，不用大网网鱼；用带有生丝线的箭射鸟，不射夜里回巢栖息的鸟。

[英译文]

The Master angled, but did not a net. He shot, but not at birds perching.

7－27

子曰：“蓋有不知而作之者，我無是也。多聞，擇其善者而從之；多見而識①之；知之次也。”

[注释]

①识：《集注》曰：“识，音志，记也……记则善恶皆当存之，以备参考。”

[白话文]

孔子说：“有的人不明白事理就妄自作为，我不会这样做的。平时遇到事情，多方面听闻别人的话，选择合理的去遵从；多方面加以观察并记在心里，这样也可以算个仅次于高智慧的人。”

[英译文]

The Master said, "There may be those who act without knowing why. I do not do so. Hearing much and selecting what is good and following it; seeing much and keeping it in memory—this is the second style of knowledge."

7－28

互鄉①難與言，童子見，門人惑。子曰：“與其進也，不與其退也，唯何甚？人潔己以進②，與其潔也，不保③其往也。”

[注释]

①互乡：地名，所处地已无考。　②人洁已以进：洁，洁身自好，不和他人同流合污。这里指不和其他人一样“难与言”。进，要求上进。　③不保：保，守、惦记的意思。

[白话文]

互乡这个地方的人，多自以为是，不大好和他们说话。一天，互乡一个小孩子来见孔子，孔子接见了他。弟子们不理解，孔子说：“我赞许他知道上进，不希望他后退,何必要拒人太甚呢? 他洁身自好,不和乡人一样而要求上进,应该鼓励他洁身上进的精神,不要老是惦记和计较他的过去。"

[英译文]

It was difficult to talk(profitably and reputably) with the people of Hu-xiang, and a lad of that place having had an interview with the Master, the disciples doubted. The Master said, "I admit people's approach to me without committing myself as to what they may do when they have retired. Why must one be so severe? If a man purify himself to wait upon me I receive him so purified, without guaranteeing his past conduct."

7-29

子曰:"仁遠乎哉? 我欲仁,斯仁至矣。"

[白话文]

孔子说:"仁,离我们何远之有? 我要寻求仁,仁就来到。"

[英译文]

The Master said, "Is virtue a thing remote? I wish to be virtuous, and virtue is at hand."

7-30

陳司敗①問,昭公②知禮乎? 孔子曰:"知禮。"孔子退,揖巫馬期③而進之,曰:"吾聞君子不黨④,君子亦黨乎? 君取於吳爲同姓,謂之吳孟子⑤。君而知禮,孰不知禮?"巫馬期以告。子曰:"丘也幸,苟有過,人必知之。"

[注释]

①陈司败:陈,陈国。司败,陈国的官名,即司寇。　②昭公:鲁国君,名裯,昭是谥号。③巫马期:孔子弟子。复姓巫马,名施,字子期。　④党:《集注》曰:"相助匿非曰党。"　⑤君取于吴为同姓,谓之吴孟子:君,指昭公。取,同"娶"。鲁君是周公后代,吴是泰伯后代,都姓姬。按周礼法,同姓不婚。昭分娶吴女,故谓吴孟子。

[白话文]

陈司败问孔子:"昭公知礼吗?"孔子说:"知礼。"孔子退出,陈司败揖请巫马期进来,说:"我听说君子不偏袒人。难道孔子会偏袒人吗? 鲁君娶了吴国的女子,是同姓,所以她改称为吴孟子。鲁君如知礼,那还有谁不知礼?"巫马期将此话转告孔子,孔子说:"我真幸运,如果有什么过错,人家必定知道。"

[英译文]

The minister of crime of Chen asked whether the duke Zhao knew propriety, and Confucius said, "He knew propriety." Confucius having retired, the minister bowed to Wu Ma-qi to come forward, and said, "I have heard that the superior man is not a partisan. May the superior man be a partisan also? The prince married a daughter of the house of Wu, of the same surname with himself, and called her 'The elder Zi of Wu'. If the prince knew propriety, who does not know it?" Wu Ma-qi reported these remarks, and the Master said, "I am fortunate! If I have any errors, people are sure to know them."

7 – 31

子與人歌，而善，必使反①之，而後和之。

[注释]

①反：复，重复一遍。

[白话文]

孔子与他人一起唱歌，如果听到他唱得好，必请他重复唱一遍，然后自己再跟着和唱。

[英译文]

When the Master was in company with a person who was singing, if he sang well, he would make him repeat the song, while he accompanied it with his own voice.

7 – 32

子曰："文，莫吾猶人①也。躬行君子，則吾未之有得②。"

[注释]

①莫吾犹人：莫，疑问词。莫吾犹人，或许我尚可及人。　②未之有得：还没有做到。

[白话文]

孔子说："学文之事，或许我还可以比得上人家；亲身履行君子之道，我实在还没有做到。"

[英译文]

The Master said, "In letters I am perhaps equal to other men, but the character of the superior man, carrying out in his conduct what he professes, is what I have not yet attained to."

7-33

子曰："若聖與仁,則吾豈敢？抑爲之①不厭,誨人不倦,則可謂云爾已矣②!"公西華曰："正唯弟子不能學也。"

[注释]

①抑为之:抑,转折词,近似但的意思。为之,即为学。　②云尔已矣:云,同"有"。尔,同"此"(这里指前面所说的为学不厌、诲人不倦)。已,而已。云尔已矣,如此而已。

[白话文]

孔子说:"若说圣人与仁人,那我怎么敢当？但是,我是在不厌其烦地学习,不知疲倦地教育人,可说只是如此而已。"公西华说:"这正是弟子们所学不到的啊!"

[英译文]

The Master said, "The sage and the man of perfect virtue; how dare I rank myself with them? It may simply be said of me, that I strive to become such without satiety, and teach others without weariness." Gong Xi-hua said, "This is just what we, the disciples, cannot imitate you in."

7-34

子疾病,子路請禱。子曰："有諸①?"子路對曰："有之。《誄》②曰:'禱爾於上下神祇③。'"子曰："丘之禱久矣④!"

[注释]

①有诸:《集注》曰:"有诸,问有此理否?"　②《诔》:诔,读 lěi,叙述死者生前事迹,表示哀悼之辞也。一说是古书篇名。　③上下神祇:上下,为天地。天神曰神,地神曰祇。祇,读 qí。④丘之祷久矣:不端的行为,会影响心理健康,成为病因。古人认为行为有达神明,招致灾祸病痛,用祈祷来消除。孔子平时作为合乎神明,故谓祷之久矣。

[白话文]

孔子病,子路请代为祈祷。孔子说:"有这种事吗?"子路回答说:"有啊!《诔》文上说:'为你向天地神祇祷告。'"孔子说:"如果是这样,那我天天都在祷告,而且祷告很久了。"

[英译文]

The Master being very sick, Zi-lu asked leave to pray for him. He said, "May such a thing be done?" Zi-lu replied, "It may, In the Eulogies it is said—prayer has been made to the spirits of the upper and lower worlds." The Master said, "My praying has been for a long time."

7 – 35

子曰:"奢,则不孙①;俭,则固②。与其不孙也,宁固。"

[注释]

①孙:同"逊"。不逊,指骄矜、不谦逊。 ②固:鄙陋。也会因陋就简而不及礼。

[白话文]

孔子说:"奢侈显得骄矜,太俭约显得固陋。与其骄矜,宁可固陋。"

[英译文]

The Master said, "Extravagance leads to insubordination, and parsimony to meanness. It is better to be mean to be insubordinate."

7 – 36

子曰:"君子坦荡荡,小人长戚戚①。"

[注释]

①戚戚:忧愁、悲哀的样子。

[白话文]

孔子说:"君子心胸广阔坦然,小人常常忧戚不安。"

[英译文]

The Master said, "The superior man is satisfied and composed; the mean man is always full of distress."

7 – 37

子温而厉,威而不猛,恭而安。

[白话文]

孔子的态度既温和又严肃;有威仪,却不凶暴、粗鲁;既恭敬而又安详。

[英译文]

The Master was mild, and yet dignified; majestic, and yet not fierce; respectful, and yet easy.

泰伯第八

本篇凡二十一章(8-1~8-21)。

8-1

子曰:"泰伯①其可謂至德也已矣! 三以天下讓②,民無得而稱焉。"

[注释]

①泰伯:周祖先古公亶父(后谥为周太王)的长子。古公生三子——泰伯、仲雍、季历。季历之子姬昌,即周文王。古公在世时,认为姬昌将来必定是个大人物,故有意传位给季历,可再传给姬昌。泰伯看出父王意图,就借口和弟仲雍外出采药去吴勾,及后来的"三以天下让",终于实现了父王传位季历的愿望。 ②三以天下让:朱子曰:"三让,谓固逊也。"一说泰伯在太王殁,不返。季历为丧主,一让也;季历赴之,不来奔丧,二让也;丧后断发文身,以避季历,三让也。

[白话文]

孔子说:"泰伯可算是至德了,再三辞让天下给他的弟弟季历,且将谦让的事迹做得隐蔽不显,百姓们不知道怎样去称颂他。"

[英译文]

The Master said, "Tai-bo may be said to have reached the highest point of virtuous action. Thrice he declined the kingdom, and the people in ignorance of his motives could not express their approbation of his conduct."

8-2

子曰:"恭而無禮則勞,慎而無禮則葸①,勇而無禮則亂,直而無禮則絞②。君子篤於親,則民興於仁,故舊不遺,則民不偷③。"

[注释]

①葸:读 xǐ,胆怯不前。 ②绞:急切、逼人。 ③偷:刻薄、不厚道。

[白话文]

孔子说:"只知道态度恭敬而不知礼,便会徒然烦劳;谨慎而不知礼,就会变得畏怯;勇武而不知礼,则必至悖乱;直爽而不知礼,就会变成急切迫人。在上位的人笃厚对待亲人,百姓也就会兴起仁爱的风气;在上位的人不遗弃故旧亲友,民间的风气也就不会冷漠、刻薄,而显得淳厚起来。"

[英译文]

The Master said, "Respectfulness, without the rules of propriety, becomes laborious bustle; carefulness, without the rules of propriety, becomes timidity; baldness without the rules of propriety, becomes insubordination; straightfor-wardness, without the rules of propriety, becomes rudeness. When those who are in high stations perform well all their duties to their relations, the people are aroused to virtue. When old friends are not neglected by them, the people are preserved form meanness."

8-3

曾子有疾,召門弟子曰:"啟予足,啟予手①!《詩》云:'戰戰兢兢,如臨深淵,如履薄冰②.'而今而後,吾知免夫? 小子!"

[注释]

①启予足,启予手:掀开被看看我的手足。其意义,一说是身体受之于父母,不敢毁伤,看看手足知"保其身"。一说是人生道路,一生行事都用手足践履实行。《集注》引范氏曰:"身体犹不可亏也,况亏其行以辱其亲乎。"本章紧接着又用《诗》句告诫弟子。当从后一说。　②《诗》云:"战战兢兢,如临深渊,如履薄冰。"参阅《诗经·雅·小雅·小旻》。

[白话文]

曾子病重,叫学生们来,说:"掀开被子看看我的脚和手吧!《诗经》上说:'小心谨慎呀!像走到深潭边,像踩在薄冰上。'从今以后,我知道自己可以不必这样了!弟子们啊!"

[英译文]

The philosopher Zeng being ill, he called to him the disciples of his school, and said, "Uncover my feet, uncover my hands. It is said in the Book of Poetry—we should be apprehensive and cautious, as if on the brink of a deep gulf, as if treading on thin ice, and so have I been. Now and hereafter, I know my escape from all injury to my person. O ye, my little children."

8-4

曾子有疾,孟敬子①問之。曾子言曰:"鳥之將死,其鳴也哀;人之將死,其言也善。君子所貴乎道者三:動容貌②,斯遠暴慢矣;正顏色③,斯近信矣;出辭氣④,斯遠鄙倍矣。籩豆⑤之事,則有司存。"

[注释]

①孟敬子:即鲁国大夫仲孙捷。孟武伯之子,平时喜欢讲究祭祀用礼器等事。　②动容貌:态度举止,要依礼而动,才能远离粗暴、放肆。　③正颜色:脸色表情要端正庄重、不轻浮,才能不妄而近于诚信。　④出辞气:言语声调,以礼出之,出言有章,合礼得体,才能远离鄙俗和悖理。　⑤笾豆:祭祀用的礼器。

[白话文]

曾子病重,孟敬子去探问。曾子对他说:"鸟将要死时,鸣叫声很悲哀;人将要死时,所说的话真心、善良。在上位的人,待人接物应讲究三件事:重视自己的态度举止,要依礼而动,这样才能远离粗暴、放肆;脸色表情,端正庄重,才能使人信任;

谈吐语辞声调,以礼而出,才能远离鄙俗和悖理。至于那些祭祀用的礼器等细节之事,自有专人在办理。"

[英译文]

The philosopher Zeng being ill, Meng Jing-zi went to ask how he was. Zeng said to him, "When a bird is about to die, its notes are mournful; when a man is about to die, his words are good. There are three principles of conduct which the man of high rank should consider specially important: that in his deportment and manner he keep from violence and heedlessness; that in regulating his countenance he keep near to sincerity; and that in his words and tones he keep far from lowness and impropriety. As to such matters as attending to the sacrificial vessels, there are the proper officers for them."

8-5

曾子曰:"以能問於不能,以多問於寡;有若無,實若虛,犯而不校①,昔者吾友②嘗從事於斯矣。"

[注释]

①校:计较。 ②昔者吾友:历来多认为是颜回。《集注》曰:"颜子之心,惟知义理之无穷,不见物我之有间,故能如此。"

[白话文]

曾子说:"有能力者去问能力差者,见识多者去问见识少者,有才能好像没有才能,学问充实好像很空虚似的,过去我的朋友是能够做到上面所说的这几件事的。"

[英译文]

The philosopher Zeng said, "Gifted with ability, and yet putting questions to those who were not so; possessed of much, and yet putting questions to those possessed of little; having, as though he had not; full, and yet counting himself as empty; offended against, and yet entering into no altercation: formerly I had a friend who pursued this style of conduct."

8-6

曾子曰:"可以託六尺之孤①,可以寄百里之命②,臨大節而不可奪③也。君子人與? 君子人也。"

[注释]

①六尺之孤:古制六尺,相当于今 138.6 厘米,指身高还在十五岁左右或以下的时候。六尺

之孤,即谓幼主。　②百里之命:百里,指国家封地面积,当时诸侯国面积不大。百里之命,乃谓国家命脉。　③夺:动摇。

[白话文]

曾子说:"可以托付他辅助幼主的重任,可以交给他摄国政的大权,遇到国之安危存亡的关头,决不屈志、动摇。这样的人可算君子吗? 当然是位君子!"

[英译文]

The philosopher Zeng said, "Suppose that there is an individual who can be entrusted with the charge of a young orphan prince, and can be commissioned with authority over a state of a hundred li, and whom no emergency however great can drive from his principles—is such a man a superior man? He is a superior man indeed."

8-7

曾子曰:"士不可以不弘毅,任重而道遠。仁以爲己任,不亦重乎? 死而後已,不亦遠乎?"

[白话文]

曾子说:"读书人的志气不可不远大,意志不可不刚毅。他责任重大,而且路途遥远。全心全意推行仁德作为自己的责任,要以身体力行之,这不是很重吗? 一息尚存,志不容懈,到死了才罢休,时间久长,这不是很远吗?"

[英译文]

The philosopher Zeng said, "The officer may not be without breadth of mind and vigorous endurance. His burden is heavy and his course is long. Perfect virtue is the burden which he considers it is his to sustain—is it not heavy? Only with death does his course stop. Is it not long?"

8-8

子曰:"興於《詩》①,立於禮,成於樂。"

[注释]

①《诗》:即指《诗经》。

[白话文]

孔子说:"鼓舞人的意志在于《诗》;人之视听、言行、仪容、举止良好,以立足社会,在于礼;怡养人之性情,使之高尚,在于乐。"

[英译文]

The Master said, "It is by the Odes that the mind is aroused. It is by the

Rules of Propriety that the character is established. It is from Music that the finish is received. "

8－9

子曰:"民可使由之,不可使知之①。"

[注释]

①民可使由之,不可使知之:由,一般都解释为"遵从",即顺从去做。本章争议颇多,有人认为这是"愚民政策";有人认为是断句的标点符号错置,应为:"民可使,由之;不可使,知之。"后一句的意义与原来的完全相反。也有人认为"不可"二字的意思是"不可能(做到)",这是在贯彻政令中的实际情况。《集注》引程子曰:"圣人设教,非不欲人家喻而户晓也,然不能使之知,但能使之由之尔。若曰圣人不使民知,则是后世朝四暮三之术也,岂圣人之心乎?"程子之谓虽未展开说明"不能使之知"的具体原委,但说明"不能使之知其所以然",并非是圣人之主观愿望,而是客观实际情况。

[白话文]

孔子说:"执行政策法令,使用民力,让百姓们遵照着去做,这还是可以做到的。但是要家喻户晓其所以然,这是不太可能的。"

[英译文]

The Master said, "The people may be made to follow a path of action, but they may not be made to understand it. "

8－10

子曰:"好勇疾①貧,亂也。人而不仁,疾之已②甚,亂也。"

[注释]

①疾:痛恨、厌恶。　②已:太过。

[白话文]

孔子说:"好勇而痛恨自己贫穷的人,必将生乱。对不仁的人,厌恶他太甚,也会激惹出乱子来的。"

[英译文]

The Master said, "The man who is fond of daring and is dissatisfied with poverty. Will proceed to insubordination. So will the man who is not virtuous, when you carry your dislike of him to an extreme. "

8－11

子曰:"如有周公之才之美,使驕且吝,其餘不足觀也已。"

[白话文]

孔子说:"如有人有周公那样美好的才能,假使他骄傲而又鄙吝,其余的也就不值得一顾了。"

[英译文]

The Master said, "Though a man have abilities as admirable as those of the duke of Zhou, yet if he be proud and niggardly, those other things are really not worth being looked at."

8-12

子曰:"三年學,不至於穀^①,不易得也。"

[注释]

①穀:俸禄。

[白话文]

孔子说:"学了三年那么久,还不想求得官禄,这种人是不容易多得的。"

[英译文]

The Master said, "It is not easy to find a man who has learned for three years without coming to be good."

8-13

子曰:"篤信好學,守死善道。危邦不入,亂邦不居^①。天下有道則見,無道則隱。邦有道,貧且賤焉,恥也;邦無道,富且貴焉,恥也。"

[注释]

①危邦不入,乱邦不居:政治纪纲已紊,谓之乱。有乱的征兆出现,谓之危。危乱之邦,君子不去。

[白话文]

孔子说:"有坚定的信念,又能好学。誓死坚守君子之道。不进入危险的国家,不居住祸乱的国家。政治清明,天下有道的时候,可以出仕行道;天下无道,不能行道的时候,就该隐退。国家政治清明,安定发展,如果仍然是贫且贱,那是可耻的;但国家离乱,政治腐败,你却既富又贵,也是可耻的。"

[英译文]

The Master said, "With sincere faith he unites the love of learning; holding firm to death, he is perfecting the excellence of his course. Such an one will not enter a tottering state, nor dwell in a disorganized one. When right principles of government prevail in the kingdom, he will show himself; when they are prostrated, he will keep concealed. When a country is well-governed, poverty and a mean condition are things to be ashamed of. When a country is ill-governed, riches and honour are things to be ashamed of."

8-14

子曰:"不在其位,不谋其政。"

[白话文]

孔子说:"不在那个职位上,就不要参与那职位上的事。"

[英译文]

The Master said, "He who is not in any particular office, has nothing to do with plans for the administration of its duties."

8-15

子曰:"師摯之始①,《關雎》之亂②,洋洋③乎盈耳哉。"

[注释]

①师摯之始:师摯,鲁国太师,名摯,太师是乐官。始,乐之开始,即升歌。 ②《关雎》之乱:关雎(读 jū),《诗经·风·周南》中的一诗篇名。乱,乐之终,即合乐。 ③洋洋:美盛的意思。

[白话文]

孔子说:"从师摯开始演奏,到结尾演奏《关雎》,音律弘美,充盈两耳,美盛极了。"

[英译文]

The Master said, "When the music-master Zhi first entered on his office, the finish of the Guan Ju was magnificent; how it filled the ears!"

8-16

子曰:"狂而不直,侗而不愿①,悾悾②而不信,吾不知之矣。"

[注释]

①侗而不愿:侗,无知的样子。愿,老实谨慎。 ②悾悾:无能的样子。

[白话文]

孔子说:"狂妄而不直率,无知而不老实、谨慎,无能又无信用,对这种人,我真不知道其结局将如何。"

[英译文]

The Master said, "Ardent and yet not upright; stupid and yet not attentive;

simple and yet not sincere—such persons I do not understand."

8－17

子曰:"學如不及,猶恐失之。"

[白话文]

孔子说:"为学的态度,好像追逐什么东西似的,惟恐追赶不上。学有所得,又惟恐失去它。"

[英译文]

The Master said, "Learn as if you could not reach your object, and were always fearing also lest you should lose it."

8－18

子曰:"巍巍①乎! 舜禹之有天下也,而不與②焉。"

[注释]

①巍巍:高大的样子。 ②不与:朱注:"不与,犹言'不相关',言其不以位为乐。"另一说为"不与求",即其位非自己求得的。又一说为"无为",即不身亲其事,而是得人善任。还有一说认为是孔子叹自己"不与禹舜并时"。以上四种解释,读了总有瑕疵感。近读南怀瑾先生《论语别裁》对本章及下一章的解读,从中得到启发:虽然尧禅让舜、舜禅让禹都是经过几十年的考验与观察,但从天命论的认知看其所以为天子,是"天之历数"所在(参阅尧曰篇)。上古,"天"字是一个抽象的代名词,天生万物,自己既不表功,也不要求回报。作为一个天子,其政治胸襟、政治器度效法天一样崇高伟大,只有付出,不期望给予,此即所谓"不与"。坐天子位,无所谓乐与不乐或是怎样求得的。

[白话文]

孔子说:"多么崇高和伟大啊! 舜禹之有天下,真正做到为天下人服务,只有付出,不期望、图谋给予自己回报。"

[英译文]

The Master said, "How majestic was the manner in which Shun and Yu held possession of the empire, as if it were nothing to them!"

8－19

子曰:"大哉,堯之爲君也,巍巍乎! 唯天爲大,唯堯則①之。蕩蕩乎②! 民無能名焉。巍巍乎! 其有成功③也。焕④乎! 其有文章⑤!"

[注释]

①则:效法。一说"则天"乃指任贤使能,无为而治。 ②荡荡乎:广而远,言其大。 ③成

功:朱子曰:"成功,事业也。"　④焕:光明的样子。　⑤文章:指礼乐法度。

[白话文]

孔子说:"伟大啊!像尧舜这样的君王,多么崇高啊!天是最高大的,只有尧舜能效法天道,泽被天下,那样的广远啊!人们都不知如何称颂他。他所成就的功业,多么崇高而伟大;他所制订的礼乐法度,多么光明而美好!"

[英译文]

The Master said, "Great indeed was Yao as a sovereign! How majestic was he! It is only Heaven that is grand, and only Yao corresponded to it. How vast was his virtue! The people could find no name for it. How majestic was he in the works which he accomplished! How glorious in the elegant regulations which he instituted!"

8—20

舜有臣五人①而天下治。武王曰:"予有亂臣十人②。"孔子曰:"才難③,不其然乎?唐虞之際④,於斯爲盛。有婦人焉,九人而已。三分天下有其二⑤,以服事殷。周之德,其可謂至德也已矣。"

[注释]

①舜有臣五人:相传有禹、稷、契、皋陶、伯益五人为舜之臣而天下大治。　②乱臣十人:乱臣,即治世之能臣。十人,乃周公旦、召公奭、太公望、毕公、荣公、大颠、闳夭、散宜生、南宫适,还有一位女性——武王后、太公女邑姜。　③才难:人才难得。④唐虞之际:唐,尧号。唐虞之际,即尧舜之际,指尧舜以下,不是尧舜之间。　⑤三分天下有其二:中国上古行政区划九州。(《春秋传》:"文王率商之畔国以事纣。"盖天下归文王者六州,荆、梁、雍、豫、徐、扬也,唯青、兖、冀尚属纣耳。)

[白话文]

虞舜有贤臣五人而天下大治。武王说:"我有治臣十人。"孔子说:"古人讲'人才难得',不是吗?尧舜之际及周,人才可算多的了。但周武王十个治臣中,一个是女性,其余的也只有九人而已。在周武王前期,文王已占有三分之二的天下,仍然以臣礼事殷王,可说是至德了(正因周之德厚,得道多助,能得治臣相辅)。"

[英译文]

Shun had five ministers, and the empire was well governed. King Wu said, "I have ten able ministers." Confucius said, "Is not the saying that talents are difficult to find. True? Only when the dynasties of Tang and Yu met, were they more abundant than in this of Zhou, yet there was a woman among them. The able ministers were no more than nine men. King Wen possessed two of the three parts of the empire, and with those he served the dynasty of Yin. The virtue of the house of Zhou may be said to have reached the highest point indeed."

8 - 21

　　子曰:"禹①,吾無間然②矣。菲③飲食,而致孝乎鬼神;惡④衣服,而致美乎黻冕⑤;卑宮室,而盡力乎溝洫⑥。禹,吾無間然矣。"

[注释]

　　①禹:即夏禹。原为上古时代夏后氏部落领袖,又叫大禹、戎禹。治水有功,且大公无私,故舜让位给他。接着,由他的儿子夏启建立了中国历史上第一个奴隶制王朝——夏朝。　　②间然:间,训为"非"。然,犹"焉",语助词。间然,非议的。　　③菲:菲薄,量少,质次。　　④恶:劣。⑤黻冕:黻,读 fú。黻冕,礼服礼帽。　　⑥沟洫:洫,读 xù。沟洫,农田中的水道。

[白话文]

　　孔子说:"大禹,我对他是无可非议的。他自己的饮食量少而质差,好喝好吃的却尽孝敬鬼神;平时穿的衣服粗劣,而祭祀用的礼服礼帽却讲究华美;自己住的宫室很简陋,却尽力于兴修农田沟渠。大禹啊! 我对他真正没有可说不好的。"

[英译文]

The Master said, "I can find no flaw in the character of Yu. He used himself coarse food and drink, but displayed. The utmost filial piety towards the spirits. His ordinary garments were poor, but he displayed the utmost elegance in his sacrificial cap and apron. He lived in a low mean house, but expended all his strength on the ditches and water channels. I can find nothing like a flaw in Yu."

子罕第九

本篇凡三十章(9－1～9－30)。

9－1

子罕言利與命,與仁^①。

[注释]

①罕言利与命,与仁:罕言,少言、不多说。《论语》全部单一谈到"利"、单一谈到"命"的各不出十章,单谈到"仁"的将近六十章,其中讲到"利"、"命"的关系,以及怎样来处理其关系者仅三四章;讲到"利"与"仁"的关系者也很少;只是讲"利"与"义"的关系者略多一些而已。

[白话文]

孔子很少谈到利与命、利与仁的关系,以及怎样来对待、处理其中的关系问题。

[英译文]

The subjects of which the Master seldom spoke were: profitableness, and also the appointments of Heaven, and perfect virtue.

9－2

達巷黨人^①曰:"大哉孔子,博學而無所成名。"子聞之,謂門弟子曰:"吾何執^②? 執御乎? 執射乎? 吾執御矣。"

[注释]

①达巷党人:达巷,小地名。党,按《周礼》五百家为一党。故达巷党是一个乡以下的居民区。党人,即乡党之人。 ②执:指专门执掌(的事项、专业)。

[白话文]

达巷这个地方的人说:"孔子真伟大啊! 他博学多才,可惜没有一项成名的专长。"孔子听后对学生们讲:"我该专做哪一项呢? 专门驾车,还是专门射箭? 我看我还是专门驾车吧!"

[英译文]

A man of the village of Da-xiang said, "Great indeed is the philosopher Kong! His learning is extensive, and yet he does not render his name famous by any particular thing." The Master heard the observation, and said to his disciples, "What shall I practise? Shall I practise charioteering, or shall I practise archery? I will practise charioteering."

9－3

子曰:"麻冕^①,禮也,今也純^②,儉^③,吾從衆。拜下^④,禮也,今拜乎上,泰^⑤也,雖違衆,吾從下。"

[注释]

①麻冕:黑色礼帽。用麻线两千四百缕,细密难成,不如用丝绸做省约。 ②纯:丝。
③俭:俭省。 ④拜下:古时臣见君先在堂下跪拜,登堂后再拜。 ⑤泰:骄慢。

[白话文]

孔子说:"祭祀时戴黑麻布做成的礼帽,这是古礼,但这种帽用很多黑麻线制成,工艺复杂,现在改用丝绸做成,比较俭省。我随从大家。臣见君,先堂下跪拜,登堂后再拜,这是古礼。现改为只在堂上拜见,显得为臣者傲慢。虽然有违大家的做法,但我仍然要按古礼跪拜。"

[英译文]

The Master said, "The linen cap is that prescribed by the rules of ceremony, but now a silk one is worn. It is economical, and I follow the common practice. The rules of ceremony prescribe the bowing below the hall, but now the practice is to bow only after ascending it. That is arrogant. I continue to bow below the hall, though I oppose the common practice."

9-4

子絶①四:毋②意③,毋必④,毋固,毋我。

[注释]

①绝:完全杜绝。 ②毋:不要。 ③意:怀疑、臆想。 ④必:成见。

[白话文]

孔子从来就杜绝下列四种思维:凭空猜想、臆测;事先有成见;固执己见;掺有私己之心。

[英译文]

There were four things from which the Master was entirely free. He had no foregone conclusions, no arbitrary predetermination, no obstinacy, and no egoism.

9-5

子畏①於匡②。曰:"文王既没,文③不在兹④乎? 天之將喪斯文也。後死者⑤不得與於斯文也。天之未喪斯文也。匡人其如予何?"

[注释]

①畏:朱子曰:"畏者,有戒心之谓。"《庄子·秋水》以"围"为说。《孔子世家》有"拘焉五日"、弟子惧等说。似宜以"围"字解较妥。 ②匡:地名,今河南省长垣县西南。春秋时为郑邑。鲁定公八年,鲁师郑,季氏家臣阳虎曾暴于匡。定公十三年,孔子过匡,匡人误认为阳虎而兵围五

日,此即所谓"子畏于匡"事。 ③文:《集注》曰:"道之显者谓之文,盖礼乐制度之谓。"孔子所说的文,就是指周文王时期设立的礼乐典章传统文化。 ④兹:此的意思。 ⑤后死者:孔子自谓,对文王而言。

[白话文]

孔子和弟子们经匡地,被匡人误认为是阳虎而被围困。弟子有惧怕,孔子对他们说:"周文王已经死了,传统的礼乐典章文化不是都在我这里吗? 如果天将要毁灭周之礼乐典章传统文化,那么也不会让我闻而知之;如果天意不想毁灭传统文化,那匡人又能将我怎么样呢?"

[英译文]

The Master was put in fear in Kuang. He said, "After the death of King Wen, was not the cause of truth lodged here in me? If Heaven had wished to let this cause of truth perish, then I, a future mortal, should not have got such a relation to that cause. While Heaven does not let the cause of truth perish, what can the people of Kuang do to me?"

9-6

大宰①問於子貢曰:"夫子聖者與! 何其多能也?"子貢曰:"固天縱之將聖,又多能也。"子聞之曰:"大宰知我乎? 吾少也賤,故多能鄙事。君子多乎哉? 不多也。"牢②曰:"子云:'吾不試③,故藝。'"

[注释]

①大宰:即太宰,官名。考其人可能是吴国太宰嚭。据《左传·哀公七年》《左传·哀公十二年》,鲁哀公三次适吴,子贡与太宰嚭语凡三次。《说苑·善说篇》亦载子贡与太宰嚭论孔子。②牢:姓琴,名牢,又名子张,字子开,卫国人,孔子的弟子。 ③试:用的意思。

[白话文]

(吴)太宰问子贡说:"你的老师是圣人吧! 不然,怎会如此多才多艺呢?"子贡说:"这本来就是天意,要他成为圣人,又让他多才多艺。"孔子听了后说:"太宰真的知道我吗? 我小的时候微贱,所以能做很多粗俗之事。君子要如此多能吗? 不用多的。"琴牢说:"孔子曾经说:'我因为未被社会所重用,所以学了许多技艺。'"

[英译文]

A high officer asked Zi-gong, "May we not say that your master is a sage? How various is his ability!" Zi-gong said, "Certainly Heaven has endowed him unlimitedly. He is about a sage. And, moreover, his ability is various." The Master heard of the conversation and said, "Does the high officer know me? When I was young, my condition was low, and therefore I acquired my ability in many things, but they were mean matters. Must the superior man have such variety of ability? He does not need variety of ability." Qin-lao said, "The Master said, 'Having no official employment, I acquired many arts.'"

9-7

子曰:"吾有知乎哉? 無知也。有鄙夫①問於我,空空如也;我叩②其兩端而竭焉。"

[注释]

①鄙夫:没知没识者。 ②叩:反问。

[白话文]

孔子说:"我很有知识吗? 没有。有个乡下人来问我,对他的问题我也不知如何回答。但我问清楚事情的正反面,尽我所知答复他。"

[英译文]

The Master said, "Am I indeed possessed of knowledge? I am not knowing. But if a mean person, who appears quite empty-like, ask anything of me, I set it forth from one end to the other, and exhaust it."

9-8

子曰:"鳳鳥①不至,河不出圖②,吾已矣乎!"

[注释]

①凤鸟:古传说中的神鸟,据说舜时来仪,文王时鸣于岐山。 ②河不出图:相传伏羲时黄河中有龙马负图而出。据说只有圣王出世时,才有此祥瑞之兆。

[白话文]

孔子说:"象征祥瑞的凤鸟不来,黄河的龙马也不背着河图出现,表示圣王不在了。我想推行的大道大概也没希望了。"

[英译文]

The Master said, "The Feng bird does not come; the river sends forth no map—it is all over with me!"

9-9

子見齊衰①者、冕衣裳②者與瞽③者。見之,雖少,必作④;過之,必趨⑤。

[注释]

①齐衰:丧服。 ②冕衣裳:冕,冠,帽。衣,上服。裳,下服。这样穿戴的人即做官者。

③瞽：盲人。　④作：起立。　⑤趋：快走。

[白话文]

　　孔子见到穿丧服的人、穿戴官冕盛服的官员，以及遇见盲人，即使是少年，也必定站起来表示敬意。要是经过他们身旁，也一定快走几步表示敬意。

[英译文]

When the Master saw a person in a mourning dress, or any one with the cap and upper and lower garments of full dress, or a blind person, on observing them approaching, though they were younger than himself, he would rise up, and if he had to pass by them, he would do so hastily.

9－10

　　颜渊喟然嘆曰：“仰之彌①高，鑽之彌堅。瞻之在前，忽焉在後！夫子循循然善誘人，搏我以文，約我以禮，欲罷不能。既竭吾才，如有所立卓爾②，雖欲從之，末由也已③！”

[注释]

　　①弥：更加。　②卓尔：高耸的样子。　③末由也已：无路可循。

[白话文]

　　颜渊叹了一声说：“夫子的道德学问越仰望它，越显得高不可及；越钻研它，越显得坚硬不能深入。看它好像就在前头，忽然间又似在后面。夫子循序渐进地引导我们，教我们广泛地学习典籍文章，用礼节来规范我们的行为，我们即使想歇下来也歇不下来。我的才力心思都用尽了，而夫子之道依然高耸地竖立在我的前面，我想要追及，却又无路可循！”

[英译文]

Yan-yuan, in admiration of the Master's doctrines, sighed and said, "I looked up to them, and they seemed to become more high; I tried to penetrate them, and they seemed to become more firm; I looked at them before me, and suddenly they seemed to be behind. The Master, by orderly method, skillfully leads men on. He enlarged my mind with learning, and taught me the restraints of propriety. When I wish to give over the study of his doctrines, I cannot do so, and having exerted all my ability, there seems something to stand right up before me; but though I wish to follow and lay hold of it. I really find no way to do so."

9－11

　　子疾病①，子路使門人爲臣②，病間③曰：“久矣哉，由之行詐也！無臣而爲有臣,吾誰欺?欺天乎?且予與其死於臣之手也,無寧死於二三子之手乎!且予縱不得大葬④,予死於道路乎?"

[注释]

①子疾病:据《四书广解》称,孔子在回鲁途中病,且病势严重。 ②子路使门人为臣:臣,指家臣。当时孔子已去职,无家臣。子路为尊敬孔子,安排几位同学充作家臣。 ③病间:病情稍瘥。 ④大葬:卿大夫的葬礼。

[白话文]

孔子在返鲁的途中得了病,且病情严重。子路安排了几位同学当孔子的家臣。孔子的病情稍瘥,他说:"我没有家臣已经很久了吧?仲由(子路)却在弄虚作假。我没有家臣,装作有家臣,我欺骗谁?欺天吗?再说,我与其死在家臣的手上,倒不如死在学生们手上。纵使我死后得不到卿大夫的大葬礼,难道我就会死在路上不成?"

[英译文]

The Master being very ill, Zi-lu wished the disciples to act as ministers to him. During a remission of his illness, he said, "Long has the conduct of You been deceitful! By pretending to have ministers when I have them not, whom should I impose upon? Should I impose upon Heaven? Moreover, than that I should die in the hands of ministers, is it not better that I should die in the hands of you, my disciples? And though I may not get a great burial, shall I die upon the road?"

9-12

子貢曰:"有美玉於斯,韞匵①而藏諸②?求善賈③而沽④諸?"子曰:"沽之哉!沽之哉!我待賈者也!"

[注释]

①韞匵:韫,读 yùn,收藏。匵,读 dú,盒子。韫匵,即收藏在盒子里。 ②诸:本句二"诸"字,均作"之乎"。 ③贾:读 gǔ,买卖称贾。贾人,即买卖人——商人。贾,又作"价"字解。 ④沽:买或卖。买,沽酒、买酒;卖,如待价而沽。

[白话文]

子贡说:"有一块美玉在这里,把它收藏在盒子里呢,还是找个好价钱卖掉它呢?"孔子说:"卖掉,卖掉!我正等待着好的买卖人来买呀!"

[英译文]

Zi-gong said, "There is a beautiful gem here. should I lay it up in a case and keep it? or should I seek for a good price and sell it?" The Master said, "Sell it!

Sell it! But I would wait for one to offer the price."

9 – 13

子欲居九夷①。或曰:"陋,如之何?"子曰:"君子居之②,何陋之有!"

[注释]

①九夷:古代中国东部各民族称"东夷"。《后汉书·东夷列传》还列出九种夷族的名称。也有人根据刘宝楠《论语正义》,认为九夷即现在的朝鲜。　②君子居之:刘氏《论语正义》指君子居之即箕子〔参阅微子篇第一章(18-1)中孔子所称的"殷有三仁"〕居之,不是孔子自称君子居之。

[白话文]

孔子想到九夷去。有人说:"那个地方偏僻、落后,怎么好去居住呢?"孔子说:"君子居住的地方,用道德、礼仪去感化,还有什么简陋、不懂礼仪呢?"

[英译文]

The Master was wishing to go and live among the nine wild tribes of the east. Some one said, "They are rude. How can you do such a thing?" The Master said, "If a superior man dwelt among them, what rudeness would there be?"

9 – 14

子曰:"吾自衛反魯①,然後樂正,《雅》、《頌》,各得其所。"

[注释]

①自卫反鲁:反,同"返"。孔子于鲁哀公十一年冬,经卫返鲁。

[白话文]

孔子说:"我从卫国返回鲁国后,把《诗》的乐曲进行整理,使《雅》乐和《颂》乐恢复原来应有的地位。"

[英译文]

The Master said, "I returned from Wei to Lu, and then the music was reformed, and the pieces in the Royal songs and praise songs all found their proper places."

9 – 15

子曰:"出則事公卿,入則事父兄,喪事不敢不勉,不爲酒困;何有於我哉?"

[白话文]

孔子说:"出仕朝廷,尽其忠勤以事公卿;回到家中,尽其孝悌以事父兄。遇到丧事,不敢不认真去办理,使它合乎礼制;喝酒有节制,以免损身废事。这些事对我来说,又有什么困难呢?"

[英译文]

The Master said, "Abroad, to serve the high ministers and nobles; at home, to server one's father and elder brothers; in all duties to the dead, not to dare not to exert one's self; and not to be overcome of wine—which one of these things do I attain to?"

9-16

子在川上曰:"逝①者如斯夫②! 不舍晝夜。"

[注释]

①逝:过去。　②夫:助词,用在句末表示感叹。

[白话文]

孔子站在河边岸上,感叹地说:"时光就像流水一样过去,不分昼夜地流去。"

[英译文]

The Master standing by a stream, said, "It passes on just like this, not ceasing day or night."

9-17

子曰:"吾未見好德如好色者也①。"

[注释]

①吾未见好德如好色者也:《史记》:"孔子居卫,灵公与夫人(南子)同车,使孔子为次乘,招摇市过之。"孔子出此言。

[白话文]

孔子说:"我没有看见过爱好美德像爱好美色那样真切的人。"

[英译文]

The Master said, "I have not seen one who loves virtue as he loves beauty."

9-18

子曰:"譬如爲山,未成一簣①,止,吾止也! 譬如平地,雖覆一簣,進,吾往也!"

[注释]

①簣:读 kuì,盛土的竹筐。"功亏一篑"的成语就是本章所说的差了一筐子十而不能完成造山

[白话文]

孔子说:"譬如用土来堆山,只差了一筐土而没有去完成它,停了下来,那是我自己要停下来的啊! 又譬如要填平一块地,虽然刚倒下一筐土,而我继续进行填覆,那也是我自己要进行下去的。"

[英译文]

The Master said, "The prosecution of learning may be compared to what may happen in raising a mound. If there want but one basket of earth to complete the work, and I stop, the stopping is my own work. It may be compared to throwing down the earth on the level ground, Though but one basketful is thrown at a time, the advancing with it is my own going forward."

9–19

子曰:"語之而不惰者,其回也與!"

[白话文]

孔子说:"告诉他以后,能够照我的话去做而不懈怠的人,只有颜回(子渊)吧!"

[英译文]

The Master said, "Never flagging when I set forth anything to him—ah! That is Hui."

9–20

子謂顏淵曰:"惜乎! 吾見其進也,吾未見其止也!"

[白话文]

孔子提到已死去的颜渊,感叹地说:"多可惜呀! 我只看到他不断地前进,从没有看到他停止下来的时候。"

[英译文]

The Master said of Yan-yuan, "Alas! I saw his constant advance. I never saw him stop in his progress."

9–21

子曰:"苗而不秀者,有矣夫! 秀而不實者,有矣夫①!"

[注释]

①苗而不秀者,有矣夫! 秀而不实者,有矣夫:秀,指开花吐穗。实,指结实。本章是孔子痛惜颜渊之喻义,也泛指任何学习是否有成,贵在自勉。

[白话文]

　　孔子说:"庄稼发苗不吐穗扬花者,是有的;抽穗后不结实的,也是有的。"

[英译文]

　　The Master said, "There are cases in which the blade springs, but the plant does not go on to flower! There are cases where it flowers, but no fruit is subsequently produced."

9－22

　　子曰:"後生可畏,焉知來者之不如今也? 四十、五十而無聞焉,斯亦不足畏也已。"

[白话文]

　　孔子说:"年轻人可畏,怎么能料到他们的将来不如今天的这辈人呢? 不过,如果到四五十岁还没有什么成就的话,这也没有什么可畏的了。"

[英译文]

　　The Master said, "A youth is to be regarded with respect. How do we know that his future will not be equal to our present? If he reach the age of forty or fifty, and has not made himself heard of then indeed, he will not be worth being regarded with respect."

9－23

　　子曰:"法語之言①,能無從乎? 改之爲貴。巽與之言②,能無説乎? 繹③之爲貴。説而不繹,從而不改,吾末如之何也已矣。"

[注释]

　　①法语之言:清楚、严正的告诫。　②巽与之言:巽,读 xùn,同"逊"。巽与之言,委婉的规劝。　③绎:读 yì,抽出或理出事物的头绪来,寻绎、抽绎。

[白话文]

　　孔子说:"正言厉色的告诫,能不接受吗? 但要改过才是最重要的;委婉劝导的话,固然悦耳,但要寻出个头绪来、抽绎出话中的意思,才是可贵的。光感觉话的好听而不去寻绎其意思,光是口头上顺从而不切实改过,那么,我也对他无可奈何了。"

[英译文]

　　The Master said, "Can men refuse to assent to the words of strict admonition? But it is reforming the conduct because of them which is valuable. Can men refuse to be pleased with words of gentle advice? But it is unfolding their aim which is valuable. If a man be pleased with these words, but does not unfold their aim, and assents to those, but does not reform his conduct, I can really do nothing with him."

9 - 24

子曰："主忠信，毋友不如己者，過則勿憚改。"

[注释]

此章重出，参阅学而篇第八章(1-8)。

9 - 25

子曰："三軍可奪帥也，匹夫^①不可奪志也。"

[注释]

①匹夫：一个人。泛指平常人。

[白话文]

孔子说："三军之勇在人多，仍然可以把他们的主帅夺取过来。一个平常人只要能够坚定自己的意志，谁也动摇不了他。"

[英译文]

The Master said, "The commander of the forces of a large state may be carried off, but the will of even a common man cannot be taken from him."

9 - 26

子曰："衣敝縕袍^①，與衣狐貉^②者立，而不恥者，其由也與？'不忮不求，何用不臧^③？'"子路終身誦之。子曰："是道也，何足以臧？"

[注释]

①衣敝縕袍：衣，动词，穿的意思。敝，破烂。縕，棉絮。敝縕袍，褴褛棉袍。　②衣狐貉：穿狐貉(读háo)皮裘。　③不忮不求，何用不臧：句出《诗经·卫风·雄雉》。忮，读zhì，嫉妒。求，贪求。臧，善、好。不忮不求，何用不臧，乃谓不嫉妒，不贪求，有何不好？

[白话文]

孔子说："穿着褴褛的棉袍，与穿狐貉皮裘的人站在一起，不感到难为情，那只有由(子路)啊！《诗经》说：'不嫉妒，不贪求，那有什么不好呢？'"子路听后，便经常念这诗句。孔子说："这仅仅是做人的起码道理，怎能算是足够的好呢？"

[英译文]

The Master said, "Dressed himself in a tattered robe quilted with hemp, yet standing by the side of men dressed in furs, and not ashamed—ah! It is You who is equal to this! 'He dislikes none, he covets nothing; what can he do but what is good?'"Zi-lu kept continually repeating these words of the ode, when the Master said,"Those things are by no means sufficient to constitute excellence."

9－27

子曰:"歲寒,然後知松柏之後彫①也。"

[注释]

①彫:"凋"的异体字。凋谢、凋落、凋零。

[白话文]

孔子说:"寒冬天冷时,更令人体会到松柏之坚贞。它们是在所有草木中最后凋零的。"

[英译文]

The Master said,"When the year becomes cold, then we know how the pine and the cypress are the last to lose their leaves."

9－28

子曰:"知者不惑,仁者不憂,勇者不懼。"

[白话文]

孔子说:"有智慧的人不会迷惑;有仁德的人不会有忧愁;勇敢的人不会有畏惧。"

[英译文]

The Master said,"The wise are free from perplexities; the virtuous from anxiety; and the bold from fear."

9－29

子曰:"可與共學,未可與適道①;可與適道,未可與立②;可與立,未可與權③。"

[注释]

①适道:向往,追求道。 ②与立:立,守道。与立,一起坚定不移于道。 ③权:秤锤,用以权衡轻重。

[白话文]

孔子说:"有人可以和他一起学道,未必可以和他一起去追求道;可以和他一起追求道,未必可以和他一起坚定不移地立于道;可以和他一起立于道,未必可以和他一起用道来权衡轻重。"

[英译文]

The Master said, "There are some with whom we may study in common, but we shall find them unable to go along with us principles. Perhaps we may go on with them to principles, but we shall find them unable to get established in those along with us. Or if we may get so established along with them, we shall find them unable to weigh occurring events along with us."

9-30

"唐棣之華,偏其反而①。豈不爾思?室是遠而。"② 子曰:"未之思也,夫何遠之有?"

[注释]

①唐棣之华,偏其反而:逸诗诗句,《诗经》无载。唐棣,一树名,无考。华,即花。偏其反而,一说是花翩翩摇动,一说是同株上的花向背而开。现从后说。　②孔子引此诗句,说明"我欲仁,斯仁至矣"。参阅述而篇第二十九章(7-29)。

[白话文]

古诗有这样的诗句:"唐棣树的花呀,向背地开着,难道我不想念你吗?只因你住得太远。"孔子说:"那是没有去想,有什么远呢?"

[英译文]

How the flowers of the aspen-plum flutter and turn! Do I not think of you? But your house is distant. The Master said, "It is the want of thought about it, how is it distant?"

乡党第十

　　本篇旧说凡一章，但各版本又按事类分成若干节，多少不等。今从《集注》所用原版，分十八个章节，其中一节重出。本篇凡十八章（10—1～10—18）。

10-1

孔子於鄉黨①,恂恂②如也,似不能言者。其在宗廟、朝廷,便便③言,唯謹爾。

[注释]

①乡党:即乡里。 ②恂恂:恂,读 xún。恂恂,诚实、恭谨的样子。 ③便便:朱注:"便便,辩也。"

[白话文]

孔子在自己乡里的时候,容貌温恭信实,好像不会说话似的。而在宗庙和朝廷上,却将要说的话都明白地表达出来,只是比较谨慎罢了。

[英译文]

Confucius, in his village, looked simple and sincere, and as if he were not able to speak. When he was in the prince's ancestorial temple, or in the court, he spoke minutely on every point, but cautiously.

10-2

朝,與下大夫①言,侃侃如也②。與上大夫言,誾誾如也③。君在,踧踖④如也,與與如也⑤。

[注释]

①大夫:官名,三卿(司徒、司马、司空)即上大夫(卿大夫);三卿以下为下大夫。 ②侃侃如也:说话时和和气气,从容不迫。 ③誾誾如也:誾,读 yín。说话时态度恭敬、中正,和悦而诤。 ④踧踖:踧,读 cù。踖,读 jí。敬畏,有些紧张不安。 ⑤与与如也:仪态合适、合礼。

[白话文]

孔子在朝廷上和下大夫谈话时,总是和和气气,说话也从容不迫;和上大夫谈话,态度恭敬、端庄中正,有诤言,态度也是委婉、和悦的;君主临朝时,又显得敬畏,虽有些紧张,但仪态仍然合适、合礼。

[英译文]

When he was waiting at court, in speaking, with the great officers of the lower grade, he spoke freely, but in a straight forward manner; in speaking with those of the higher grade, he did so blandly, but precisely. When the ruler was present, his manner displayed respectful uneasiness; it was grave, but self-possessed.

10－3

君召使擯①，色勃②如也。足躩③如也，揖所與立，左右手，衣前後，襜④如也。趨進，翼如⑤也。賓退，必復命，曰："賓不顧⑥矣。"

[注释]

①擯：同"儐"。迎接宾客者。　②勃：变色。这里指变色起敬。　③躩：读 jué，快步行走。④襜：读 chān，衣服摇动的样子。　⑤翼如：快步走而小心翼翼，谨慎的样子。　⑥宾不顾：将宾客送到门外之后，均言"宾不顾"。

[白话文]

国君派孔子做接待来宾的傧相。他的面色就显得庄敬认真，走起路来脚步快而慎重，向其他站在一起的同为傧者举左、右手，向两边拱手作揖，他穿的衣服前后摇动着。他在庭上快步走动，小心翼翼地接待着宾客。等送走宾客之后，一定回来复命，向君主报告说："宾客已离开出门了。"

[英译文]

When the prince called him to employ him in the reception of a visitor, his countenance appeared to change, and his legs to move forward with difficulty. He inclined himself to the other officers among whom he stood, moving his left or right arm, as their position required, but keeping the skirts of his robe before and behind evenly adjusted. He hastened forward, with his arms like the wings of a bird. When the guest had retired, he would report to the prince, "The visitor is not turning round any more."

10－4

入公門，鞠躬①如也，如不容。立不中門，行不履閾②。過位③，色勃如也，足躩如也，其言似不足者。攝齊升堂④，鞠躬如也，屏氣似不息者。出，降一等，逞顏色，怡怡如也⑤。沒階，趨進，翼如也。復其位，踧踖如也⑥。

[注释]

①鞠躬：将身子弯着一些。公门虽高大而若不容，这是敬之至。　②行不履阈：阈，读 yù，门坎。行不履阈，走路不踏门坎。　③过位：位，指君主的位置。君虽未在座，但经过其位仍应敬之，不可轻慢。　④摄齐升堂：摄齐，撩起衣服的下摆。升堂，进入君主日常听政议事之堂。撩衣，以策跨步安全。　⑤逞颜色，怡怡如也：逞，放、开。逞颜色，脸色放松，舒缓而开颜。怡怡如也，显示出和悦的样子。　⑥复其位：指再回到堂下自己的位置。

[白话文]

孔子进入朝廷的大门时，弯着身子，好像公门低矮容不下他似的，站立时不敢站在门正中。行走时脚不踩在门坎上。经过君王平时座位时,脸色立即庄重起来,加快了脚步;讲话放低声音,好像说不出来似的。撩起衣服下摆,走进大堂,恭敬地弯着腰,屏着气,好像没有呼吸似的。当他出大堂,走下一级台阶,脸色就放松起来,显出和悦的样子。走完台阶,小心翼翼,赶快走。再回到自己的位置时,又显得有些急促不安的样子。

[英译文]

When he entered the palace gate, he seemed to bend his body, as if were not sufficient to admit him, when he was standing, he did not occupy the middle of the gate-way; when he passed in or out, he did not tread upon the threshold. When he was passing the vacant place of the prince, his countenance appeared to change, and his legs to bend under him, and his words came as if he hardly had breath to utter them. He ascended the reception hall, holding up his robe with both his hands, and his body bent; holding in his breath also, as if he dared not breathe. When he came out from the audience, as soon as he had descended one step, he began to relax his countenance, and had a satisfied look. When he had got to the bottom of the steps, he advanced rapidly to his place, with his arms like wings, and on occupying it, his manner still showed respectful uneasiness.

10 - 5

执圭①,鞠躬如也,如不胜②,上如揖,下如授③。勃如战色④,足蹜蹜如有循⑤。享礼,有容色⑥。私觌⑦,愉愉⑧如也。

[注释]

①圭,读 guī,一种上尖(或圆)下方的玉,诸侯举行朝会或祭祀典礼时、大夫受命出使别国时执着它。 ②如不胜:拿着圭,像力不能胜的样子。 ③上如揖,下如授:指执圭的高低。朱注云:"谓执圭平衡,手与心齐,高不过揖,卑不过授。" ④勃如战色:勃如,参阅本篇第三章(10-3)注。战色,战栗的样子。 ⑤足蹜蹜如有循:足蹜蹜,小步行走,不敢放开大步走。如有循,如循依轨道而行。 ⑥享礼,有容色:享礼,即献礼。有容色,乃指献礼之后,礼物罗列庭中,这时不再有战栗之色,态度从容。 ⑦私觌:私下相见。 ⑧愉愉:轻松愉快。

[白话文]

孔子拿着君主交给他作信物的圭玉,出使到别的邦国,在典礼上他躬着身子,恭敬谨慎,好像不胜重负似的。他拿着圭玉向上举,好像在作揖;向下摆,像是授受什么东西似的。面色凝重,小步走路,像是沿着轨道走。献礼以后,面色就舒展开来。以私人身份再与对方国君见面时,显得轻松愉快、和颜悦色。

[英译文]

When he was carrying the sceptre of his ruler, he seemed to bend his body, as if he were not able to bear its weight. He did not hold it higher than the position of the hands in making a bow, nor lower than their position in giving anything to another. His countenance seemed to change, and look apprehensive, and he dragged his feet along as if they were held by something to the ground. In presenting the presents with which he was charged, he wore a placid appearance. At his private audience, he looked highly pleased.

10 - 6

君子不以紺緅飾①，紅紫不以爲褻服②。當暑，袗絺綌，必表而出之③。緇衣，羔裘；素衣，麑裘；黃衣，狐裘④。褻裘長，短右袂。必有寝衣⑤，長一身有半。狐貉之厚以居⑥。去喪，無所不佩。非帷裳，必殺之⑦。羔裘玄冠不以弔⑧。吉月⑨，必朝服而朝。

[注释]

①君子不以绀缌饰：君子，指在上位者。绀，深青带红的颜色；缌，读 zōu，黑里带红的颜色。饰，领口、袖口滚边。不以绀缌饰，即不用这两种颜色滚领、袖口的边。　②亵服：家居时穿的衣服。下面所说的"亵裘"，亦即家居时穿的裘衣。　③袗絺绤，必表而出之：袗，读 zhěn，单衣。绤，读 chī，细葛布。绤，读 xì，粗葛布。表，上衣。表而出之，出门时穿着上衣。　④缁衣，羔裘；素衣，麑裘；黄衣，狐裘：缁，读 zī，黑色。羔裘，羊皮裘。素，白色。麑裘，小鹿皮裘。狐裘，狐皮裘。　⑤寝衣：小卧被。　⑥狐貉之厚以居：以狐貉的厚皮作坐垫。　⑦非帷裳，必杀之：帷裳，朝服，用正幅布裁剪。杀，斜裁。非帷裳，必杀之，指除了朝服，别的都斜裁缝制。　⑧羔裘玄冠不以吊：古人以白色为素服。羔裘、玄（黑色）冠是吉服，不用以吊丧。　⑨吉月：农历每月初一日。

[白话文]

君子不用深青带红或黑色带红的颜色衣料做领口、袖口的滚边，不用红、紫色做在家穿的便服。暑天，穿葛布单衣；出门，一定穿有上衣，不能赤膊。冬天，穿黑色的衣服搭配黑羊皮裘，白色衣服搭配小麑皮裘，黄衣搭配狐貉皮裘。在家穿的裘衣较长，但右边袖子要短一些，以方便做事。睡觉盖的被子，其长过身子一半。冬天，用狐貉的厚皮作坐垫。服丧期满，脱去丧服，可佩带各种饰物。除了朝服之外，其余的衣服要斜幅裁剪缝制。不能穿戴黑裘、黑帽去吊丧。每逢吉日，要穿朝服上朝。

[英译文]

The superior man did not use a deep purple, or a puce colour, in the ornaments of his dress. Even in his undress, he did not wear anything of a red or red-dish colour. In warm weather, he had a single garment either of coarse or fine texture, but he wore it displayed over an inner garment. Over lamb's fur he wore a garment of black; over fawn's fur one of white; and over fox's fur one of yellow. The fur robe of his undress was long, with the right sleeve short. He required his sleeping dress to be half as long again as his body. When staying at home, he used thick furs of the fox or the badger. When he put off mourning, he wore all the appendages of the girdle. His under-garment, except when it was required to be of the curtain shape, was made of silk cut narrow above and wide below. He did not wear lamb's fur or a black cap, on a visit of condolence. On the first day of the month, he put on his court robes, and presented himself at court.

10－7

齊①，必有明衣，布。齊，必變食，居必遷坐。

［注释］

①齐：斋戒。

［白话文］

斋戒时，必须沐浴更衣，穿明亮洁净的布制衣服；改变饮食习惯，不吃荤，不吃气味厚重的食物，不饮酒；改换居住处，和妻室分居。

［英译文］

When fasting, he thought it necessary to have his clothes brightly clean and made of linen cloth. When fasting, he thought it necessary to change his food, and also to change the place where he commonly sat in the apartment.

10－8

食不厭精，膾①不厭細。食饐②而餲③，魚餒④而肉敗，不食。色惡，不食。臭惡，不食。失飪，不食。不時，不食⑤。割不正，不食。不得其醬，不食。肉雖多，不使勝食氣。惟酒無量，不及亂。沽酒市脯⑥不食。不撤薑食。不多食。祭於公，不宿肉。祭肉不出三日。出三日，不食之矣。食不語，寢不言。雖疏食⑦、菜羹、瓜祭，必齊如也⑧。

［注释］

①脍：读 kuài，切得很细或很薄的肉或鱼。　②饐：读 yì，食物腐败变味。　③餲：读 ài，食物馊腐，饭发馊。　④餒：读 něi，鱼腐烂。　⑤不时，不食：这里指食物生产还不到收成季节的，

不吃。一说不到吃饭时不吃。　⑥脯:肉干、果干。　⑦疏食:粗粮。　⑧必齐如也:齐,同"斋"。必齐如也,必同斋祭一样恭敬。

[白话文]

粮食不嫌精细,肉脍不嫌切得细薄。饭食馊腐变味、鱼肉腐烂变质,不食。食物变色,不食。食物发臭,不食。半生不熟或煮焦了的不食。食物尚未生长成熟、不到季节的,不食。肉切割不方正、乱切一通的不食。没有适合的酱料,不食。肉虽多,其量不得比饭多。喝酒虽无限量,但不能喝醉。街上零沽的酒或肉干、菜脯,怕不清洁,不吃。姜,永远不撤,但也不宜吃得太多。祭祀分的肉,当天就分掉,不经宿。分到的祭肉,过了三天就不吃了。吃饭时,不交谈,睡觉时,不讲话。虽然吃的是粗饭、菜羹和瓜类,也要先匀出一些祭供先人,像祭祀那样恭敬,不忘先人恩德。

[英译文]

He did not dislike to have his rice finely cleaned, nor to have his minced meat cut quite small. He did not eat rice which had been injured by heat or damp and turned sour, nor fish or flesh which was gone. He did not eat what was discoloured, or what was of a bad flavour, nor anything which was ill-cooked, or was not in season. He did not eat meat which was not cut properly, nor what was served without its proper sauce. Though there might be a large quantity of meat, he would not allow what he took to exceed the due proportion for the rice. It was only in wine that he laid down no limit for himself, but he did not allow himself to be confused by it. He did not partake of wine and dried meat bought in the market. He was never without ginger when he ate. He did not eat much. When he had been assisting at the prince's sacrifice, he did not keep the flesh which he received over night. The flesh of his family sacrifice he did not keep over three days. If kept over three days, people could not eat it. When eating, he did not converse. When in bed, he did not speak. Although his food might be coarse rice and vegetable soup, he would offer a little of it in sacrifice with a grave respectful air.

10－9

席①不正,不坐。

[注释]

①席:坐席。古无椅凳,席地而坐。

[白话文]

坐席没有摆端正,不坐。

[英译文]

If his mat was not straight, he did not sit on it.

10－10

乡人飲酒,杖者^①出,斯出矣。乡人儺^②,朝服而立於阼階^③。

[注释]

①杖者:持拐杖者,指年老者。　②儺:古时民间一种迎神驱疫的赛会。　③阼阶:东面的台阶,主人站立处。

[白话文]

乡里举行酒礼时,孔子必等年长者出去了,自己才出去。乡里举行迎神驱疫的赛会时,孔子必穿着朝服,立在家庙东阶之上,表示诚敬。

[英译文]

When the villagers were drinking together, on those who carried staffs going out, he went out immediately after. When the villagers were going through their ceremonies to drive away pestilential influences, he put on his court robes and stood on the eastern steps.

10－11

問人於他邦,再拜而送之。康子饋藥,拜而受之。曰:"丘未達,不敢嘗。"

[白话文]

派往他国访问的使者,出使时要两次相拜送行。季康子派人送药来问候,孔子拜谢受之,又对来者说:"在我还未弄清楚这药的药性之前,暂时还不敢尝试它。"

[英译文]

When he was sending complimentary inquiries to any one in another state, he bowed twice as he escorted the messenger away. Ji-kang having sent him a present of physic, he bowed and received it, saying, "I do not know it, I dare not taste it."

10－12

廄焚。子退朝,曰:"傷人乎?"不問馬。

[白话文]

孔子家中的马房失火了。孔子退朝回来,说:"烧伤了人没有?"不问有没有烧伤马。

[英译文]

The stable being burned down, when he was at court, on his return he said, "Has any man been hurt?" He did not ask about the horses.

10－13

君賜食,必正席先嘗之;君賜腥①,必熟而薦之②;君賜生③,必畜之。侍食於君,君祭,先飯④。疾,君視之,東首,加朝服,拖紳⑤。君命召,不俟駕行矣。

[注释]

①腥:生的肉或鱼。　②荐之:进献给先祖,向先祖祭供。　③生:活物。　④君祭,先饭:陪君主用餐,君王行祭祀时,自己先尝一下饭。　⑤绅:朝服上的衣带。

[白话文]

国君所赐的熟食,必定摆正席位先尝,然后再以余下的分赐他人;所赐生的食物,必煮熟后献祭给先祖;所赐的活物,必定蓄养着;陪国君用餐,在国君献祭时,先替国君试尝一下饭。孔子生病,国君来探望,不能起床,必面朝东躺着,披着朝服,又将朝服的大带拖在朝服上。君有命召唤,不待仆者驾车,立即徒步前往。

[英译文]

When the prince sent him a gift of cooked meat, he would adjust his mat, first taste it, and then give it away to others. When the prince sent him a gift of undressed meat, he would have it cooked, and offer it to the spirits of his ancestors. When the prince sent him a gift of a living animal, he would keep it alive. When he was in attendance on the prince and joining in the entertainment, the prince only sacrificed. He first tasted everything. When he was ill and the prince came to visit him, he had his head to the east, made his court robes be spread over him, and drew his girdle across them. When the prince's order called him, without waiting for his carriage to be yoked, he went at once.

10－14

入太廟,每事問。

[注释]

本章重出。参阅八佾篇第十五章(3-15)。

10－15

朋友死，無所歸①。曰：“於我殯。”朋友之饋，雖車馬，非祭肉，不拜②。

[注释]

①无所归：乃指无人来收殓殡葬。　②非祭肉，不拜：朋友馈送的礼品，其祭肉是用来祭神、祭先人的。不拜，则表示敬重朋友的先人。

[白话文]

有朋友死了，没有人来收殓殡葬。孔子说：“由我来料理殡殓吧！”朋友馈送礼品给孔子，即使是车马之类的重礼，他在接受时也不拜谢；除非是祭祀的肉才拜谢，以表示对友人祭祀的先人和神表示敬畏。

[英译文]

When any of his friends died, if he had no relations who could be depended on for the necessary offices. He would say, "I will bury him." When a friend sent him a present, though it might be a carriage and horses, he did not bow. The only present for which he bowed was that of the flesh of sacrifice.

10－16

寢不尸①，居不容②。見齊衰者③，雖狎④，必變。見冕者與瞽者⑤，雖褻⑥，必以貌。凶服者式之⑦。式負版者⑧。有盛饌，必變色而作。迅雷、風烈，必變。

[注释]

①寝不尸：《集注》曰：“谓偃卧似死人也。”　②居不容：居，居家；容，容仪。居不容，指居住在家时，不讲究如祭祀或会见宾客那套礼节仪式和严肃的样子。　③齐衰者：参阅子罕篇第九章(9-9)注。　④狎：亲热(的朋友)。　⑤冕者与瞽者：参阅子罕篇第十九章(9-19)注。　⑥褻：同“狎”。　⑦凶服者式之：凶服者，服丧服的人。式，车前横木。凶服者式之，乃指坐在车上看见这种人，必俯横木而凭之，以表示敬意。　⑧负版者：负邦国图籍的人。

[白话文]

睡觉时，不挺直着四肢像个死尸；平时闲居在家，不讲究像祭祀或接见宾客那样的礼节仪式。见到服丧的人，即使平素是十分亲近的人，也一定要改变容貌以表示同情与哀悼。看见穿戴礼服礼帽的人或盲人，即使是很熟悉、亲近的人，也必定以礼相待，让开一步。如坐车在路上遇见穿丧服的人，一定要俯身扶着车前横木致意。看到负着邦国图籍的人也是这样。朋友盛宴招待，一定要动容站起来对主人表示谢意。遇迅雷、大风，变容而显不安。

126

[英译文]

In bed, he did not lie like a corpse. At home, he did not put on any formal deportment. When he saw any one in a mourning dress, though it might be an acquaintance, he would change countenance; when he saw any one wearing the cap of full dress, or a blind person, though he might be in his undress, he would salute them in a ceremonious manner. To any person in mourning he bowed forward to the crossbar of his carriage; he bowed in the same way to any one bearing the tables of population. When he was at an entertainment where there was an abundance of provisions set before him, he would change countenance and rise up. On a sudden clap of thunder, or a violent wind, he would change countenance.

10－17

升車,必正立,執綏①。車中,不內顧,不疾言②,不親指。

[注释]

　　①绥:上车的绳索。　　②疾言:高声说话。一说急促说话。

[白话文]

　　上车时,先端正站好,然后拉住车绳引身上车。坐在车内,不回头张望,不大声疾呼,不用手指东点西。

[英译文]

When he was about to mount his carriage, he would stand straight, holding the cord. When he was in the carriage, he did not turn his head quite round, he did not talk hastily, he did not point with his hands.

10－18

色斯舉矣,翔而後集①。曰:"山梁②雌雉③,時哉! 時哉!"子路共之,三嗅而作④。

[注释]

　　①色斯举矣,翔而后集:色,指鸟见人,警觉的样子。举,起飞。翔,飞翔。集,集落。　　②山梁:两岩间的石梁。　　③雉:野鸡,有的地区叫山鸡,形状似鸡。雄雉长尾美羽,多为赤铜色或深绿色;雌雉尾短,灰褐色,善走,不能久飞。　　④三嗅而作:三搏两翅而起飞离去。

[白话文]

　　孔子在山间走,看见石梁上有几只野鸡。见孔子脸色一变,野鸡惊速飞起,盘旋一阵后,又落回到了石梁上。孔子说:"山梁上的雌雉也懂得时宜啊! 也懂得时宜啊！看清楚后再飞落下来！"子路向它们拱拱手，它们便张开两翅，三搏而起，又迅速飞去了。

[英译文]

　　Seeing the countenance, it instantly rises. It flies round, and by and by settles. The Master said, "There is the hen-pheasant on the hill bridge. At its season! At its season!" Zi-lu made a motion to it. Thrice it smelt him and then rose.

先进第十一

本篇凡二十五章(11—1～11—25)。

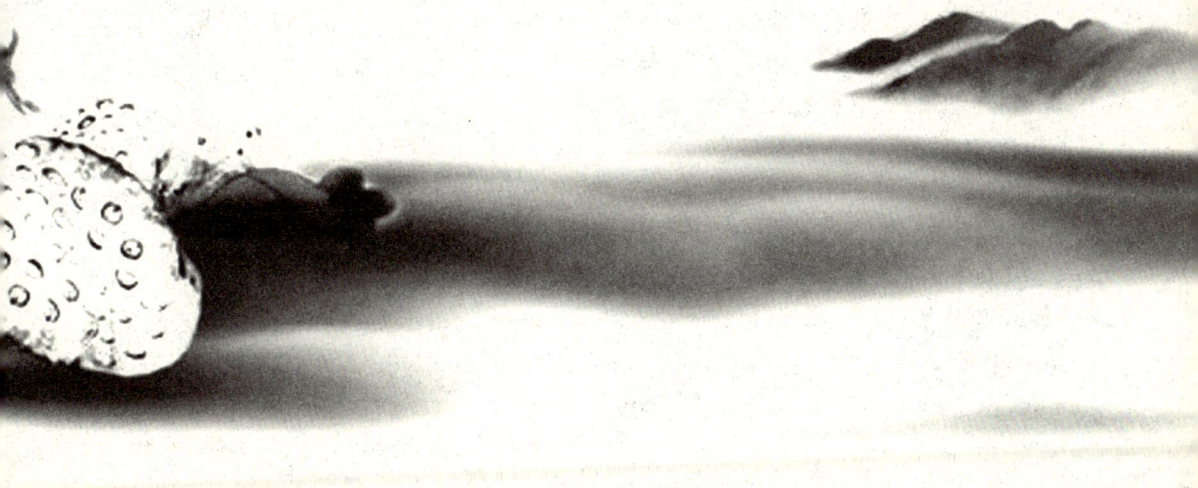

11－1

子曰：“先進於禮樂，野人也；後進於禮樂，君子也①。如用之，則吾從先進。”

[注释]

①先进于礼乐，野人也；后进于礼乐，君子也：句中“先进”、“后进”，乃指前辈、后辈；“野人”、“君子”，指在野（不仕）或在位的仕人。礼乐教化为治国的重要举措。先进之礼乐，文质相配适宜；后进之礼乐，重文轻质〔“质”和“文”参阅雍也篇第十六章(6-16)〕。当时，后进者出仕在朝，先进者反而在野，故圣人有感慨。

[白话文]

孔子说：“先辈的礼乐文质相宜，但当朝者不用他们；后辈的礼乐重文轻质，反而出仕在位。如果要我用的话，则选先辈。”

[英译文]

The Master said, "The men of former times, in the matters of ceremonies and music, were rustics, it is said, while the men of these latter times, in ceremonies and music, are accomplished gentlemen. If I have occasion to use those things, I follow the men of former times."

11－2

子曰：“從吾於陳、蔡者，皆不及門也。”德行：顏淵、閔子騫、冉伯牛、仲弓；言語：宰我、子貢；政事：冉有、季路；文學：子游、子夏。

[白话文]

孔子说：“跟随我在陈、蔡时绝粮患难的弟子，现在都不在我门下了。”杰出的弟子中，德行好的有颜渊、闵子骞、冉伯牛、仲弓；言语好的有宰我、子贡；善于政事的有冉有、季路；文学方面好的有子游、子夏。

[英译文]

The Master said, "Of those who were with me in Chen and Cai, there are none to be found to enter my door."

Distinguished for their virtuous principles and practice, there were Yan-yuan, Min Zi-qian, Ran Bo-niu, and Zhong-gong; for their ability in speech, Zai-wo and Zi-gong; for their administrative talents, Ran-you and Ji-lu; for their literary acquirements, Zi-you and Zi-xia.

11-3

子曰:"回也,非助我者也。於我言無所不说。"

[白话文]

孔子说:"颜回啊!不是对我有所助益的人。他对我所说的话无不悦服、句句听从。"

[英译文]

The Master said, "Hui gives me no assistance. There is nothing that I say in which he does not delight."

11-4

子曰:"孝哉闵子骞①! 人不間於其父母昆弟之言。"

[注释]

①闵子骞:参阅雍也篇第七章(6-7)注。《太平御览》引《说苑》云:"闵子骞母死,其父更娶,复有二子,子骞为其父御车,失辔,父持其手,衣甚单。父归,呼其后母儿,持其手,衣甚温厚……欲去。子骞曰:'母在一子寒,母去三子寒。'"故有"孝者闵子骞,一言以还母,再言三子温"句。

[白话文]

孔子说:"闵子骞真孝顺啊!他的父母兄弟都说他孝顺,与人们所称赞的没有不同。"

[英译文]

The Master said, "Filial indeed is Min Zi-qian! Other people say nothing of him different from the report of his parents and brothers."

11-5

南容①三復白圭②,孔子以其兄之子妻之。

[注释]

①南容:孔子弟子南宫适,字子容。 ②三复白圭:白圭,是一种玉器。这里是指《诗经·大雅·抑》篇中关于白圭的诗句:"白圭之玷(读 diàn,白玉上的斑点),尚可磨也,斯言之玷,不可为也。"乃言说话要谨慎。三复是虚数,言多次复诵这四句诗。

[白话文]

南容经常把《诗经》里关于白圭的诗句反复诵读。孔子觉得他这样做能谨慎自己的言论,于是把自己的侄女嫁给了他。

[英译文]

Nan-rong was frequently repeating the lines about a white sceptre-stone. Confucius gave him the daughter of his elder brother to wife.

11 – 6

季康子問："弟子孰爲好學?"孔子對曰："有顏回者好學,不幸短命死矣! 今也則亡。"

[注释]

本章与雍也篇第二章(6-2)中的字句多重复。

[白话文]

季康子问孔子:"弟子中谁最好学?"孔子回答说:"颜回最好学,不幸短命死了,如今没有这样好学的人了。"

[英译文]

Ji Kang-zi asked which of the disciples loved to learn. Confucius replied to him, "There was Yan-hui; he loves to learn. Unfortunately his appointed time was short, and he died. Now there is no one who loves to learn, as he did."

11 – 7

顏淵死,顏路①請子之車以爲之椁②。子曰："才不才,亦各言其子也。鯉③也死,有棺而無椁。吾不徒行以爲之椁。以吾從大夫之後,不可徒行也。"

[注释]

①颜路:颜渊的父亲。　②椁:读 guǒ,外棺。　③鲤:孔子的儿子,字伯鱼。死时年五十岁,当时孔子七十岁。

[白话文]

颜渊死了,他的父亲颜路请求孔子把车子卖掉,替颜渊买个外棺。孔子说:"不论才能高低,你我的儿子都一样。鲤死了,也只用内棺而没有外棺。我没有卖掉车子为儿子做外棺,而自己步行。因为我是大夫,按礼,出门时不能步行。别的大夫都坐车子,我总不能步行跟在人后跑。"

[英译文]

When Yan-yuan died, Yan-lu begged the carriage of the Master to sell and get an outer shell for his son's coffin. The Master said, "Every one calls his son, whether he has talents or has not talents. There was Li; when he died, he had a coffin but no outer shell. I would not walk on foot to get a shell for him, because, having followed in the rear of the great officers, it was not proper that I should walk on foot."

11-8

颜渊死。子曰:"噫! 天丧予! 天丧予!"

[白话文]

颜渊死了,孔子哀叹说:"唉! 老天爷要丧亡我呀! 老天爷要丧亡我呀!"

[英译文]

When Yan-yuan died, the Master said, "Alas! Heaven is destroying me! Heaven is destroying me!"

11-9

颜渊死,子哭之恸①。從者②曰:"子恸矣!"曰:"有恸乎? 非夫人③之爲恸而誰爲?"

[注释]

①恸:极悲哀,大哭。 ②从者:指随从孔子去颜渊家的弟子。 ③夫人:夫,在这里作指示词,这。夫人,就是这个人,即指颜渊。

[白话文]

颜渊死,孔子哭得非常悲哀。跟随去的弟子说:"老师哭得太悲伤了!"孔子说:"真的很悲痛啊! 我不为这个人这样悲痛,还为谁这样悲痛呢?"

[英译文]

When Yan-yuan died, the Master bewailed him exceedingly, and the disciples who were with him said, "Master, your grief is excessive." "Is it excessive?" said he, "If I am not to mourn bitterly for this man, for whom should I mourn?"

11-10

颜渊死,門人欲厚葬之。子曰:"不可。"門人厚葬之。子曰:"回也,視予猶父也。予不得視猶子也。非我也,夫二三子也。"

[白话文]

颜渊死,孔子的学生们想隆重地安葬他。孔子说:"不可。"结果,学生们仍然隆重地安葬了颜渊。孔子说:"回(颜渊)啊! 对我当父亲一样,我不能像安葬自己的儿子那样来安葬他,这不是我要违礼,是你的那些同学要这样做的呀!"

[英译文]

When Yan-yuan died, the disciples wished to give him a great funeral, and the Master said, "You may not do so." The disciples did bury in great style. The

Master said, "Hui behaved towards me as his father. I have not been able to treat him as my son. The fault is not mine; it belongs to you, my disciples."

11－11

季路問事鬼神。子曰："未能事人，焉能事鬼？"曰："敢問死。"曰："未知生，焉知死？"

［白话文］

季路(子路)问奉事鬼神的事。孔子说："还没有奉事好人，怎么能奉事鬼神？"子路又问："我大胆地再问问死的道理。"孔子说："不懂得生的道理，怎么能知道死的道理？"

［英译文］

Ji-lu asked about serving the spirits of the dead. The Master said, "While you are not able to serve men, how can you serve their spirits?"Ji-lu added, "I venture to ask about death?" He was answered, "While you do not know life, how can you know about death?"

11－12

閔子侍側，誾誾①如也。子路行行②如也。冉有、子貢侃侃③如也。子樂。"若由也，不得其死然④。"

［注释］

①誾誾：辩论的态度好。恭敬、中正、和悦的样子。　②行行：《集注》曰："行行，刚强之貌。"③侃侃：说话和和气气，从容不迫。　④若由也，不得其死然：由，即子路。不得其死然，即不得善终(后来，子路果在卫卷入一场内乱，不幸遇难)。然，语气词。

［白话文］

闵子骞侍立于孔子身旁，态度恭敬和悦；子路显得刚强的样子；冉有、子贡，表现出理壮气直、从容不迫的样子。孔子心情很快乐。但看到子路过于刚直勇敢，于是关切而忧虑地说："像由呀！真怕他将来得不到正常死亡。"

［英译文］

The disciple Min was standing by his side, looking bland and precise; Zi-lu, looking bold and soldierly; Ran-you and Zi-gong, with a free and straight forward manner. The Master was pleased. He said, "You there! He will not die a natural death."

11-13

鲁人為長府①。閔子騫曰："仍舊貫②，如之何？何以改作？"子曰："夫人③不言，言必有中。"

[注释]

①为长府：长府，鲁国的仓库名。为长府，将为长府计划改建。 ②仍旧贯：仍，依照着。贯，事例，旧例。仍旧贯，依照着老样子。 ③夫人：参阅本篇第九章(11-9)注。

[白话文]

鲁国人计划改建长府库。闵子骞说："保持原有的样子怎么样？何必要来翻修、改建？"孔子说："闵子骞这个人，平常不轻易说话，他一说话便很中肯。"

[英译文]

Some parties in Lu were going to take down and rebuild the Long treasury. Min Zi-qian said, "Suppose it were to be repaired after its old style; why must it be altered and made a new?" The Master said, "This man seldom speaks; when he does, he is sure to hit the point."

11-14

子曰："由之瑟①，奚為於丘之門②？"門人不敬子路。子曰："由也升堂矣，未入於室也。"

[注释]

①瑟：古代的一种拨弦的乐器。 ②奚为于丘之门：孔子指子路所奏有杀伐之声，岂能算出自他的门下？

[白话文]

孔子说："仲由(子路)的鼓瑟，怎么能算出自我的门下呢？"弟子因此对子路不尊敬。孔子于是又说："他的水平，已经登堂，尚未入室。也就是说，已经入门，但没有深入到更高的境界。"

[英译文]

The Master said, "What has the lute of You to do in my door?" The other disciples began not to respect Zi-lu. The Master said, "You has ascended to the hall, though he has not yet passed into the inner apartments."

11-15

子貢問："師與商也孰賢？"子曰："師也過，商也不及。"曰："然則師愈與？"子曰："過猶不及。"

[白话文]

子贡问:"师(子张)和商(子夏)谁比较好?"孔子说:"子张太过,子夏不及。"子贡说:"那么是子张胜过一些吗?"孔子说:"太过与不及,还不都一样?"

[英译文]

Zi-gong asked which of the two, Shi or Shang, was the superior. The Master said, "Shi goes beyond the due mean, and Shang does not come up to it." "Then," said Zi-gong, "the superiority is with Shi, I suppose." The Master said, "To go beyond is as wrong as to fall short."

11－16

季氏富於周公,而求也爲之聚斂而附益之。子曰:"非吾徒也。小子鳴鼓而攻之,可也。"

[白话文]

鲁卿季康子比周天子卿的周公还要富裕,而作为季氏家臣的冉求,却还在帮他想办法搜括财富。孔子说:"他不再算是我的学生了。你们可以去声讨他。"

[英译文]

The head of the Ji family was richer than the duke of Zhou had been, and yet Qiu collected his imposts for him, and increased his wealth. The Master said, "He is no disciple of mine. My little children, beat the drum and assail him."

11－17

柴①也愚,参也鲁,师②也辟,由也喭。

[注释]

①柴:高柴,字子羔,孔子弟子,比孔子小三十岁。　②师:颛孙师,即子张。参阅为政篇第十八章(2-18)注。

[白话文]

高柴比较愚笨,曾参比较迟钝,子张有些固执、偏激,子路个性鲁莽。

[英译文]

Chai is simple, Can is dull, Shi is specious, You is coarse.

11－18

子曰:"回也其庶①乎! 屡空②。赐不受命,而货殖③焉,億④则屡中。"

[注释]

①庶:近,差不多。这里指近于道。　②屡空:屡,屡次,经常。空,贫穷。　③货殖:居积生财,即现称之"做生意"。　④亿:同"臆",揣度、猜测。

[白话文]

孔子说:"颜回差不多已近于道了,可是却经常闹穷。端木赐(子贡)不安受天命而去做生意,猜测市场行情,屡次猜中,赚了钱。"

[英译文]

The Master said, "There is Hui! He has nearly attained to perfect virtue. He is often in want. Ci does not acquiesce in the appointments of Heaven, and his goods are increased by him. Yet his judgments are often correct."

11－19

子張問善人①之道。子曰:"不踐迹,亦不入於室。"

[注释]

① 善人:《集注》曰:"善人,质美而未学者也。"

[白话文]

子张问怎么作为善人。孔子说:"善人,不循着前人的路子走,但也不能进入高深的境界。"

[英译文]

Zi-zhang asked what were the characteristics of the good man. The Master said, "He does not tread in the footsteps of others, but, moreover, he does not enter the chamber of the sage."

11－20

子曰:"論篤是與,君子者乎? 色莊者乎?"

[白话文]

孔子说:"只听他的言论笃实就赞许他,是靠不住的,他究竟是个君子呢,还只是外表上庄重的人呢?"

[英译文]

The Master said, "It, because a man's discourse appears solid and sincere, we allow him to be a good man, is he really a superior man? or is his gravity only in appearance?"

11－21

子路问：“闻斯行诸①？”子曰：“有父兄在，如之何其闻斯行之？”冉有问：“闻斯行诸？”子曰：“闻斯行之。”公西华曰：“由也问：‘闻斯行诸？’子曰：‘有父兄在。’求也问：‘闻斯行诸？’子曰：‘闻斯行之。’赤也惑，敢问。”子曰：“求也退②，故进之；由也兼人③，故退之。”

[注释]

①闻斯行诸：听到这些说的，就立即去行动吗？诸，“之乎”的合音，表示疑问。　②退：做事畏缩退让。　③兼人：超过人家，一人胜两人。

[白话文]

子路问：“听到一个道理，就马上去实行吗？”孔子说：“家有父兄在，怎么听到了就立即去做呢？”冉有也问：“听到一个道理就该立即去做吗？”孔子说：“是的，应该马上去做。”公西华向孔子提问说：“由（子路）也问：‘听到一个道理就该马上去做吗？’老师回答他：‘家有父兄在。’求（冉有）也问：‘听到一个道理就该马上去做吗？’老师回答他：‘应该马上去做。’赤（公西华）实在弄不清楚为什么同一个问题有不同的回答。敢请问个明白。”孔子说：“冉有做事总是畏缩不前，所以鼓励他进取；子路好勇过人，所以要他稍加抑制，让他先问问父兄的意见，懂得谦逊，不要冒失。”

[英译文]

Zi-lu asked whether he should immediately carry into practice what he heard. The Master said, "There are your father and elder brothers to be consulted; why should you act on that principle of immediately carrying into practice what you hear?" Ran-you asked the same, whether he should immediately carry into practice what he heard, and the Master answered, "Immediately carry into practice what you hear." Gong Xi-hua said, "You asked whether he should carry immediately into practice what he heard, and you said, 'There are your father and elder brothers to be consulted.' Qiu asked whether he should immediately carry into practice what he heard, and you said, 'Carry it immediately into practice.' I, Chi, am perplexed, and venture to ask you for an explanation." The Master said, "Qiu is retiring and slow; therefore, I urged him forward. You has more than his own share of energy; therefore, I kept him back."

11－22

子畏於匡，颜渊后。子曰：“吾以女为死矣！”曰：“子在，回何敢死？”

[白话文]

孔子在匡这个地方遭到围困，解围后失散的弟子复集，颜渊最后来到。孔子说:"我以为你被杀死了!"颜渊说:"老师还在,我哪敢轻易地死了呢?"

[英译文]

The Master was put in fear in Kuang and Yan-yuan fall behind. The Master, on his rejoining him, said, "I thought you had died." Hui replied, "While you were alive, how should I presume to die?"

11-23

季子然①問:"仲由、冉求可爲大臣與?"子曰:"吾以子爲異之問,曾②由與求之問!所謂大臣者,以道事君,不可則止。今由與求也,可謂具臣矣!"曰:"然則從之者與?"子曰:"弑父與君,亦不從也。"

[注释]

①季子然:季氏子弟,何人不详。　②曾:《集注》曰:"曾,犹乃也。"即乃是的意思。这里是承上句"吾以子为异(非常)之问",原来是问由与求的事(其时,由、求二人已为季氏家臣)。

[白话文]

季子然问:"仲由(子路)、冉求(子有)可算是大臣吗?"孔子说:"我以为你要问什么特殊的问题,原来是问子路、冉求两个人。所谓大臣,应该以正道为国君做事。如果不行,就应该辞去。现在,仲由和冉求只是备位充数的臣子而已。"季子然又问:"那么他们是不是会完全听从(季氏的话)去做呢?"孔子说:"要是有大逆不道的事,如弑父弑君这类事,他们是不会听从的。"

[英译文]

Ji Zi-ran asked whether Zhong-you and Ran-qiu could be called great ministers. The Master said, "I thought you would ask about some extraordinary individuals, and you only ask about You and Qiu! What is called a great minister, is one who serves his prince according to what is right, and when he finds he cannot do so, retires. Now as to You and Qiu, they may be called ordinary ministers." Zi-ran said, "Then they will always follow their chief; will they?" The Master said, "In an act of parricide or regicide, they would not follow him."

11-24

子路使子羔爲費宰①。子曰:"賊夫人之子②!"子路曰:"有民人焉,有社稷焉,何必讀書,然後爲學?"子曰:"是故惡夫佞者③。"

[注释]

①子路使子羔为费宰:子路,其时为季氏家宰。子羔,孔子弟子,姓高,名柴,卫国人。费,季

氏的邑地。全句的意思是,子路举荐子羔到费邑去当地方首长。　②贼夫人之子:贼,害的意思。夫,代词,作"他"。全句的意思是,害他人之子。这里指子羔。　③是故恶夫佞者:恶,憎恶。佞者,能说会道的人。全句的意思是,所以憎恶强词夺理者。

[白话文]

　　子路举荐子羔当费邑宰。孔子说:"你这样不等于害了人家的儿子吗?"子路辩道:"那里有人民,也有社稷,可以学的很多,何必要读书才算是做学问呢?"孔子说:"你自以为能说会道而强词夺理,这就是我为什么厌恶没道理而喜欢强辩的人啊!"

[英译文]

　　Zi-lu got Zi-gao appointed governor of Ji. The Master said, "You are injuring a man's son." Zi-lu said, "There are common people and officers; there are the altars of the spirits of the land and grain. Why must one read books before he can be considered to have learned?" The Master said, "It is on this account that I hate your glib-tongued people."

11－25

　　子路、曾晳①、冉有、公西华侍坐。子曰:"以吾一日長乎爾,毋吾以也②!居③則曰:'不吾知也。'如或知爾,則何以哉?"

　　子路率爾④而對曰:"千乘之國,攝⑤乎大國之間,加之以師旅,因之以饑饉,由也爲之,比及⑥三年,可使有勇,且知方⑦也。"夫子哂之。

　　"求!爾何如?"對曰:"方六七十,如⑧五六十,求也爲之,比及三年,可使足民。如其禮樂,以俟君子。"

　　"赤!爾何如?"對曰:"非曰能之,願學焉。宗廟之事⑨,如會同⑩,端章甫⑪,願爲小相⑫焉。"

　　"點!爾何如?"鼓瑟希,鏗爾⑬,舍瑟而作⑭,對曰:"異乎三子者之撰。"子曰:"何傷乎?亦各言其志也。"曰:"莫春⑮者,春服既成,冠者⑯五六人,童子六七人,浴乎沂⑰,風乎舞雩⑱,詠而歸。"夫子喟然嘆曰:"吾與⑲點也!"

　　三子者出,曾晳後。曾晳曰:"夫三子者之言何如?"子曰:"亦各言其志也已矣!"曰:"夫子何哂由也?"曰:"爲國以禮,其言不讓,是故哂之。""唯求則非邦也與?""安見方六七十,如五六十,而非邦也者?""唯赤則非邦也與?""宗廟會同,非諸侯而何?赤也爲之小,孰能爲之大?"

[注释]

　　①曾晳:晳,读xī。曾晳,名点,孔子的弟子,曾参的父亲。　②毋吾以也:毋,不要。以,同

"已",止的意思。毋吾以也,不要因为我年长而拘束。　③居:平时闲居。　④率尔:不假思考,轻率,草率。　⑤摄:夹处。　⑥比及:等到。　⑦知方:方,义的意思。知方,民知道义。⑧如:或。　⑨宗庙之事:宗庙里祭祀事宜。　⑩如会同:如,与。会同,诸侯相会。　⑪端章甫:端,礼服。章甫,礼冠。　⑫小相:相,赞礼的人。小相,自谦做一个小小的司仪人。　⑬鼓瑟希,铿尔:希,同"稀"。鼓瑟希,弹瑟的节奏渐渐稀少。铿尔:铿然一声,停住。铿,读 kēng,象声词。　⑭舍瑟而作:舍瑟,推开瑟。作,站立起来。　⑮莫春:莫,同"暮"。莫春,即暮春。⑯冠者:古时一个人到二十岁就要行冠礼,算是成人了。　⑰沂:水名,在山东曲阜县南。⑱舞雩:祈雨的祭坛,在沂水之上。　⑲与:这里作"赞同"解。

[白话文]

　　子路、曾皙(点)、冉有(求)、公西华(赤)陪侍着孔子坐。孔子说:"不要因为我年纪比你们大些,你们就拘束起来。平时,你们不是常常说'没人知道我'吗? 如果有人要知道你们、任用你们,你们将怎么做呢?"

　　子路立即回答说:"假使有个千乘之国,夹在大国之间,外有入侵的军队,内又闹饥荒。让我来治理这个国家,大约等三年时间,可以使老百姓很勇敢,并且明白道义。"孔子对他笑一笑。

　　孔子又问:"求,你怎么样?"冉有回答说:"假如有六七十里见方,或五六十里见方的国土让我来治理,差不多三年时间,可以使老百姓吃饱穿暖。至于礼乐教化方面,那就得等待有才德的君子来推动了。"

　　孔子又问:"赤,你怎么样?"公西华回答说:"我不敢说我能做好什么,只是愿意学习罢了。像宗庙祭祀及诸侯盟会,我愿意穿着礼服,戴着礼帽,在那里做一个赞礼的小相。"

　　孔子又对曾皙说:"点,你怎么样?"曾皙正在鼓瑟,瑟声渐稀,"铿"的一声止住了。他推开瑟,站起来说:"我和他们三位的抱负不一样。"孔子说:"那有什么妨碍呢? 不过各人谈谈自己的志趣而已。"曾皙说:"当三月暮春,穿上春服,邀同青年五六人,孩子六七人,沐浴于沂水,再到舞雩上去,任春风吹拂,然后唱着歌回家。"孔子感叹道:"我赞同曾点的话啊!"

　　子路、冉有、公西华走了,曾皙留在后头,问孔子说:"他们三位的话说得怎么样?"孔子说:"不过各人谈谈自己的志向罢了!"曾皙说:"老师为什么对着子路笑呢?"孔子说:"治国要讲求礼让,他的讲话一点也不懂礼让,所以我笑他。"曾皙又说:"那冉有所说好像不是治理一个国家?"孔子说:"有地六七十里或五六十里见方,怎见得不算一个国家呢?"曾皙说:"那么,公西华所说的就不能算是治理一个国家了吧?"孔子说:"有宗庙祭祀,有诸侯盟会,不是国家又是什么? 如果公西华只能做一个小相,那么谁又能够做大相呢?"

[英译文]

Zi-lu, Zeng-xi, Ran-you, and Gong Xi-hua were sitting by the Master, He said to them, "Though I am a day or so older than you, do not think of that. From day to day you are saying, 'We are not known.' If some ruler were to know you, what would you like to do?"

Zi-lu hastily and lightly replied, "Suppose the case of a state of ten thousand chariots; let it be straitened between other large states; let it be suffering from invading armies; and to this let there be added a famine in corn and in all vegetables—if I were intrusted with the government of it, in three years' time I could make the people to be bold, and to recognise the rules of righteous conduct." The Master smiled at him.

Turning to Ran-you, he said, "Qiu, what are your wishes?" Qiu replied, "Suppose a state of sixty or seventy li square, or one of fifty or sixty, and let me have the government of it—in three years' time, I could make plenty to abound among the people. As to teaching them the principles of propriety, and music, I must wait for the rise of a superior man to do that."

"What are your wishes, Chi," said the Master next to Gong Xi-hua. Chi replied, "I do not say that my ability extends to these things, but I should wish to learn them. At the services of the ancestral temple, and at the audiences of the princes with the sovereign, I should like, dressed in the dark square-made robe and the black linen cap, to act as a small assistant."

Last of all, the Master asked Zeng-xi, "Dian, what are your wishes?" Dian, pausing as he was playing on his lute, while it was yet twanging, laid the instrument aside, and rose. "My wishes," he said, "are different from the cherished purposes of these three gentlemen." "What harm is there in that?" said the Master, "do you also, as well as they, speak out your wishes." Dian then said, "In this, the last month of spring, with the dress of the season all complete, along with five or six young men who have assumed the cap, and six or seven boys. I would wash in the Yi, enjoy the breeze among the rain altars, and return home singing." The Master heaved a sigh and said, "I give my approval to Dian."

The three others having gone out, Zeng-xi remained behind, and said, "What do you think of the words of these three friends?" The Master replied, "They simply told each one his wishes." Xi pursued, "Master, why did you smile at You?" He answered, "The management of a state demands the rules of propriety. His words were not humble; therefore I smiled at him." Xi again said, "But was it not a state which Qiu proposed for himself?" The reply was, "Yes;

did you ever see a territory of sixty or seventy li, or one of fifty or sixty, which was not a state?" Once more, Xi inquired, "And was it not a state which Chi proposed for himself?" The Master again replied, "Yes; who but princes have to do with ancestral temples, and with audiences but the sovereign? If Chi were to be a small assistant in these services, who could be a great one?"

颜渊第十二

本篇凡二十四章(12—1~12—24)。

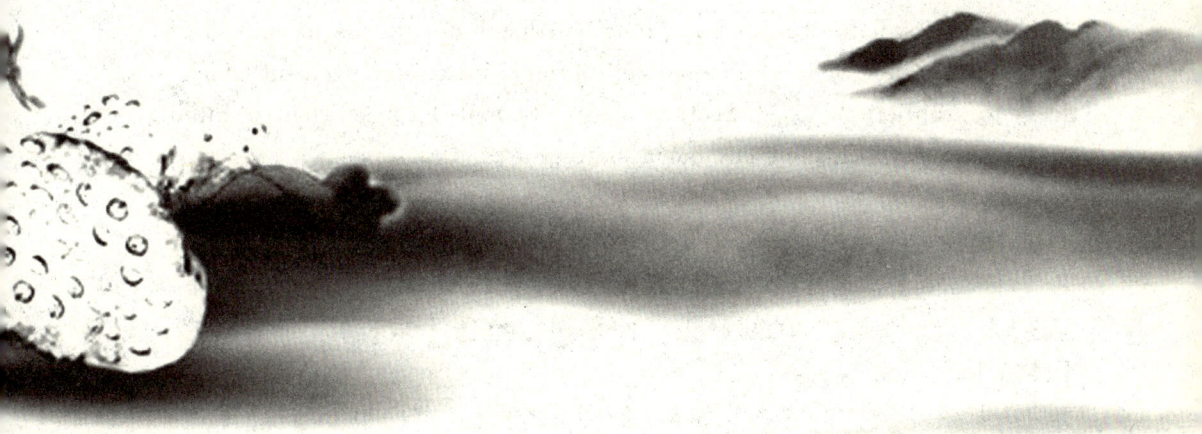

12-1

颜渊问仁。子曰:"克己復禮爲仁①。一日克己復禮,天下歸仁②焉。爲仁由己,而由人乎哉?"颜渊曰:"請問其目③。"子曰:"非禮勿視,非禮勿聽,非禮勿言,非禮勿動。"颜渊曰:"回雖不敏,請事斯語矣。"

[注释]

①克己复礼为仁:是孔子教导弟子要约束自己的言行、符合社会公德的规范、遵守各种典章制度和法规,才能实行仁德。礼,就是国家各种典章制度和行为礼仪规范、法规。随着时代的发展,礼也有所变化、发展。此即孔子回答子张问"十世可知也"的礼的沿袭和损益〔参阅为政篇第二十三章(2-23)〕。 ②归仁:归,称。仁,指实行仁德者。归仁,以仁之名称赞他。 ③目:条目,细目。这里也可认为颜渊问"具体应做些什么"。

[白话文]

颜渊问怎样才算是仁。孔子说:"能够克服自己的私欲、约束言行使之符合礼的要求,这就是仁。一旦这样做了,天下人都会称他为仁人。实践仁完全在自己,难道还要靠别人吗?"颜渊又问:"怎样具体地去实践仁?"孔子说:"不合于礼的不要看;不合于礼的不要听;不合于礼的不要讲;不合于礼的不要做。"颜渊说:"我虽然笨,但一定能遵照这些话去做。"

[英译文]

Yan-yuan asked about perfect virtue. The Master said, "To subdue one's self and return to propriety, is perfect virtue. If a man can for one day subdue himself and return to propriety. All under Heaven will ascribe perfect virtue to him. Is the practice of perfect virtue from a man himself, or is it from others?" Yan-yuan said, "I beg to ask the steps of that process." The Master replied, "Look not at what is contrary to propriety; listen not to what is contrary to propriety; speak not what is contrary to propriety; make no movement which is contrary to propriety." Yan-yuan then said, "Though I am deficient in intelligence and vigour, I will make it my business to practise this lesson."

12-2

仲弓问仁。子曰:"出門如見大賓,使民如承大祭①。己所不欲,勿施於人。在邦無怨,在家無怨。"仲弓曰:"雍雖不敏,請事斯語矣!"

[注释]

①出门如见大宾,使民如承大祭:这两句在比孔子早约百年的晋臼季曾说过:"臣闻之,出门如宾,承事如祭,仁之则也。"(参阅《春秋左氏传·僖公三十三年》)古有此语,臼季及夫子引用。

［白话文］

仲弓问："怎样才算是仁?"孔子说："出门,像要接待贵宾那样恭敬。派用老百姓做事,也要像举行重大祭祀那样敬诚。自己不喜欢的,不要施加给别人。无论出仕于诸侯的邦国或在卿大夫家做事,大家对他都没有怨言(此即敬与恕之效,亦即行仁之效)。"仲弓说："雍虽然不聪明,一定遵照这些话去做。"

［英译文］

Zhong-gong asked about perfect virtue. The Master said, "It is when you go abroad, to behave to every one as if you were receiving a great guest; to employ the people as if you were assisting at a great sacrifice; not to do to others as you would not wish done to yourself; to have no murmuring against you in the country, and none in the family." Zhong-gong said, "Though I am deficient in intelligence and vigour, I will make it my business to practise this lesson."

12 - 3

司馬牛①問仁。子曰："仁者,其言也訒②。"曰："其言也訒,斯謂之仁已乎?"子曰:"爲之難,言之得無訒乎?"

［注释］

①司马牛:孔子弟子,复姓司马,名耕(一说名犁),字子牛。他是宋桓魋(司马向魋)的弟弟,平时多言而躁。孔子对他讲的话,也是对他缺点而言。　②訒:读 rèn,言语迟钝。这里是指不要轻易说话。

［白话文］

司马牛问怎样实践仁? 孔子说："有仁德的人,说起话来有耐性,不轻易说话。"司马牛说："说话有耐性,不轻易说话。这就算是仁吗?"孔子说："因为事情说说容易,做起来往往困难,所以说话时,怎能不好好考虑而轻易出口呢?"

［英译文］

Si Ma-niu asked about perfect virtue. The Master said, "The man of perfect virtue is cautious and slow in his speech."

"Cautious and slow in his speech!" said Niu, "Is this what is meant by perfect virtue?" The Master said, "When a man feels the difficulty of doing, can he be other than cautious and slow in speaking?"

12 - 4

司馬牛問君子。子曰："君子不憂不懼①。"曰:"不憂不懼,斯謂之君子已乎？”子曰：“内省不疚^②，夫何忧何惧？”

［注释］

①君子不忧不惧：向魋作乱，司马牛常忧惧，故孔子语之以此。　②疚：惭愧、悔恨。

［白话文］

　　司马牛问：“怎样才算是个君子？”孔子说：“君子不忧愁、不恐惧。”司马牛又问：“不忧愁、不恐惧，那就算是个君子吗？”孔子说：“自我反省而内心没有惭愧、悔恨，那还有什么好忧愁、恐惧的呢？”

［英译文］

　　Si Ma-niu asked about the superior man. The Master said, "The superior man has neither anxiety nor fear." "Being without anxiety or fear!" said Niu, "Does this constitute what we call the superior man?" The Master said, "When internal examination discovers nothing wrong, what is there to be anxious about, what is there to fear?"

12－5

　　司馬牛憂曰：“人皆有兄弟，我獨亡^①。”子夏曰：“商聞之矣：‘死生有命，富貴在天。’君子敬而無失，與人恭而有禮，四海之内，皆兄弟也。君子何患乎無兄弟也？”

［注释］

①人皆有兄弟，我独亡：司马牛之兄司马向魋（桓魋）谋反，牵累及几个串通一气的兄弟，只有司马牛不参与，因而感到孤独。亡，同“无”。

［白话文］

　　司马牛忧伤地说：“人家都有兄弟，只有我没有。”子夏说：“我听人家说：‘生死由命中注定的，富贵也是由上天安排的。’一个有才德的君子，做事谨慎而没有过失，对人恭敬有礼，那么天下的人都会是你的兄弟。作为一个君子，何必担忧自己没有好兄弟呢？”

［英译文］

　　Si Ma-niu, full of anxiety, said, "Other men all have their brothers, I only have not." Zi-xia said to him, "There is the following saying which I have heard—death and life have their determined appointment; riches and honours depend upon Heaven. Let the superior man never fail reverentially to order his own conduct and let him be respectful to others and observant of propriety; then all within the four seas will be his brothers. What has the superior man to do with being distressed because he has no brothers?"

12 - 6

子張問明。子曰:"浸潤之譖①,膚受之愬②,不行焉,可謂明也已矣。浸潤之譖,膚受之愬,不行焉,可謂遠也已矣。"

[注释]

①浸润之谮:像水逐渐渗透进来的谗言,使人在不知不觉中接受了他的中伤之言。谮,读zèn,诬陷、中伤。　②肤受之愬:愬,读sù,同"诉",诬告,指控。肤受之愬,就是像有切肤之痛那样急骤而来的诬告,使人迫不及防、不知所措。

[白话文]

子张问如何明察人事。孔子说:"像水一样逐渐渗透进来的谗言,像切肤之痛那样骤烈的指控,在你面前行不通,这可算是有知人之明;像水一样逐渐渗透进来的馋言,像切肤之痛那样骤烈的指控,在你面前行不通,这可说是看得深远。"

[英译文]

Zi-zhang asked what constituted intelligence. The Master said, "He with whom neither slander that gradually soaks into the mind, nor statements that startle like a wound in the flesh, are successful, may be called intelligent indeed. Yea, he with whom neither soaking slander, nor startling statements, are successful, may be called far-seeing."

12 - 7

子貢問政。子曰:"足食,足兵,民信之矣。"子貢曰:"必不得已而去,於斯三者何先?"曰:"去兵。"子貢曰:"必不得已而去,於斯二者何先?"曰:"去食。自古皆有死,民無信不立。"

[白话文]

子贡问政治上最重要的事项是什么。孔子说:"要有足够的粮食,要有充实的军备,要有人民的信任。"子贡说:"不得已要舍弃的时候,这三项中放弃哪一项呢?"孔子说:"去军备。"子贡说:"不得已还要舍弃,这两项中又放弃哪一项呢?"孔子说:"减去粮食。自古以来,人都是要死的,但若政府失去了人民的信任,这个国家还能立吗?"

[英译文]

Zi-gong asked about government. The Master said, "The requisites of government are that there be sufficiency of food, sufficiency of military equipment, and the confidence of the people in their ruler." Zi-gong said, "If it cannot be helped, and one of these must be dispensed with, which of the three should be foregone first?" "The military equipment," said the Master. Zi-gong again asked, "If it cannot be helped, and one of the remaining two must be dispensed with, which of them should be foregone?" The Master answered, "Part with the food. From of old, death has been the lot of all men; but if the people have no faith in their rulers, there is no standing for the state."

12-8

棘子成①曰:"君子質而已矣,何以文爲?"子貢曰:"惜乎! 夫子之説君子也。駟不及舌②。文猶質也,質猶文也。虎豹之鞟③,猶犬羊之鞟。"

[注释]

①棘子成:卫国大夫。 ②驷不及舌:驷,四匹马。不及,追不上。舌,讲的话。 ③鞟:读kuò,去毛的兽皮。

[白话文]

棘子成说:"一个君子,只要本质好,何必去讲求外在的礼乐文饰呢?"子贡听后说:"可惜啊! 你老夫子这样解说君子的言论就差了,就是用四匹马拉的车子也追不回来了。一个君子应该内在外表都一致,本质和文饰都一样重要。就像虎豹皮如果把毛都去掉,那不就和去掉毛的狗皮羊皮难以区分了吗?"

[英译文]

Ji Zi-cheng said, "In a superior man it is only the substantial qualities which are wanted; why should we seek for ornamental accomplishments?" Zi-gong said, "Alas! Your words, sir, show you to be a superior man, but four horses cannot overtake the tongue. Ornament is as substance; substance is as ornament. The hide of a tiger or leopard stripped of its hair, is like the hide of a dog or goat stripped of its hair."

12-9

哀公問於有若曰:"年饑,用不足,如之何?"有若對曰:"盍徹①乎?"曰:"二,吾猶不足,如之何其徹也?"對曰:"百姓足,君孰與不足? 百姓不足,君孰與足?"

[注释]

①盍徹:盍,读 hé,何不的意思。徹,古时田税名,取十分之一曰彻。

[白话文]

鲁哀公问有若说:"年成不好,国家用度不够,怎么办呢?"有若说:"何不实施十分抽一分的税制呢?"哀公说:"抽二分,我还觉得不够,如何只收一分呢?"有若说:"百姓富足,君王怎会不富足? 百姓不富足,君王又怎能富足?"

[英译文]

The duke Ai inquired of You-ruo, "The year is one of scarcity, and the returns for expenditure are not sufficient; what is to be done?" You-ruo replied to him, "Why not simply tithe the people?" "With two-tenths," said the duke, "I find them not enough; how could I do with that system of one-tenth?" You-ruo answered, "If the people have plenty, their prince will not be left to want alone. If the people are in want, their prince cannot enjoy plenty alone."

12 – 10

子张问崇德辨惑。子曰:"主忠信①,徙义②,崇德也。爱之欲其生,恶之欲其死:既欲其生,又欲其死,是惑也。'诚不以富,亦祇以异③。'"

[注释]

①主忠信:亲近忠信的人。　②徙义:徙,迁移。徙义,迁移向义,即按照道义去实行。　③诚不以富,亦只以异:句出《诗经·小雅·我行其野》。《集注》引程子曰:"此错简。"当在季氏篇第十二章(16-12)中,"其斯之谓与句"之前,这里仍按原版排列。

[白话文]

子张问怎么样崇尚品德、辨别迷惑。孔子说:"亲近忠信的人,按照道义去行事,这样就能提高品德。当爱一个人,就希望他永远活下去;一旦讨厌他,就希望他死了。既希望他活,又希望他死,这便是迷惑。'这样,对自己毫无好处,只是让人觉得奇怪罢了。'"

[英译文]

Zi-zhang having asked how virtue was to be exalted, and delusions to be discovered. The Master said, "Hold faithfulness and sincerity as first principles, and be moving continually to what is right; this is the way to exalt one's virtue. You love a man and wish him to live; you hate him and wish him to die. Having wished him to live, you also wish him to die. This is a case of delusion. 'It may not be on account of her being rich, yet you come to make a difference.'"

12 – 11

齐景公①问政于孔子。孔子对曰:"君君,臣臣,父父,子子。"公曰:

"善哉！信如君不君,臣不臣,父不父,子不子,雖有粟,吾得而食諸?"

[注释]

①齐景公:齐国君主,名杵臼。景是谥号。鲁昭公末年时,孔子适齐,作了这段对话。齐景公当时失政,在君臣父子之间皆失其道,虽善孔子之言而不能用,终遭大夫陈氏弑君篡国之祸。

[白话文]

齐景公问孔子如何处理政事。孔子说了八个字——君君、臣臣、父父、子子。也就是说做君主的要像个君主;为臣的像个臣;做父亲的像个父亲;为子女的像个子女。齐景公说:"好极了! 如果君不君,臣不臣,父不父,子不子,纵使有充足的粮食,我这做君主的又怎能享受呢?"

[英译文]

The duke Jing of Qi, asked Confucius about government. Confucius replied, "There is government, when the prince is prince, and the minister is minister; when the father is father, and the son is son." "Good!" said the duke, "If, indeed; the prince be not prince, the minister not minister, the father not father, and the son not son, although I have my revenue, can I enjoy it?"

12－12

子曰:"片言可以折獄①者,其由也與?"子路無宿諾。

[注释]

①片言可以折狱:折狱,即断案。这里是指子路忠信明决,得人信任,所以不待诉讼双方说完就断案。

[白话文]

孔子说:"不待诉讼双方说完就断案的,那只有由(子路)吧!"子路答应人家的事,诺言不留宿(不会拖延很长时间)就会兑现的。

[英译文]

The Master said, "Ah! It is You, who could with half a word settle litigation!" Zi-lu never slept over a promise.

12－13

子曰:"聽訟①,吾猶人也。必也使無訟乎!"

[注释]

①听讼:审判案件。

[白话文]

孔子说:"审判案件,我可以做得跟别人一样。然而更重要的是怎样使百姓知礼义,减少或不发生诉讼,使社会更为安定、和谐。"

[英译文]

The Master said, "In hearing litigation, I am like any other body. What is necessary, however, is to cause the people to have no litigation."

12－14

子張問政。子曰:"居之無倦,行之以忠。"

[白话文]

子张问怎样才能治理政事。孔子说:"居于官位要敬事不倦、始终如一,不可初勤终怠;行使政令要忠实,不徇私歪曲、不做表面文章。"

[英译文]

Zi-zhang asked about government, The Master said, "The art of governing is to keep its affairs before the mind without weariness, and to practise them with undeviating consistency."

12－15

子曰:"博學於文,約之以禮,亦可以弗畔矣夫。"

[注释]

本章重出,参阅雍也篇第二十五章(6-25)。

12－16

子曰:"君子成人之美,不成人之惡;小人反是。"

[白话文]

孔子说:"君子成全别人的好事,不成全别人的坏事;小人则相反。"

[英译文]

The Master said, "The superior man seeks to perfect the admirable qualities of men, and does not seek to perfect their bad qualities. The mean man does the opposite of this."

12－17

季康子問政於孔子。孔子對曰:"政者,正也。子帥① 以正,孰敢不正?"

[注释]

①帅:同"率",率先。

[白话文]

季康子问孔子怎样治理政事。孔子回答说:"政,就是中正的正。执政的人,自己先行中正之道,以作表率,那么下属谁敢不依循中正之道呢?"

[英译文]

Ji Kang-zi asked Confucius about government. Confucius replied, "To govern means to rectify. If you lead on the people with correctness, who will dare not to be correct?"

12－18

季康子患盗,問於孔子。孔子對曰:"苟^①子之不欲,雖賞之不竊。"

[注释]

①苟:假使、如果。

[白话文]

季康子担心国内盗贼多,问孔子怎么办。孔子回答说:"假使作为领导的你自己不贪心、取之有度,老百姓安居乐业,你就是悬赏他们去偷盗,他们也不会去的。"

[英译文]

Ji Kang-zi, distressed about the number of thieves in the state, inquired of Confucius how to do away with them. Confucius said, "If you, sir, were not covetous, although you should reward them to do it, they would not steal."

12－19

季康子問政於孔子,曰:"如殺無道,以就有道,何如?"孔子對曰:"子爲政,焉用殺? 子欲善,而民善矣。君子之德風,小人之德草。草上之風,必偃^①。"

[注释]

①君子之德风,小人之德草。草上之风,必偃:据南怀瑾释,句中的"德"字,是总称,可以理解为人的行为思想所形成的社会风气。君子乃指上位者,小人乃指庶民。他们在社会风气中扮演的角色分别犹风或草。草上风如何吹向,草就如何倒向。

[白话文]

季康子向孔子问为政之道,说:"如果杀掉坏人以成就好人,你看怎样?"孔子说:"你是主政者,何必用杀人的办法? 你向善,百姓也就会跟着向善。在上位的人好像风,老百姓好像草。风向哪个方向吹,草必定向哪个方向倒。"

[英译文]

Ji Kang-zi asked Confucius about government, "What do you say to killing the unprincipled for the good of the principled?" Confucius replied, "Sir, in carrying on your government, why should you use killing at all? Let your evinced desires be for what is good, and the people will be good. The relation between superiors and inferiors, is like that between the wind and the grass. The grass must bend, when the wind blows across it."

12 - 20

子張問：“士何如斯可謂之達矣？”子曰：“何哉？爾所謂達①者。”子張對曰：“在邦必聞，在家必聞②。”子曰：“是聞也，非達也。夫達也者，質直而好義，察言而觀色，慮以下人③。在邦必達，在家必達。夫聞也者，色取仁而行違，居之不疑。在邦必聞，在家必聞。”

[注释]

①达：即通达。通于处人处己之道，所行无阻违。 ②在邦必闻，在家必闻：邦，诸侯之国。家，卿大夫家。闻，即名声。 ③虑以下人：指思虑周详，所以态度谦逊，无自高自大。

[白话文]

子张问：“读书人怎样方可叫做通达？”孔子说：“你指的通达到底是什么意思？”子张说：“在邦国做官一定有名声；在卿大夫家做事也一定有名声。”孔子说：“你所说的是声望，不是通达呀！所谓通达，是心存正直而好义；善于分析别人的话，又能观察别人的脸色；待人谦虚；能想到退让于别人之下。这样的人，在邦国或在卿大夫家都会通达。至于所谓有名声者，表面装得仁德而行为相背；自以为是，不怀疑自己是否有过失，这种人在邦国、在大夫家的虚誉浮名，就是‘闻’（不是‘达’）人。”

[英译文]

Zi-zhang asked, "What must the officer be, who may be said to be distinguished?" The Master said, "What is it you call being distinguished?" Zi-zhang replied, "It is to be heard of through the state, to be heard of throughout his clan." The Master said, "That is notoriety, not distinction. Now the man of distinction is solid and straightforward, and loves righteousness. He examines people's words, and looks at their countenances. He is anxious to humble himself to others. Such a man will be distinguished in the country; he will be distinguished in his clan. As to the man of notoriety, he assumes the appearance of virtue, but his actions are opposed to it, and he rests in this character without any doubts about himself. Such a man will be heard of in the country; he will be heard of in the clan."

12-21

樊迟從遊於舞雩①之下，曰："敢問崇德、修慝②、辨惑。"子曰："善哉問。先事後得③，非崇德與？攻其惡，無攻人之惡④，非修慝與？一朝之忿，忘其身以及其親⑤，非惑與？"

[注释]

①舞雩：雩，读yú。舞雩，求雨祭祀的坛，下植树木，可供游玩之地。　②修慝：慝，读tè。罪恶、邪恶、恶念。修，治也。修慝，去除恶念。　③先事后得：先劳心劳力做好该做的事，然后取得报酬。　④攻其恶，无攻人之恶：攻其恶，即反省自己。无攻人之恶，不攻击别人。　⑤忘其身以及其亲：忘记了自己生命安危，甚至忘掉父母亲人的牵累。

[白话文]

樊迟跟从着孔子闲游于祈雨的祭坛之下，他说："请问如何崇尚品德、去除恶念、明辨迷惑？"孔子说："问得很好。先做好该做的事，然后取得报酬，这不是崇尚品德吗？勇于反省自己的坏处，而不攻击人的坏处，这不是去除自己的恶念吗？一旦愤怒，就忘了自己的安危甚至忘掉父母亲人的安危，这不就是迷惑吗？"

[英译文]

Fan-chi rambling with the Master under the trees about the rain altars, said, "I venture to ask how to exalt virtue, to correct cherished evil, and to discover delusions." The Master said, "Truly a good question! If doing what is to be done be made the first business, and success a secondary consideration; is not this the way to exalt virtue? To assail one's own wickedness and not assail that of others; is not this the way to correct cherished evil? For a morning's anger to disregard one's own life, and involve that of his parents; is not this a case of delusion?"

12-22

樊遲問仁。子曰："愛人。"問知。子曰："知人。"樊遲未達。子曰："舉直錯諸枉①，能使枉者直。"樊遲退，見子夏曰："鄉②也，吾見於夫子而問知，子曰'舉直錯諸枉，能使枉者直'，何謂也？"子夏曰："富哉言乎！舜有天下，選於眾，舉皋陶③，不仁者遠矣。湯有天下，選於眾，舉伊尹④，不仁者遠矣。"

[注释]

①举直错诸枉：参阅为政篇第十九章(2-19)注。　②乡：昔，过去、刚才的意思。　③皋陶：舜之贤相。　④伊尹：汤之贤相。

[白话文]

樊迟问什么是仁。孔子说："爱人。"又问什么是智。孔子说："知人。"樊迟还没有弄明白。孔子又说:"举用正直的人,让邪曲的人靠边,可使不正直者变得正直。"樊迟退出,去见子夏。樊迟说:"我刚才请教老师什么是智,老师说'举用正直的人,可使邪曲的人变得正直',这是什么意思啊?"子夏说:"这话说得真富有意义!当舜有了天下,他从众人中选拔、使用了皋陶,那些不仁德的人就远离了;当汤有了天下,在众人中选拔、举用了伊尹,那些不仁德的人也就远离而去了。"

[英译文]

Fan-chi asked about benevolence. The Master said, "It is to love all men." He asked about knowledge. The Master said, "It is to know all men." Fan-chi did not immediately understand these answers. The Master said, "Employ the upright and put aside all the crooked; in this way the crooked can be made to be upright." Fan-chi retired, and, seeing Zi-xia, he said to him, "A little while ago, I had an interview with our master, and asked him about knowledge. He said, 'Employ the upright, and put aside all the crooked; in this way, the crooked can be made to be upright.' What did he mean?" Zi-xia said, "Truly rich is his saying! Shun, being in possession of the kingdom, selected from among all the people, and employed Gao-tao, on which all who were devoid of virtue disappeared. Tang, being in possession of the kingdom, selected from among all the people, and employed Yi-yin, and all who were devoid of virtue disappeared."

12－23

子貢問友。子曰:"忠告而善道①之,不可則止,毋自辱焉②。"

[注释]

①道:劝导。 ②毋自辱焉:毋,不要。自辱,自己反而受耻辱(对方反而以为你不是)。焉,在这里作代词,相当于"之"。

[白话文]

子贡问怎样交朋友。孔子说:"朋友有过错,要尽心劝导他,好好地引导他向善。朋友要是不接受,也就算了,不要自讨耻辱。"

[英译文]

Zi-gong asked about friendship. The Master said, "Faithfully admonish your friend, and skillfully lead him on. If you find him impracticable, stop. Do not disgrace yourself."

12－24

曾子曰:"君子以文會友,以友輔仁。"

[白话文]

曾子说:"君子以礼乐文章来聚会朋友,以朋友的帮助来修养自己的仁德。"

[英译文]

The philosopher Zeng said, "The superior man on grounds of culture meets with his friends, and by their friendship helps his virtue."

子路第十三

本篇凡三十章（13—1～13—30）。

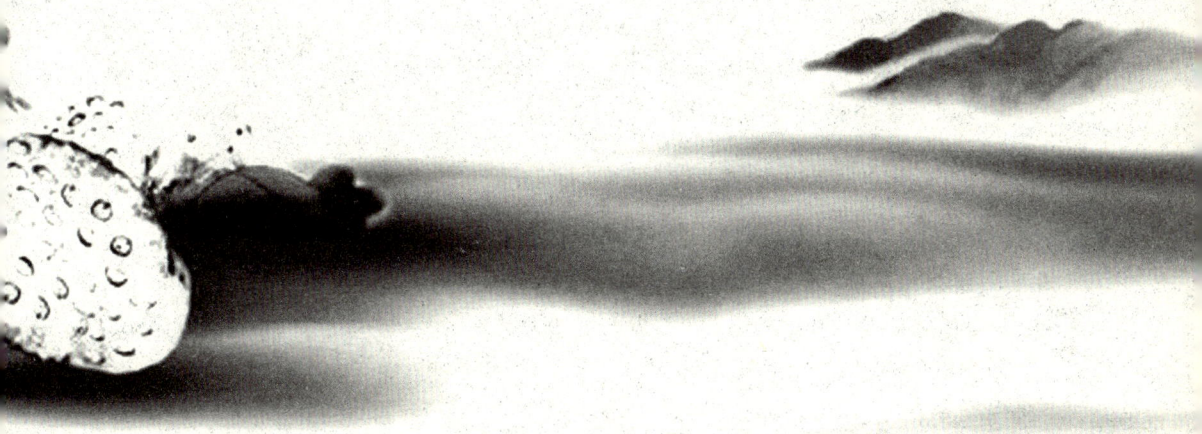

13－1

子路問政。子曰："先之勞之^①。"請益^②。曰："無倦。"

[注释]

①先之勞之：《集注》引苏氏曰："凡民之行,以身先之,则不令而行。凡民之事,以身劳之,则虽勤不怨。"意谓要先其民而劳、以身作则。 ②益：增的意思。这里指请再多说一点。

[白话文]

子路问治国之道。孔子说："凡事要以身作则,不辞辛劳,先做出榜样。这样,人民再劳苦也不会有怨恨。"子路请求再多说一点。孔子说："永不倦怠。"

[英译文]

Zi-lu asked about government. The Master said, "Go before the people with your example, and be laborious in their affairs." He requested further instruction, and was answered, "Be not weary(in these things)."

13－2

仲弓爲季氏宰^①,問政。子曰："先有司^②,赦小過,舉賢才。"曰："焉知賢才而舉之?"曰："舉爾所知。爾所不知,人其舍諸?"

[注释]

①仲弓为季氏宰：仲弓,即冉雍〔参阅雍也篇第一章(6-1)、颜渊篇第二章(12-2)〕。宰,家臣、总管。 ②先有司：有司,指宰的属官。先,一说先整饬官吏职司,规定权责。一说,以身率之。以从后一说为多。

[白话文]

仲弓做了鲁国卿大夫季氏的家宰,求问孔子怎样为政。孔子说："先要为下属做出表率;为政以宽,不斤斤计较下属的小过失;举用有德有能的人。"仲弓接着说："怎样知道谁有德有能而提拔他呢?"孔子说："提拔你所知道的贤才。你所不知道的,难道别人会舍弃他而不推荐给你吗?"

[英译文]

Zhong-gong, being chief minister to the Head of the Ji family, asked about government. The Master said, "Employ first the services of your various officers, pardon faults, and raise to office men of virtue and talents." Zhong-gong said, "How shall I know the men of virtue and talent, so that I may raise them to office?" He was answered, "Raise to office those whom you know. As to those whom you do not know, will others neglect them?"

13 - 3

　　子路曰：“衞君①待子而爲政，子將奚先？”子曰：“必也正名乎！”子路曰：“有是哉，子之迂②也，奚其正？”子曰：“野③哉，由也！君子於其所不知，蓋闕如也。名不正，則言不順；言不順，則事不成；事不成，則禮樂不興；禮樂不興，則刑罰不中；刑罰不中④，則民無所措手足。故君子名之必可言也，言之必可行也。君子於其言，無所苟而已矣。”

[注釋]

　　①卫君：《集注》曰：“卫君，卫出公辄也。是时，鲁哀公之十年，孔子自楚反乎卫。”据《春秋左氏传》记载，哀公二年夏，卫灵公卒，立逃亡在晋的卫世子蒯聩的儿子辄为国君，而蒯聩又在晋赵鞅的帮助下返卫，于是出现了父子争国。父不父，子不子。故孔子就说出了“必也正名乎”的话。②迂：迂腐固执。　③野：蛮横不讲理，粗鲁无礼貌。这里是孔子批评子路（但子路终不悟）。④中：得当。

[白话文]

　　子路对孔子说：“如果卫国国君要老师去辅政，老师先从什么事情做起？”孔子说：“必先要正名分。”子路说：“有这个必要吗？老师真是迂执。”孔子说：“你真是粗鲁不懂啊！君子对于自己所不知道的事情，是不随便乱说的。要知道，名分不正，说话就不会合理。说话不合理，政务就无法施行。政务无法施行，礼乐教化就无法建立。礼乐制度建立不起来，法律、刑罚的执行就不得当。法律、刑罚执行不得当，人民就无所适从。所以，君子要立名分，必须在道理上说得过去；说出来的话，一定要行得通。君子所说任何一句话，都不能随随便便的啊！”

[英译文]

　　Zi-lu said, "The ruler of Wei has been waiting for you, in order with you to administer the government. What will you consider the first thing to be done?" The Master replied, "What is necessary is to rectify names." "So, indeed!" said Zi-lu, "You are wide of the mark! Why must there be such rectification?" The Master said, "How uncultivated you are, You! A superior man, in regard to what he does not know, shows a cautious reserve. If names be not correct, language is not in accordance with the truth of things, If language be not in accordance with the truth of things, affairs cannot be carried on to success. When affairs cannot be carried on to success, proprieties and music will not flourish. When proprieties and music do not flourish, punishments will not be properly awarded. When punishments are not properly awarded, the people do not know how to move hand or foot. Therefore a superior man considers it necessary that the names he uses may be spoken appropriately, and also that what he speaks may be carried out appropriately. What the superior man requires, is just that in his words there may be nothing incorrect."

13－4

　　樊遲請學稼①。子曰:"吾不如老農。"請學爲圃。曰:"吾不如老圃。"樊遲出。子曰:"小人哉,樊須②也! 上好禮,則民莫敢不敬;上好義,則民莫敢不服;上好信,則民莫敢不用情③。夫如是,則四方之民襁負其子而至矣④,焉用稼?"

[注释]

　　①稼:朱注云:"种五谷曰稼;种蔬菜曰圃。"　　②须:樊迟之名。　　③用情:以诚实对上。
④四方之民襁负其子而至矣:四面八方的人,用布裹负着小孩子来到。乃指从事农业的劳动力由于政府的好礼、好义而归顺。

[白话文]

　　樊迟想学种五谷。孔子说:"我不如老农。"樊迟又想学种菜。孔子说:"我不如菜农。"樊迟离开后,孔子说:"樊须真是个小人物啊! 在上位者好礼,则百姓不敢不谦让;在上位者好义,则百姓不会不顺服;在上位者好信,则百姓必诚实以对上。如果能这样,则各地的人民就会背着小孩前来归顺,为什么还要自己去种庄稼呢?"

[英译文]

Fan-chi requested to be taught husbandry. The Master said, "I am not so good for that as an old husbandman." He requested also to be taught gardening, and was answered, "I am not so good for that as an old gardener." Fan-chi having gone out. The Master said, "A small man, indeed, is Fan-xu! If a superior man love propriety, the people will not dare not to be reverent. If he love righteousness, the people will not dare not to submit to his example. If he love good faith, the people will not dare not to be sincere. Now, when these things obtain, the people from all quarters will come to him, bearing their children on their backs; what need has he of a knowledge of husbandry?"

13－5

　　子曰:"誦《詩》三百①,授之以政,不達②;使於四方,不能專對③,雖多,亦奚以爲?"

[注释]

　　①《诗》三百:即三百零五篇的《诗经》。三百,是个大约数。　　②不达:在为政上不能通情达

理。　③专对:独立应对。

[白话文]

　　孔子说:"读了《诗经》三百多篇诗,把政事托付给他,却不能治理得好;派他出使诸侯诸国,不能独立应对,这样的人,即使读诗再多,又有什么用呢?"

[英译文]

The Master said "Though a man may be able to recite the three hundred odes, yet if, when intrusted with a governmental charge, he knows not how to act, or if, when sent to any quarter on a mission, he cannot give his replies unassisted, notwithstanding the extent of his learning, of what practical use is it?"

13－6

　　子曰:"其身正,不令而行。其身不正,雖令不從。"

[白话文]

　　孔子说:"为政者自己行为正当,就是不等他下达命令,人民也会各行其是。反之,本身行为不正当,即使是三申五令,人民也不会听从。"

[英译文]

The Master said, "When a prince's personal conduct is correct, his government is effective without the issuing of orders. If his personal conduct is not correct, he may issue orders, but they will not be followed."

13－7

　　子曰:"魯、衛①之政,兄弟也。"

[注释]

　　①魯、卫:始祖本是兄弟。鲁是周武王弟周公的封国,卫是武王弟康叔的封国。

[白话文]

　　孔子说:"鲁、卫两国的政治情况,好像兄弟一样。"

[英译文]

The Master said, "The governments of Lu and Wei are brothers."

13－8

　　子謂衛公子荊①:"善居室。始有,曰:'苟②合矣。'少有,曰:'苟完矣。'富有,曰:'苟美矣。'"

[注释]

①卫公子荆：卫献公子，字南楚。卫国的卿大夫，善于治理家业，不尚奢侈。　②苟：朱子曰："苟，聊且粗略之意。"

[白话文]

孔子谈论卫公子荆："他善于治理家业。当他开始有一点家产时，他说：'能凑合着可用就行了。'稍多时，他说：'差不多就完备了。'富有时，他说：'够完美了。'"

[英译文]

The Master said of Jing, "A scion of the ducal family of Wei, that he knew the economy of a family well. When he began to have means, he said, 'Ha! Here is a collection!' When they were a little increased, he said, 'Ha! This is complete!' When he had become rich, he said, 'Ha! This is admirable!'"

13－9

子适①卫，冉有仆②。子曰："庶矣哉！"冉有曰："既庶③矣，又何加焉？"曰："富之。"曰："既富矣，又何加焉？"曰："教之。"

[注释]

①适：去，往。　②仆：御车。　③庶：人民众多。

[白话文]

孔子到卫国去，冉有为孔子驾车。孔子说："卫国的人民真多啊！"冉有问："人口已经这么多，进一步该怎么办？"孔子说："使他们富足起来。"冉有又问："人民富足了，进一步要做什么呢？"孔子说："让他们受教育。"

[英译文]

When the Master went to Wei, Ran-you acted as driver of his carriage. The Master observed, "How numerous are the people!" You said, "Since they are thus numerous, what more shall be done for them?" "Enrich them", was the reply. "And when they have been enriched, what more shall be done?" The Master said, "Teach them."

13－10

子曰："苟①有用我者，期月②而已可也，三年有成。"

[注释]

①苟：如果。　②期月：期，读 jī。期月，一整年之岁月。

[白话文]

孔子说："如果有人任用我来治国，一年就可以见成效，三年便可以成功。"

[英译文]

The Master said, "If there were any of the princes who would employ me, in the course of twelve months, I should have done something considerable. In three years, the government would be perfected."

13 - 11

子曰:"'善人爲邦百年,亦可以勝殘去殺^①矣。'誠哉是言也!"

[注释]

①胜残去杀:胜残,教化残暴凶恶者,不再作恶。去杀,化民为善,不再用刑杀。

[白话文]

孔子说:"古人说'善人相继主政历百年,也就能够感化残暴凶恶的人,而废去杀戮的刑罚。'这话说得真不错啊!"

[英译文]

The Master said, "'If good men were to govern a country in succession for a hundred years, they would be able to transform the violently bad, and dispense with capital punishments.' True indeed is this saying!"

13 - 12

子曰:"如有王者^①,必世^②而後仁。"

[注释]

①王者:行王道仁政者。一说,圣人为天子者。　②世:三十年为一世。不同于为政篇第二十三章(2-23)中所说世代的世。

[白话文]

孔子说:"如果推行王道者治理天下,也要以三十年才能德化而行仁政。"

[英译文]

The Master said, "If a truly royal ruler were to arise, it would still require a generation, and then virtue would prevail."

13 - 13

子曰:"苟正其身矣,於從政乎何有? 不能正其身,如正人何?"

[白话文]

孔子说:"如果自身正,从政有什么困难呢? 如果自身不正,又如何匡正别人呢?"

[英译文]

The Master said, "If a minister make his own conduct correct, what difficulty will he have in assisting in government? If he cannot rectify himself, what has he to do with rectifying others?"

13－14

冉子退朝。子曰："何晏①也?"對曰："有政。"子曰："其事②也。如有政,雖不吾以③,吾其與聞之。"

[注释]

①晏:晚。　②事:这里指季氏的家事。　③虽不吾以:以,用。虽不吾以,虽然不用我。

[白话文]

冉有从季氏家的朝会回来。孔子说:"为什么这么晚才回来?"冉有说:"因为讨论国政。"孔子说:"恐怕是季氏的家事吧! 如果真有国政,即使没有人用我,人家也会征询我的意见。"

[英译文]

The disciple Ran returning from the court. The Master said to him, "How are you so late?" He replied, "We had government business." The Master said, "It must have been family affairs. If there had been government business, though I am not now in office, I should have been consulted about it."

13－15

定公問："一言而可以興邦,有諸①?"孔子對曰："言不可以若是,其幾②也。人之言曰:'爲君難,爲臣不易。'如知爲君之難也,不幾乎一言而興邦乎?"曰："一言而喪邦,有諸?"孔子對曰："言不可以若是,其幾也。人之言曰:'予無樂乎爲君,唯其言而莫予違也。'如其善而莫之違也,不亦善乎? 如不善而莫之違也,不幾乎一言而喪邦乎?"

[注释]

①诸:"之于"的合音,"之"是代词。或相当于"之乎","乎"作疑问语气词。　②几:期望。

[白话文]

鲁定公问:"一句话可以兴邦,有这样的话吗?"孔子回答说:"话不能这样讲,不能期望一句话有如此大的效果。不过,有人说:'为君难,为臣子也不易。'如果能理解做国君的困难,不几乎是一句话而兴邦吗?"定公又问:"有一句话可以丧邦的吗?"孔子说:"话也不能这样说,不可能期望一句话有这么大的作用。不过,有人

166

说:'做国君没有什么乐趣,只是说话没人敢违背而感到有兴趣!'如果国君说的话正确,没人违背,那不是很好吗? 但若说的话是错的,而没有人敢违背,岂不是近乎于一句话可以丧邦?"

[英译文]

The duke Ding asked whether there was a single sentence which could make a country prosperous. Confucius replied, "Such an effect cannot be expected from one sentence. There is a saying, however, which people have, 'To be a prince is difficult; to be a minister is not easy.' If a ruler knows this—the difficulty of being a prince, may there not be expected from this one sentence the prosperity of his country?" The duke then said, "Is there a single sentence which can ruin a country?" Confucius replied, "Such an effect as that cannot be expected from one sentence. There is, however, the saying which people have, 'I have no pleasure in being a prince, but only in that no one can offer any opposition to what I say!' If a ruler's words be good, is it not also good that no one oppose them? But if they are not good, and no one opposes them, may there not be expected from this one sentence the ruin of his country?"

13 – 16

葉公^①問政。子曰:"近者説,遠者來。"

[注释]

①叶公:参阅述而篇第十八章(7-18)注。

[白话文]

叶公问为政的道理。孔子说:"使近处的人民能安居乐业、生活欢悦,则远处的人民自然而然地会来归顺。"

[英译文]

The duke of Xie asked about government. The Master said, "Good government obtains, when those who are near are made happy, and those who are far off are attracted."

13 – 17

子夏爲莒父宰^①,問政。子曰:"無欲速,無見小利。欲速則不達,見小利則大事不成。"

[注释]

①莒父宰:莒,读 jǔ。莒父,鲁国的一个小邑。宰,即邑宰,地方长官。

[白话文]

子夏做了莒父的邑宰,求问孔子为政之道。孔子说:"不要求速成,不要只看到小利。想要求快,反而达不到目的;贪图小利,就不能成大事。"

[英译文]

Zi-xia, being governor of Ju-fu, asked about government. The Master said, "Do not be desirous to have things done quickly; do not look at small advantages. Desire to have things done quickly prevents their being done thoroughly. Looking at small advantages prevents great affairs from being accomplished."

13－18

葉公語孔子曰:"吾黨①有直躬②者,其父攘③羊,而子證之。"孔子曰:"吾黨之直者異於是:父爲子隱④,子爲父隱,直在其中矣⑤。"

[注释]

①吾党:党,乡党,即乡里。吾党,即我乡。　②直躬:一说"直率的人";一说"直人名弓"。从前说。　③攘:偷盗。　④隐:隐瞒。　⑤直在其中矣:孔子的伦理观念基于家族制度和家族观念,重视亲情,父慈子孝,将子(父)为父(子)隐作为"理顺"。然而,随着社会的发展,应以公义在前,以事实、公正为原则,动员犯错者"怀刑自首"、"不惮改",但当今社会却又同时存在着种种隐瞒、包庇的现象。所以,这是一个很值得讨论的问题。

[白话文]

叶公对孔子说:"我们乡里有个直率的人,他父亲偷了羊,儿子出来作证。"孔子说:"在我们那里,直率的人不会这样做,父亲为儿子隐瞒,儿子为父亲隐瞒,直率的道理就在其中了。"

[英译文]

The duke of Xie informed Confucius, "Among us here there are those who may be styled upright in their conduct. If their father have stolen a sheep, they will bear witness to the fact."

Confucius said, "Among us, in our part of the country, those who are upright are different from this. The father conceals the misconduct of the son, and the son conceals the misconduct of the father. Uprightness is to be found in this."

13－19

樊遲問仁。子曰:"居處恭①,執事敬,與人忠。雖之夷狄,不可棄也。"

[注释]

①居处恭：日常生活起居不可放肆无礼。

[白话文]

樊迟问怎样才算是仁。孔子说：“日常生活起居不可放肆，做事要认真，待人要忠诚。即使到了夷狄之邦，也不可舍弃这些处世为人的品德。”

[英译文]

Fan-chi asked about perfect virtue. The Master said, "It is, in retirement, to be sedately grave; in the management of business, to be reverently attentive; in intercourse with others, to be strictly sincere. Though a man go among rude, uncultivated tribes, these qualities may not be neglected."

13 – 20

子贡问曰：“何如斯可谓之士矣？”子曰：“行己有耻①，使於四方，不辱君命，可谓士矣。”曰：“敢问其次？”曰：“宗族称孝焉，乡党称弟焉。”曰：“敢问其次？”曰：“言必信，行必果，硁硁然②，小人哉！抑亦可以为次矣。”曰：“今之从政者何如？”子曰：“噫！斗筲之人③，何足算也？”

[注释]

①行己有耻：操守廉洁而知耻。　②硁硁然：朱注：“硁，小石之坚确者。”硁硁然，指小石坚确之状，比喻庶民也讲求言必信、行必果。　③斗筲之人：斗，容量名。筲，竹器。比喻这些从政者都是量小的容器，是气量和才识浅薄的人。

[白话文]

子贡问孔子说：“怎样可以算作士呢？”孔子说：“自己操守廉洁，行为知耻；出使他邦，不辱使命。这样的人，便可称为士。”子贡说：“请问次一等的又如何？”孔子说：“宗族中的人都称赞他孝顺，乡里的人都称赞他友爱兄弟。”子贡说：“请问再次一等的如何？”孔子说：“说话讲信用，行事有结果，自守执著，虽然是识浅量狭的小人物，也可称为次一等的士了。”子贡说：“现在从政的人怎样？”孔子说：“唉！这些人才识短浅、器量狭小，算得上什么呢？”

[英译文]

Zi-gong asked, "What qualities must a man possess to entitle him to be called an officer?" The Master said, "He who in his conduct of himself maintains a sense of shame, and when sent to any quarter will not disgrace his prince's commission, deserves to be called on officer." Zi-gong pursued, "I venture to ask who may be placed in the next lower rank?" and he was told, "He whom the circle of his relatives pronounce to be filial, whom his fellow villagers and neighbours pronounce to be fraternal." Again the disciple asked, "I venture to ask about the class still next in order." The Master said, "They are determined to be sincere in what they say, and to carry out what they do. They are obstinate little men. Yet perhaps they may make the next class." Zi-gong finally inquired, "Of what sort are those of the present day, who engage in government?" The Master said, "Pooh! They are so many pecks and hampers, not worth being taken into account."

13 – 21

子曰:"不得中行①而與之,必也狂狷②乎! 狂者進取,狷者有所不爲也。"

[注释]

①中行:依中庸之道而行。　②狂狷:狂者,虽好高骛远,但富进取精神。狷,读 juàn,狷者,洁身自好而无为的人。

[白话文]

孔子说:"如果找不到与行中庸之道的人交朋友,也必和狂狷之人为伍。狂者志气高大,有进取心;狷者洁身自好,不做非分之事。"

[英译文]

The Master said, "Since I cannot get men pursuing the due medium, to whom I might communicate my instructions, I must find the ardent and the cautiously-decided. The ardent will advance and lay hold of truth; the cautiously-decided will keep themselves from what is wrong."

13 – 22

子曰:"南人有言曰:'人而無恒,不可以作巫醫①。'善夫!""不恒其德,或承之羞②。"子曰:"不占而已矣。"

[注释]

①巫医:古代以占卜、祈祷等方法为人治病。故"医"字古有"毉"字。　②不恒其德,或承之羞:语出《易经·恒卦》。不恒其德,指其德行不能持之以恒。或,经常。承,接续。

[白话文]

孔子说:"南方人有句话:'没有恒心的人,不可以做巫医。'这话说得真好!"《易经》说:"立德无恒毅,羞辱就接踵而来。"孔子又说:"'不恒'的原因没有别的,只不过自己无恒心。没恒心的人什么事都办不成,占卜有什么用呢? 不必占卜了。"

[英译文]

The Master said, "The people of the south have a saying, 'A man without constancy cannot be either a wizard or a doctor.' Good!" "Inconstant in his virtue, he will be visited with disgrace." The Master said, "This arises simply from not attending to the prognostication."

13-23

子曰:"君子和而不同,小人同而不和①。"

[注释]

①和而不同,同而不和:不同,是人与事物之间客观存在的差异、矛盾。和,乃指保持事物对立统一,和谐、平衡、完美、稳定地发展。同而不和,是要取消事物的差异、矛盾,不容对立面的存在,为结党营私,为小团体的同,强调单方面的同,消灭异己,促使事物单方面极端化发展而引起社会动荡、战乱。《春秋左氏传·昭公二十年》载晏子对答齐景公以调和五味为美,调谐不同琴瑟之音为乐喻为和;以梁丘据(人名)的一味迎合为同,指出和而不同以防止事物向极端发展,是一个非常值得重视的历史经验。

[白话文]

孔子说:"君子与人和谐相处,亲切友善,却不谄媚逢迎,做到和而不同;小人结党营私,却不能与人和谐相处,同而不和。"

[英译文]

The Master said, "The superior man is affable, but not adulatory; the mean man is adulatory, but not affable."

13-24

子贡问曰:"乡人皆好之,何如?"子曰:"未可也。""乡人皆恶之,何如?"子曰:"未可也,不如乡人之善者好之,其不善者恶之。"

[白话文]

子贡问孔子说:"乡里的人都喜欢他,这个人如何?"孔子说:"还不可以说他是好人。""乡里的人都厌恶他,这个人如何?"孔子说:"还不能说他是坏人,总不如乡里的好人都喜欢他,乡里的坏人都厌恶他,这才能确信他是个好人。"

[英译文]

Zi-gong asked, "what do you say of a man who is loved by all the people of his neighbourhood?" The Master replied, "We may not for that accord our approval of him." "And what do you say of him who is hated by all the people of his neighbourhood?"The Master said, "We may not for that conclude that he is bad. It is better than either of these cases that the good in the neighbourhood love him, and the bad hate him."

13－25

子曰:"君子易事而難説①也。説之不以道,不説也。及其使人也,器之②。小人難事而易説也。説之雖不以道,説也。及其使人也,求備③焉。"

[注释]

①难说:难以取悦。　②器之:量才而用。　③求备:求全责备。

[白话文]

孔子说:"与君子共事是容易的,但不容易取悦他,不以正当的方法去取悦他,他是不会高兴的,但他在用人的时候,却会衡量其人的才能而分配工作。在小人下面做事很难,但却容易取悦他,就是用不正当的方法去讨好他,他也会高兴。但他使用人做事的时候,却处处求全责备、苛刻挑剔。"

[英译文]

The Master said, "The superior man is easy to serve and difficult to please. If you try to please him in any way which is not accordant with right, he will not be pleased. But in his employment of men, he uses them according to their capacity. The mean man is difficult to serve, and easy to please. If you try to please him, though it be in a way which is not accordant with right, he may be pleased. But in his employment of men, he wishes them to be equal to everything."

13－26

子曰:"君子泰而不驕,小人驕而不泰。"

[白话文]

孔子说:"君子(因自重重人、循理行事、无挂无碍)所以安舒而不骄;小人(因自以为是、藐视他人、器小贪欲)所以骄而不得安舒。"

[英译文]

The Master said, "The superior man has a dignified ease without pride. The mean man has pride without a dignified ease."

13－27

子曰:"剛、毅、木、訥①,近仁。"

[注释]

①刚、毅、木、讷：刚，无欲。毅，果敢坚忍。木，质朴。讷，慎言。

[白话文]

孔子说："公正无欲，果敢坚忍，性情质朴，慎言少语的人，近于仁德。"

[英译文]

The Master said, "The firm, the enduring, the simple, and the modest are near to virtue."

13-28

子路问曰："何如斯可谓之士矣？"子曰："切切偲偲^①，怡怡^②如也，可谓士矣。朋友切切偲偲，兄弟怡怡。"

[注释]

①切切偲偲：切磋，督促。偲，读 sī。 ②怡怡：快乐、愉快。

[白话文]

子路问："怎样才能叫作士？"孔子说："互相切磋，互相督促，愉快相处，便可以叫作士了。朋友之间要互相切磋、督促，兄弟间要和乐、愉快。"

[英译文]

Zi-lu asked, "What qualities must a man possess to entitle him to be called a scholar?" The Master said, "He must be thus—earnest, urgent, and bland. Among his friends, earnest and urgent; among his brothers, kind and bland."

13-29

子曰："善人教民七年，亦可以即戎^①矣。"

[注释]

①教民七年，亦可以即戎：《集注》曰："教民者，教之以孝弟忠信之行，务农讲武之法。即，就也。戎，兵也。"

[白话文]

孔子说："善人主政，教化百姓七年，然后可以言军事，当兵作战。"

[英译文]

The Master said, "Let a good man teach the people seven years, and they may then likewise be employed in war."

13-30

子曰："以不教民战，是谓弃之。"

［白话文］

孔子说："让未经受训练的人民去打仗，就等于抛弃他们。"

［英译文］

The Master said, "To lead an uninstructed people to war, is to throw them away."

宪问第十四

本篇凡四十七章(14—1~14—47)。

14-1

憲^①問恥。子曰："邦有道，穀^②；邦無道，穀，恥^③也。"

[注释]

①宪：孔子的弟子，在七十二贤人中，是一位清高之士。姓原，名宪，字子思，鲁国人。本章不称他的字，也不加姓，故有人怀疑恐系其自记。 ②穀：做官的俸禄。 ③耻：《集注》曰："邦有道不能有为，邦无道不能独善，而但知食禄，皆可耻也。"

[白话文]

原宪问什么是耻。孔子说："国家政治清明的时候，出仕为官司，只知享用俸禄而无建树；国家政治昏乱的时候，也只知享用俸禄而不能洁身自好，都是可耻的。"

[英译文]

Xian asked what was shameful. The Master said, "When good government prevails in a state, to be thinking only of salary; and when bad government prevails, to be thinking in the same way, only of salary—this is shameful."

14-2

"克、伐、怨、欲^①，不行焉，可以爲仁矣？"子曰："可以爲難矣！仁則吾不知也。"

[注释]

①克、伐、怨、欲：克，好胜。伐，自矜。怨，愤恨。欲，贪欲。

[白话文]

（原宪又问）："好胜、自矜、怨恨、贪欲，这四种不良的思想和行为，如果去除掉，就可算是仁吗？"孔子说："可以说是难能可贵的了。至于说是不是仁，我就不知道了。"

[英译文]

"When the love of superiority, boasting, resentments, and covetousness are repressed, this may be deemed perfect virtue." The Master said, "This may be regarded as the achievement of what is difficult. But I do not know that it is to be deemed perfect virtue."

14-3

子曰："士而懷居^①，不足以爲士矣！"

[注释]

①怀居：怀，思怀、留恋。居，所涵甚广，凡居室之安，口体之奉，皆居也。又一说，怀居，等于

所谓"问舍求田,原无大志"的问舍,指一个人就是追求自己的房产田地。

[白话文]

孔子说:"作为一个读书人,如果只贪恋生活的安乐,而忘怀事业和社会责任,就不配称为士。"

[英译文]

The Master said, "The scholar who cherished the love of comfort is not fit to be deemed a scholar."

14－4

子曰:"邦有道,危言危行①;邦無道,危行言孫②。"

[注释]

①危言危行:正直、端正。危言,据理直言。危行,行为端正,不同流合污。 ②孙:同"逊",逊避、退逊。

[白话文]

孔子说:"国家政治清明的时候,应该言语正直、行为正直;国家政治昏乱的时候,行为仍应正直,不可失理,而在言语文字上,不但忠言逆耳,且易无端触犯忌讳,故应该慎言寡言,言必谦逊。"

[英译文]

The Master said, "When good government prevails in a state, language may be lofty and bold, and actions the same. When bad government prevails, the actions may be lofty and bold, but the language may be with some reserve."

14－5

子曰:"有德者必有言;有言者不必有德。仁者必有勇,勇者不必有仁。"

[白话文]

孔子说:"有德行的人,一定能说出有意义的话;但是能说出有意义的话的人,不一定是有德行的人。有仁德的人,一定有勇气;但是有勇气的人,不一定有仁德。"

[英译文]

The Master said, "The virtuous will be sure to speak correctly, but those whose speech is good may not always be virtuous. Men of principle are sure to be bold, but those who are bold may not always be men of principle."

14-6

南宫适^①問於孔子曰:"羿善射^②,奡盪舟^③,俱不得其死然。禹稷^④躬稼而有天下。"夫子不答。南宫适出。子曰:"君子哉若人! 尚德哉若人!"

[注释]

①南宫适:即南容,孔子的弟子,后为孔子的侄婿。参阅公冶长篇第一章(5-1)。适,读 kuò,不是"適"的简化字。亦有将南宫适写成南宫括的,盖"适"、"括"读音同。 ②羿善射:羿,读 yì,相传是夏代有穷国的君主,善射,后为其臣寒浞所杀。 ③奡荡舟:奡,读 ào,夏代寒浞的儿子,力大,善水战,曾伐斟氏,左右冲杀而覆其舟,后为少康所杀。 ④禹稷:禹,即夏禹,善治水,受舜禅位而为夏代第一个君主。稷即后稷,名弃,周民族的祖先,教民种田,其后武王建立了周朝。

[白话文]

南宫适问孔子说:"羿和奡二人,一个善射,一个力大能覆舟,皆以勇力见称,但都被杀而失败;禹和稷二人,一个治水,一个教民务农,安分修德,终得天下。老师认为怎样?"孔子知道南宫适所问的意思是将禹、稷拟比自己,所以未作正面回答。南宫适退出后,孔子说:"此人有君子之气度,此人知崇德之能成大功啊!"

[英译文]

Nan Gong-kuo, submitting an inquiry to Confucius, said, "Yi was skillful at archery, and Ao could move a boat along upon the land, but neither of them died a natural death. Yu and Ji personally wrought at the toils of husbandry, and they became possessors of the kingdom." The Master made no reply; but when Nan Gong-kuo went out, he said, "A superior man indeed is this! An esteemer of virtue indeed is this!"

14-7

子曰:"君子而不仁者有矣夫! 未有小人而仁者也。"

[白话文]

孔子说:"君子偶尔违仁,这种情况是有的。但小人行仁,这种事是不会有的。"

[英译文]

The Master said, "Superior man, and yet not always virtuous, there have been, alas! But there never has been a mean man, and, at the same time, virtuous."

14-8

子曰:"愛之,能勿勞乎? 忠焉,能勿誨乎?"

[白话文]

孔子说："爱一个人,能不使他勤劳、懂得创造和人生的艰辛吗(即所谓'禽犊之爱')? 忠于某个人,包括人家忠于我或我忠于人,其有错误时,能不给他教诲吗?"

[英译文]

The Master said, "Can there be love which does not lead to strictness with its object? Can there be loyalty which does not lead to the instruction of its object?"

14-9

子曰:"爲命①,裨諶②草創之,世叔③討論之,行人④子羽⑤修飾之,東里⑥子産潤色之。"

[注释]

①为命:命,指郑国当时应对诸侯的外交辞令。一说国家立法颁令。为命,即撰作辞令(或立法制令)。 ②裨谌:郑国大夫,也叫裨灶。他是子产所任的贤臣。 ③世叔:郑国大夫游吉。 ④行人:官名,掌出使各国之官。 ⑤子羽:郑国大夫公孙挥。 ⑥东里:地名,郑国大夫子产的居地。

[白话文]

孔子说："郑国所撰应对各国的外交辞令(或立法颁令),先由裨谌起草稿,再由世叔研究审议;外交事务官子羽修饰文字,子产润色。如此经过四贤的合作撰写,详审精密,便很少会败事。"

[英译文]

The Master said, "In preparing the governmental notifications, Bi-chen first made the rough draft; Shi-shu examined and discussed its contents; Zi-yu, the manager of foreign intercourse, then polished the style; and finally, Zi-chan of Dong-li gave it the proper elegance and finish."

14-10

或問子産①。子曰:"惠人也。"問子西②。曰:"彼哉! 彼哉!"問管仲③。曰:"人也。奪伯氏④駢邑⑤三百,飯疏食,没齒⑥無怨言。"

[注释]

①子产:孔子之前,郑国大夫,姓公孙,名侨,字子产,是郑国著名政治家、外交家。对内政、外交作出许多成就。参阅公冶长篇第十五章(5-15)。 ②子西:楚国大夫公子申,字子西。 ③管仲:齐国的上卿,春秋初期著名政治家。他的政绩、治国思想在《春秋·左传》中有记载。他辅佐齐桓公成为诸侯的盟主。但他曾帮助齐国公子纠与齐桓公争位,失败,后来又去辅助桓公,

故有人认为他不仁,对他颇有争议。参阅公冶长篇第十五章(5-15)、本篇第十七章(14-17)、本篇第十八章(14-18)。 ④伯氏:齐国大夫,名偃。 ⑤骈邑:骈,读 pián。邑,古时县的别称。骈邑,齐国的地名。 ⑥没齿:终生。

[白话文]

有人问子产这个人怎样。孔子说:"他是个专施恩惠给人民的人。"又问到子西。孔子说:"他呀! 他呀! 没有什么可取的。"又问到管仲。孔子说:"他是一个人才呀! 齐桓公将伯氏在骈邑的封地夺了三百户给管仲,使伯氏穷到吃粗粮蔬菜,到死也没有出怨言。"

[英译文]

Some one asked about Zi-chan. The Master said, "He was a kind man." He asked about Zi-xi. The Master said, "That man! That man!" He asked about Guan-zhong. "For him," said the Master, "The city of Pian, with three hundred families, was taken from the chief of the Bo family, who did not utter a murmuring word, though to the end of his life, he had only coarse rice to eat."

14-11

子曰:"貧而無怨難,富而無驕易。"

[白话文]

孔子说:"贫穷却不怨恨,是较难的;富裕却不骄傲,是比较容易做到的。"

[英译文]

The Master said, "To be poor without murmuring is difficult. To be rich without being proud is easy."

14-12

子曰:"孟公綽爲趙、魏老則優①,不可以爲滕、薛②大夫。"

[注释]

①孟公绰为赵、魏老则优:孟公绰,鲁国的大夫,是与孔子同时期的人,廉静寡欲,而短于才。赵、魏,皆晋国卿。老,家臣之长。优,有余。本句的意思是让孟公绰做赵、魏的家臣,才能绰绰有余。 ②滕、薛:鲁国附近的两个小诸侯国。

[白话文]

孔子说:"孟公绰要是做晋卿赵、魏的家臣之长(家老望尊,无官守之责),他的才能是绰绰有余的,但他却不能胜任滕、薛等小国政繁责重的大夫。"

[英译文]

The Master said, "Meng Gong-chuo is more than fit to be chief officer in the families of Zhao and Wei, but he is not fit to be great officer to either of the states Teng or Xue."

14－13

　　子路問成人①。子曰:"若臧武仲②之知,公綽③之不欲,卞莊子④之勇,冉求⑤之藝,文之以禮樂,亦可以爲成人矣!"曰:"今之成人者何必然? 見利思義,見危授命,久要⑥不忘平生之言,亦可以爲成人矣!"

[注释]

　　①成人:才德完善的人。　　②臧武仲:鲁国大夫臧孙纥。他曾逃去齐国,预料齐庄公不会长久,故拒绝接受齐庄公给他的封地。后齐庄公被杀,他也未受牵连,故人誉其智。　　③公綽:即孟公绰。参阅上章(14-12)。　　④卞莊子:卞,邑名。卞莊子是一位勇士,历史上流传有卞庄刺虎的故事。　　⑤冉求:孔子弟子,多才艺。雍也篇第六章(6-6)有"求也艺"句。　　⑥久要:要,同"约"。久要,即旧有之约。

[白话文]

　　子路问如何方可称为一个才德兼备的完人。孔子说:"要像臧武仲那样的智慧、孟公绰那样的清高廉洁、卞庄子的勇敢、冉求的技艺,并且熟习礼和乐,这也就可算是个才德完美的人了。"又说:"现在要成为一个完美的人何必要这样呢? 只要在见到财利时,先想想是否合乎义理;遇到危难时是否有献身精神;跟人的旧约,虽过了长久时间,仍不忘当时的诺言,这也就是人格完美的人了。"

[英译文]

Zi-lu asked what constituted a complete man. The Master said, "Suppose a man with the knowledge of Zang Wu-zhong, the freedom from covetousness of Gong-chuo, the bravery of Bian Zhuang-zi, and the varied talents of Ran-qiu; add to these the accomplishments of the rules of propriety and music—such an one might be reckoned a complete man." He then added, "But what is the necessity for a complete man of the present day to have all these things? The man, who in the view of gain thinks of righteousness; who in the view of danger is prepared to give up his life; and who does not forget an old agreement however far back it extends—such a man may be reckoned a complete man."

14－14

　　子問公叔文子①於公明賈②曰:"信乎? 夫子③不言、不笑、不取乎?"公明賈對曰:"以④告者過也。夫子時然後言,人不厭其言;樂然後笑,人不厌其笑；義然後取，人不厭其取。"子曰："其然？豈其然乎？"

[注释]

①公叔文子：卫国大夫，公叔是氏，名发，文是谥号。人称他是卫国的贤人。传闻他有不言、不笑、不取的德行。孔子初到卫国，就此问于公明贾。　②公明贾：卫国人，姓公明，名贾。　③夫子：孔子称指公叔文子。　④以：因的意思。

[白话文]

孔子向公明贾问卫大夫公叔文子的为人，说："是真的吗？听说公孙夫子平常不太讲话、不笑、不取财。"公明贾回答说："那是告诉你的人说得太过分了。公孙大夫是应该说话的时候才说话，人家就不讨厌他说的话；快乐的时候才笑，人家就不讨厌他的笑；对应该接受的财物才收取，人家就不讨厌他的取。"孔子（存疑地）说："是这样吗？难道真是这样吗？"

[英译文]

The Master asked Gong Ming-jia about Gong-shu Wen-zi, saying, "Is it true that your master speaks not, laughs not, and takes not?" Gong Ming-jia replied, "This has arisen from the reporters going beyond the truth. My master speaks when it is the time to speak, and so men do not get tired of his speaking. He laughs when there is occasion to be joyful, and so men do not get tired of his laughing. He takes when it is consistent with righteousness to do so, and so men do not get tired of his taking." The Master said, "So! But is it so with him?"

14-15

子曰："臧武仲以防求爲後於魯①，雖曰不要②君，吾不信也。"

[注释]

①臧武仲以防求为后于鲁：臧武仲，鲁国大夫。防，地名，位于山东费城东北。鲁襄公二十三年，臧武仲从鲁出奔到邾（蜀）国，继而从邾到防，据守防邑，并向君主要求立后封邑。　②要：要挟。

[白话文]

孔子说："臧武仲据守防邑，要求鲁君立他的后代。虽然有人说他并没有要挟君主，我是不相信的。"

[英译文]

The Master said, "Zang Wu-zhong, keeping possession of Fang, asked of duke of Lu to appoint a successor to him in his family. Although it may be said that he was not using force with his sovereign, I believe he was."

14－16

子曰：“晋文公^①谲^②而不正；齐桓公^③正而不谲。”

［注释］

①晋文公：晋献公的儿子，名重耳。献公因听信谗言，逼死太子申生，又派人去攻打重耳的封地蒲城，重耳出逃。十九年后，在秦穆公派兵护送下回国，先取得军队，又派人杀了晋怀公而成为国君，用诡道又成为诸侯盟主，是春秋五霸之一。伐楚，用阴谋取胜。　②谲：读 jué，欺诈、诡谲。　③齐桓公：姓姜，名小白，春秋五霸之一。他因不记射钩（与公子纠争位时，管仲奉纠命射中桓公衣带钩）而重用管仲为相，在内政、外交方面建树颇多。伐楚时，仗义执言，不用诡道。

［白话文］

孔子说：“晋文公诡谲，不走正道；齐桓公走正道，不行诡谲。”

［英译文］

The Master said, "The duke Wen of Jin was crafty and not upright. The duke Huan of Qi was upright and not crafty."

14－17

子路曰：“桓公杀公子纠，召忽死之^①，管仲不死。”曰：“未仁乎？”子曰：“桓公九合诸侯^②，不以兵车，管仲之力也。如其仁！ 如其仁！”

［注释］

①桓公杀公子纠，召忽死之：齐僖公生诸儿、纠、小白。僖公卒，立诸儿为襄公。襄公无道。齐大夫鲍叔牙知将乱，奉小白奔莒（读 jǔ，地名，今山东莒县）。僖公的表弟公孙无知弑襄公自立。齐大夫召忽——纠之师傅奉纠奔鲁，不久，齐大夫雍杀掉无知，小白自莒先入，立为桓公。纠又从鲁来战，管仲亦曾帮助纠与齐桓公争位。败，后奔鲁。齐使逼鲁庄公于次年杀纠，召忽自杀。管仲被囚至齐，齐桓公因鲍叔牙之竭力推荐，释管仲，委以重任，让他做了宰相。因此，子路问：“未仁乎？”　②九合诸侯：一说九次会合诸侯；一说九与纠通。疑为“纠合诸侯”，亦通。

［白话文］

子路说：“齐桓公杀了公子纠，召忽殉忠，管仲却不死。”接着说：“管仲不算是个仁人吧！”孔子说：“齐桓公多次召集各国诸侯会盟，不用武力，使天下太平几十年，老百姓避免了战乱祸害，这都是管仲的功劳。谁有如他这样的仁德？ 谁有如他这样的仁德？”

［英译文］

Zi-lu said, "The duke Huan caused his brother Jiu to be killed, when Zhao-hu died with his master, but Guan-zhong did not die. May not I say that he was wanting in virtue?" The Master said, "The duke Huan assembled all the princes together, and that not with weapons of war and chariots—it was all through the influence of Guan-zhong. Whose beneficence was like his?"

14－18

子贡曰:"管仲非仁者与①?桓公殺公子糾,不能死,又相②之。"子曰:"管仲相桓公,霸③諸侯,一匡④天下,民到於今受其賜。微⑤管仲,吾其被髮左衽⑥矣。豈若匹夫匹婦⑦之爲諒⑧也,自經⑨於溝瀆,而莫之知也?"

[注释]

①与:同"欤",表示疑问。跟"吗"或"呢"相同。 ②相:辅。 ③霸:古代诸侯联盟的首领。 ④匡:正。 ⑤微:无。 ⑥被发左衽:被,同"披"。左衽,衣襟向左开。被发左衽,是描述当时有些少数民族披着头发、衣襟开的打扮。 ⑦匹夫匹妇:指平常人,或指无知男女。 ⑧谅:遵守信用,这里指小信。 ⑨自经:自缢。

[白话文]

子贡说:"管仲恐不能称为仁者吧?齐桓公杀了公子纠,管仲不守节殉主,反而去辅佐桓公。"孔子说:"管仲辅佐桓公,成为诸侯的盟主,匡正了混乱的天下,老百姓到现在还享受到他的好处。倘若没有管仲,中国恐怕已沦亡于被发左衽的夷狄。他难道也该如无知的匹夫匹妇,只知守小信小节,自缢在水沟里,死了还没有人知道吗?"

[英译文]

Zi-gong said, "Guan-zhong, I apprehend, was wanting in virtue. When the duke Huan caused his brother Jiu to be killed, Guan-zhong was not able to die with him. Moreover, he became prime minister to Huan." The Master said, "Guan-zhong acted as prime minister to the duke Huan, made him leader of all the princes, and united and rectified the whole kingdom. Down to the present day, the people enjoy the gifts which he conferred. But for Guan-zhong, we should now be wearing our hair unbound, and the lappets of our coats buttoning on the left side. Will you require from him the small fidelity of common men and common women, who would commit suicide in a stream or ditch, no one knowing anything about them?"

14－19

公叔文子之臣大夫僎①,與文子同升諸公。子聞之曰:"可以爲'文'矣。"

［注释］

①僎：读 zhuàn，卫国大夫，原是公叔文子之家臣，由于其贤能，被公叔文子荐于公朝，同列公卿之位。

［白话文］

公叔文子的家臣僎，由文子举荐升为大夫，与文子同上公朝。孔子知道这件事后，说："公叔文子真可以为'文'的谥号了。"

［英译文］

The great officer, Zhuan, who had been family-minister to Gong-shu Wen-zi, ascended to the prince's court in company with Wen. The Master, having heard of it, said, "He deserved to be considered Wen (the accomplished)."

14－20

子言衞靈公之無道也，康子①曰："夫如是，奚而不喪②？"孔子曰："仲叔圉③治賓客，祝鮀治宗廟，王孫賈治軍旅。夫如是，奚其喪？"

［注释］

①康子：即季康子。参阅为政篇第二十章(2-20)。　②奚而不丧：奚，疑问词，为什么。丧，丧亡。这里指的是国家丧亡。　③仲叔圉：圉，读 yǔ。仲叔圉，即孔文子，卫国大夫〔参阅公冶长篇第十四章(5-14)〕。他和祝鮀〔字子鱼，亦为卫国大夫，参阅雍也篇第十四章(6-14)〕、王孙贾〔卫国大夫，参阅八佾篇第十三章(3-13)〕三个人都是卫国有才能的重臣。卫灵公无道而未致亡国，正是因为善用这三位的才能。

［白话文］

孔子谈论到卫灵公无道的事，季康子就问："既然如此，他的国家怎么不丧亡呢？"孔子说："卫国还有人才，像仲叔圉掌管外交，祝鮀掌管宗庙祭祀，王孙贾统率军队。能这样善于用人，怎么会亡国呢？"

［英译文］

The Master was speaking about the unprincipled course of the duke Ling of Wei, when Ji Kang-zi said, "Since he is of such a character, how is it he does not lose his state?" Confucius said, "The Zhong Shu-yu has the superintendence of his guests and of strangers; the litanist, Zhu-tuo, has the management of his ancestral temple; and Wang Sun-jia has the direction of the army and forces—with such officers as these, how should he lose his state?"

14－21

子曰："其言之不怍①，則爲之也難。"

[注释]

①怍:读 zuò,惭愧。

[白话文]

孔子说:"一个人如果大言不惭,那么,要实现他的话一定是很难的。"

[英译文]

The Master said, "He who speaks without modesty will find it difficult to make his words good."

14-22

陈成子弑简公①。孔子沐浴而朝②,告於哀公曰:"陈恒弑其君,请讨之。"公曰:"告夫三子③!"孔子曰:"以吾从大夫之後,不敢不告也。君曰'告夫三子'者!"之三子告,不可。孔子曰:"以吾从大夫之後,不敢不告也。"

[注释]

①陈成子弑简公:陈成子,齐国大夫,名恒,又名田成子(古时陈、田同音)。简公,齐国君主,名壬。弑,读 shì,臣杀死君或子女杀死父母,称弑。陈成子弑君,事在鲁哀公十四年。 ②孔子沐浴而朝:其时孔子已告退在家,对此事件十分重视,特地沐浴去朝见鲁哀公。孔子之所以如此重视,一是弑君罪大,齐鲁又为邻,按周制邻邦有弑逆者,诸侯当不请而讨;二是本国三子掌握重权,且现轻君僭越现象。 ③三子:指鲁国的季孙、仲孙、孟孙。

[白话文]

齐国大夫陈成子杀死了齐君简公。孔子沐浴斋戒,去朝见鲁哀公说:"陈恒杀了他的国君,请发兵讨伐他。"哀公说:"你去向三位大夫报告吧!"孔子退出,自言自语说:"因为我做过大夫,所以不敢不将此事报告国君!而君主不自命三家大夫,却说'你去告诉三家大夫吧!'真令人费解。"孔子转而去向三家大夫报告,他们不同意发兵讨伐。孔子说:"因为我曾做过大夫,所以知道了这件事,不敢不依礼来报告啊!"

[英译文]

Chen Cheng-zi murdered the duke Jian of Qi. Confucius bathed, went to court, and informed the duke Ai, saying, "Chen Heng has slain his sovereign, I beg that you will undertake to punish him." The duke said, "Inform the chiefs of the three families of it." Confucius retired, and said, "Following in the rear of the great officers, I did not dare not to represent such a matter, and my prince says, 'Inform the chiefs of the three families of it.'" He went to the chiefs, and informed them, but they would not act. Confucius then said, "Following in the rear of the great officers, I did not dare not to represent such a matter."

14 – 23

子路問事君。子曰:"勿欺也,而犯之。"

[白话文]

子路问怎样侍奉君主。孔子说:"要忠诚,不可欺骗;进谏时,不要怕触犯他,要直言敢谏。"

[英译文]

Zi-lu asked how a ruler should be served. The Master said, "Do not impose on him, and, moreover, withstand him to his face."

14 – 24

子曰:"君子上達,小人下達①。"

[注释]

①上达、下达:达,通达。通达仁义,谓之上;通达财利,谓之下。朱熹所谓"循天理",就是行仁义。"日进乎高明",求上进,就是上达;而"徇人欲",甚至为谋财利而"日究乎污下",就是下达。本章述义与里仁篇第十六章(4-16)相近。

[白话文]

孔子说:"君子循天理,行仁义,日求上进;小人追求私欲,甚至为谋财利而不惜合污下流。"

[英译文]

The Master said, "The progress of the superior man is upwards; the progress of the mean man is downwards."

14 – 25

子曰:"古之學者爲己,今之學者爲人。"

[白话文]

孔子说:"古代求学的人为了充实和提高自己的学问道德;今之求学者是为了让别人知道自己、炫耀于人而学习。"

[英译文]

The Master said, "In ancient times, men learned with a view to their own improvement. Nowadays, men learn with a view to the approbation of others."

14－26

蘧伯玉①使人於孔子。孔子與之坐而問焉，曰："夫子②何爲?"對曰："夫子欲寡其過而未能也。"使者出。子曰："使乎③! 使乎!"

[注释]

①蘧伯玉：蘧，读 qú，姓蘧，字伯玉，名瑗，谥号成子。卫国有名的贤大夫，孔子在卫时常住其家。　②夫子：孔子指称蘧大夫。　③使乎：称赞语。孔子对使者能言之卑谦，其主之贤盖彰，回答得体而加以赞叹。重复"使乎"，加重语气。

[白话文]

卫国大夫蘧伯玉，派了一个使者来鲁国，问候孔子。孔子让他坐下并问他说："蘧夫子近来在干些什么?"使者回答说："他老先生想要减少自己的过失，但总觉得未能做到。"使者告辞出去后，孔子连加称赞："好个使者呀! 好个使者呀!"

[英译文]

Qu Bo-yu sent a messenger with friendly inquiries to Confucius.

Confucius sat with him, and questioned him. "What," said he, "is your master engaged in?" The messenger replied, "My master is anxious to make his faults few, but he has not yet succeeded." He then went out, and the Master said, "A messenger indeed! A messenger indeed!"

14－27

子曰："不在其位，不謀其政。"

[注释]

此章重出，参阅泰伯篇第十四章(8-14)。

14－28

曾子曰："君子思不出其位①。"

[注释]

①君子思不出其位：此句是曾子接上章引用《易经》艮卦的象辞加以伸展的。有的版本将此章合并入上章。本书仍从朱熹《集注》版本排列。

[白话文]

曾子说："君子所思考的是他所任的职责范围内的事。"

[英译文]

The philosopher Zeng said, "The superior man, in his thoughts, does not go out of his place."

14 - 29
子曰:"君子耻其言而过其行。"

[白话文]

孔子说:"君子认为,说的比做的多是可耻的。"

[英译文]

The Master said, "The superior man is modest in his speech, but exceeds in his actions."

14 - 30
子曰:"君子道者三,我无能焉:仁者不忧①,知者不惑,勇者不惧。"子贡曰:"夫子自道②也。"

[注释]

①仁者不忧:参阅子罕篇第十八章(9-18)。我无能焉,乃孔子自己说"我没有做到"。《集注》曰:"自责以勉人。" ②自道:同"自谦"。

[白话文]

孔子说:"君子之道有三:仁者不忧,智者不惑,勇者不惧。但是,我却没有做到。"子贡说:"这些话正是老师的自谦之辞。"

[英译文]

The Master said, "The way of the superior man is threefold, but I am not equal to it. Virtuous, he is free from anxieties; wise, he is free from perplexities; bold, he is free from fear." Zi-gong said, "Master, that is what you yourself say."

14 - 31
子贡方人①。子曰:"赐②也贤乎哉?夫我则不暇。"

[注释]

①方人:方,比方。方人,论人长短。 ②赐:子贡姓端木,名赐。

[白话文]

子贡喜欢议论别人的长短。孔子说:"赐呀!你就那么好吗?我却没有这些闲工夫去唠叨别人!"

[英译文]

Zi-gong was in the habit of comparing men together. The Master said, "Ci, must have reached a high pitch of excellence! Now, I have not leisure for this."

14－32

子曰："不患人之不己知，患其不能也①。"

[注释]

①不患人之不己知，患其不能也：按学而篇第十六章(1-16)、里仁篇第十四章(4-14)、卫灵公篇第十八章(15-18)及本章，共四次且意义相同(或文字有小异者)。故朱熹曰："盖屡言之，其丁宁之意，亦可见矣。"

[白话文]

孔子说："不愁别人不知道自己，只愁自己有没有真才实学。"

[英译文]

The Master said, "I will not be concerned at men's not knowing me; I will be concerned at my own want of ability."

14－33

子曰："不逆①诈，不億②不信，抑③亦先覺④者，是賢乎！"

[注释]

①逆：预料。 ②亿：臆度，主观猜测。 ③抑：转折词，相当于"可是"、"然而"。 ④先觉：先发觉。朱熹曰："言虽不逆不亿，而于人之情伪自然先觉，乃为贤也。"又引杨氏曰："君子一于诚而已。然未有诚而不明者，故虽不逆诈，不亿不信而常先觉也。"

[白话文]

孔子说："不要预先怀疑别人骗我，也不要预先臆度别人会对我失信，并不特别去顾虑这些，但却能早先发觉，这不就是个贤明之人吗！"

[英译文]

The Master said, "He who does not anticipate attempts to deceive him, nor think beforehand of his not being believed, and yet apprehends these things readily(when they occur)—is he not a man of superior worth?"

14－34

微生畝①謂孔子曰："丘何爲是栖栖②者與？無乃爲佞③乎？"孔子曰："非敢爲佞也，疾固④也！"

[注释]

①微生亩：姓微生，名亩，鲁国的一位隐士(一说是道家人物)。他和孔子对话直呼孔子之名，故有人怀疑他可能是孔子的前辈。 ②栖栖：忙忙碌碌，不安其居。 ③佞：读 nìng，有口才、才智。惯用花言巧语谄媚人，称佞人。 ④疾固：疾，痛恨的意思。固，固陋。疾固，痛恨固陋者。

[白话文]

微生亩对孔子说："丘,你为什么这样忙碌、不安居,到处游说？莫非要卖弄你的口才吗？"孔子说："我不敢卖弄口才,只是痛恨那些固陋者昧于仁义之道,想改变他们而已！"

[英译文]

Wei Sheng-mu said to Confucius, "Qiu, how is it that you keep roosting about? Is it not that you are an insinuating talker?" Confucius said, "I do not dare to play the part of such a talker, but I hate obstinacy."

14－35

子曰："骥不称其力,称其德也。"

[白话文]

孔子说："好马之所以受称赞,并不是因为它有好的脚力,而是因为它的德性驯良。"

[英译文]

The Master said, "A horse is called a Ji, not because of its strength, but because of its other good qualities."

14－36

或曰："以德①報怨,何如？"子曰："何以報德？ 以直②報怨,以德報德。"

[注释]

①德:朱注曰:"谓恩惠也。""以德报怨"语出老子。　②直:朱注曰:"爱憎取舍,一以至公而无私。"故"直"应作"公正"解。

[白话文]

有人问："用恩惠去报答和我有仇恨的人,怎么样？"孔子说："那么,用什么来报答对你有恩惠的人呢？ 应该以公正来报答怨恨,用恩惠来报答恩惠。"

[英译文]

Some one said, "What do you say concerning the principle that injury should be recompensed with kindness?" The Master said, "With what then will you recompense kindness? Recompense injury with justice, and recompense kindness with kindness."

14－37

子曰："莫我知也夫!"子貢曰："何爲其莫知子也?"子曰："不怨天,不尤人,下學而上達。知我者其天乎!"

[白话文]

孔子说:"没有人知道我的用心了吧!"子贡问:"何以没人知道老师的用心呢?"孔子说:"我既不怨恨天,也不责怪人,只是下学人事,从浅近处下工夫,因循序进而上达,领悟天理。恐怕也只有天晓得了吧!"

[英译文]

The Master said, "Alas! there is no one that knows me." Zi-gong said, "What do you mean by thus saying—that no one knows you?" The Master replied, "I do not murmur against Heaven. I do not grumble against men. My studies lie low, and my penetration rises high. But there is Heaven—that knows me!"

14－38

公伯寮①愬②子路於季孫。子服景伯③以告,曰："夫子④固有惑志於公伯寮,吾力猶能肆⑤諸⑥市朝。"子曰："道之將行也與⑦,命也;道之將廢也與,命也。公伯寮其如命何!"

[注释]

①公伯寮:复姓公伯,名寮,鲁国人。一说他是孔子弟子。 ②愬:诉说坏话。 ③子服景伯:子服,名何,字伯,景是谥,鲁国大夫。一说他也是孔子弟子。 ④夫子:指季孙。春秋时卿大夫亦称夫子。 ⑤肆:杀而陈其尸曰"肆"。 ⑥诸:"之于"二字的合音。 ⑦与:同"欤",表示感叹。

[白话文]

公伯寮在季孙面前说子路的坏话。鲁国大夫子服景伯将此事告诉孔子,他说:"季孙听了公伯寮的话,对子路自然会生疑心,但对公伯寮,我有力量能够杀掉他,并将他陈尸于街市示众。"孔子说:"我所主张的治世之道如果能够实行,这是天命;如果不能实行,这也是天命。公伯寮能对天命怎么样?"

[英译文]

Gong Bo-liao, having slandered Zi-lu to Ji-sun, Zi-fu Jing-bo informed Confucius of it, saying, "Our master is certainly being led astray by the Gong Bo-liao, but I have still power enough left to cut Liao off, and expose his corpse in the market and in the court."

The Master said, "If my principles are to advance, it is so ordered. If they are to fall to the ground, it is so ordered. What can the Gong Bo-liao do where such ordering is concerned?"

14－39

子曰："賢者辟^①世，其次辟地，其次辟色，其次辟言。"

［注释］

①辟：同"避"。

［白话文］

孔子说："贤人看到天下无道，政治昏乱，就避开世俗，隐居不仕；次一等的人避开混乱的社会到治理好的地方去；再次一等的人不愿看到某些人的脸色而避开；再次一等的人不愿听到某些人的妄语危言而违避了。"

［英译文］

The Master said, "Some men of worth retire from the world. Some retire from particular states. Some retire because of disrespectful looks. Some retire because of contradictory language."

14－40

子曰："作者七人矣。"^①

［注释］

①本章连接上一章。较多的版本与上章合为一章。本书从朱熹《集注》版本排列。句中的"作"字，即起而为之。七人，据《集解》包曰："为之者凡七人。谓长沮、桀溺、丈人、石门、荷蒉、仪封人、楚狂接舆。"

［白话文］

孔子说："起而隐居的已有七个人了。"

［英译文］

The Master said, "Those who have done this are seven men."

14－41

子路宿於石門^①。晨門^②曰："奚自？"子路曰："自孔氏。"曰："是知其不可而爲之者與？"

［注释］

①石门：鲁国都城外门。　②晨门：早晨看守城门的人。

193

[白话文]

子路在石门外住了一夜。翌晨进城，看守城门的人问他："你从哪里来?"子路回答："从孔家来。"守城门的人说："就是那位明知其事之不可为而仍欲为之者吗?"

[英译文]

Zi-lu happening to pass the night is Shi-men, the gate-keeper said to him "Whom do you come from?" Zi-lu said, "From Mr. Kong." "It is he—is it not?" said the other, "Who knows the impracticable nature of the times, and yet will be doing in them."

14－42

子击磬①於衞，有荷蕢②而過孔氏之門者，曰："有心哉，擊磬乎!"既而曰："鄙③哉! 硜硜④乎! 莫己知⑤也，斯己而已矣⑥。深則厲，淺則揭⑦。"子曰："果哉⑧! 末之難矣。"

[注释]

①磬:读 qìng。一种打击乐器，状如曲尺，玉制或石制。　②荷蕢:荷，负、担。蕢，草筐。③鄙:狭、固执。　④硜硜:硜，读 kēng，击磬声。　⑤莫己知:指人家不知道自己。　⑥斯己而已矣:"斯己"的"己"作"止"字解。"而已矣"，语助词。　⑦深则厉，浅则揭:句出《诗经·邶风·匏有苦叶》(朱注误为"卫风"，应更正)。本句的意思是:涉水时遇到深水，索性就穿着衣徒步涉水过去;水浅，不妨撩起衣走过去。其含义是讥孔子的莫己知(人不知己)而不止(还在固执地奔波)。用涉水当视深浅而用不同的方式来比喻道之可行则行、不可则止、可以已矣。　⑧果哉:果然、果敢。

[白话文]

孔子在卫国，有一天正在击磬消遣，有位负着草筐的人经过孔子的门前，说:"真是位有心人在击磬!"听了一会儿又说:"这硜硜声是多么鄙狭、固执呀! 没人知道自己，就算了吧! 水深处就干脆和衣徒步涉水过去，水浅就撩起衣服走过去。"孔子说:"果敢于忘掉世事，那就没有什么难的了。"

[英译文]

The Master was playing, one day, on a musical stone in Wei, when a man, carrying a straw basket, passed the door of the house where Confucius was, and said, "His heart is full who so beats the musical stone." A little while after, he added, "How contemptible is the one ideaed obstinacy those sounds display! When one is taken no notice of he has simply at once to give over his wish for public employment. Deep water must be crossed with the clothes on; shallow water may be crossed with the clothes held up." The Master said, "How determined is he in his purpose! But this is not difficult!"

14－43

子張曰:"《書》①云:'高宗諒陰②,三年不言.'何謂也?"子曰:"何必高宗? 古之人皆然. 君薨③,百官總己④以聽於冢宰⑤三年."

[注释]

①《书》:指《尚书》。　②高宗谅阴:高宗,即商朝第二十二任君王武丁。谅阴,古代天子居丧的名称。　③薨:读 hōng,古代诸侯或大官死亡称薨。　④总己:总管自己职事。　⑤冢宰:冢,读 zhǒng。冢宰,后世所称宰相。

[白话文]

子张说:"《尚书》说:'商代高宗居丧,三年不问政。'这是什么意思?"孔子说:"不仅高宗是这样,古代帝王都如此。君主死了,三年之内各官员总管自己的职事而听命于宰相。"

[英译文]

Zi-zhang said, "What is meant when the Shu says that Gao-zong, while observing the usual imperial mourning, was for three years without speaking?" The Master said, "Why must Gao-zong be referred to as an example of this? The ancients all did so. When the sovereign died, the officers all attended to their several duties, taking instructions from the prime minister for three years."

14－44

子曰:"上好禮,則民易使也."

[白话文]

孔子说:"在上位者崇尚礼,事事遵礼而行,则下属和人民也会敬重上位者而听从使命。"

[英译文]

The Master said, "When rulers love to observe the rules of propriety, the people respond readily to the calls on them for service."

14－45

子路問君子. 子曰:"脩己以敬①."曰:"如斯而已乎?"曰:"脩己以安人②."曰:"如斯而已乎?"曰:"脩己以安百姓,脩己以安百姓. 堯、舜其猶病③諸!"

［注释］

①脩己以敬:脩,同"修"。脩己,修养自己的品德。敬,严肃认真的态度。　②人:这里指周围的人。　③病:缺陷,不完整。

［白话文］

　　子路问怎样才算是君子。孔子说:"用严肃认真的态度来修养自己的品德。"子路说:"这样就可以吗?"孔子说:"修养自己使周围的人安定。"子路说:"这样就可以吗?"孔子说:"修养自己,使百姓安定。修养自己,使百姓都安定,恐怕连尧、舜也忧虑没有完全做到呢!"

［英译文］

　　Zi-lu asked what constituted the superior man. The Master said, "The culti-vation of himself in reverential carefulness." "And is this all?" said Zi-lu. "He cultivates himself so as to give rest to others," was the reply. "And is this all?" again asked Zi-lu. The Master said, "He cultivates himself so as to give rest to all the people. He cultivates himself so as to give rest to all the people—even Yao and Shun were still solicitous about this."

14－46

　　原壤①夷②俟③。子曰:"幼而不孫弟,長而無述焉,老而不死,是爲賊④."以杖叩其脛⑤。

［注释］

①原壤:孔子的故友,是一个放浪形骸、乏善可陈的人。《礼记·檀弓下》篇里有其母死,孔子帮着整理棺材,原壤却不哭而歌的记载。　②夷:蹲踞。　③俟:等待。　④贼:害。　⑤胫:小腿。

［白话文］

　　原壤蹲踞在那儿等候孔子,见到孔子也不相迎。孔子说:"你小时候不知道谦顺孝悌,长大后又没有作为,如今老了还不死,真是一个祸害呀!"既责之,又用拐杖敲他的小腿。

［英译文］

　　Yuan-rang was squatting on his heels, and so waited the approach of the Master, who said to him, "In youth, not humble as befits a junior; in manhood, doing nothing worthy of being handed down; and living on to old age—this is to be a pest." With this he hit him on the shank with his staff.

14－47

阙党①童子将命②。或问之曰："益者③与?"子曰："吾见其居於位④也,见其與先生并行⑤也。非求益者也,欲速成者也。"

[注释]

①阙党:一个地方团体名称。 ②将命:将,带着。命,命令、通知。这里指传达主宾之间的话。 ③益者:学问上进者。 ④居于位:按礼节,童子隅坐无位(隅坐,只能坐边、角,或只能站在主人后,无正式席位),居于正式席位是一种不知礼的行为。 ⑤与先生并行:先生,指长辈或对年龄大于自己者尊称。并行,并肩而行。按礼节,童子应跟在长辈身后行。

[白话文]

阙党的一个童子,孔子叫他去向客人传话。有人问孔子:"这大概是个学问有进步的童子吧?"孔子说:"我看他坐在成年人的位子上,又看见他和长辈并肩地走着,这不是个要求上进的人,而是个急于求成的人。"

[英译文]

A youth of the village of Que was employed by Confucius to carry the messages between him and his visitors. Some one asked about him, saying, "I suppose he has made great progress." The Master said, "I observe that he is fond of occupying the seat of a full-grown man; I observe that he walks shoulder to shoulder with his elders. He is not one who is seeking to make progress in learning. He wished quickly to become a man."

卫灵公第十五

本篇凡四十一章（15—1～15—41）。

15－1

衛靈公問陳^①於孔子。孔子對曰:"俎豆之事^②,則嘗^③聞之矣;軍旅之事,未之學也。"明日遂行。

在陳^④絕糧,從者病,莫能興^⑤。子路慍見曰:"君子亦有窮乎?"子曰:"君子固窮,小人窮斯濫^⑥矣。"

[注释]

①陈:战阵。　②俎豆之事:俎,读 zǔ,古代祭祀时盛牛、羊祭品的器具。豆,也是盛食的器具,状如高座的盆子。俎豆之事,这里指以礼制祭祀的事。　③尝:曾经。　④陈:这里乃指诸侯国的陈国,今河南省淮阳一带的小国。孔子离卫后,经曹、宋、郑,约在鲁哀公六年到陈。
⑤兴:起来。　⑥滥:溢,指溢出做人的范围——放溢为非。

[白话文]

卫灵公向孔子问作战布阵的事。孔子回答说:"礼制祭祀方面的事,我曾经听到过。军队打仗一类事情,我没有学过。"第二天,孔子就离开了卫国。

孔子到了陈国(实际是在陈、蔡边境上。吴正伐陈,楚派兵救陈并派人聘请孔子,但陈、蔡又怕孔子去楚,孔子被围困于荒郊),粮食断绝了,从行的弟子也饿成病,起不来了。子路懊恼地来见孔子,说:"君子也会有这样穷困的时候吗?"孔子说:"有的,只是君子有穷困能把持自己,若是小人就会胡作非为了。"

[英译文]

The duke Ling of Wei asked Confucius about tactics. Confucius replied, "I have heard all about sacrificial vessels, but I have not learned military matters." On this, he took his departure the next day.

When he was in Chen, their provisions were exhausted, and his followers became so ill that they were unable to rise. Zi-lu, with evident dissatisfaction, said, "Has the superior man likewise to endure in this way?" The Master said, "The superior man may indeed have to endure want, but the mean man, when he is in want, gives way to unbridled license."

15－2

子曰:"賜^①也,女以予爲多學而識^②之者與?"對曰:"然,非與?"曰:"非也,予一以貫之。"

[注释]

①赐:端木赐,即子贡。　②识:读 zhì,同"记"。

[白话文]

孔子说:"赐呀! 你以为我是个博学而强记的人吗?"子贡回答说:"是的。难道不是这样的吗?"孔子说:"不是的。我是以一个基本的道理贯穿在自己所学之中的。"

[英译文]

The Master said, "Ci! You think, I suppose, that I am one who learns many things and keeps then in memory?" Zi-gong replied, "Yes, but perhaps it is not so?" "No," was the answer, "I seek a unity all-pervading."

15-3

子曰:"由,知德者鲜矣。"

[白话文]

孔子说:"仲由(子路)呀! 懂得道德的人太少了!"

[英译文]

The Master said, "You, those who know virtue are few."

15-4

子曰:"無爲而治①者,其舜也與! 夫②何爲哉? 恭己正南面而已矣。"

[注释]

①无为而治:舜继尧,任贤能,制礼仪,为政以德,顺应自然,让社会按本身规律发展,得以天下大治,而表面上只看到舜面南恭坐而已。 ②夫:作指示词,那、这。也可作代词,他。亦可作助词,用在一句话之前,如在句末或句中停顿处,表示感叹。

[白话文]

孔子说:"无所作为而把天下治理好的,大概只有舜吧! 他做了些什么呢? 只是恭敬地面南端坐在朝廷上罢了。"

[英译文]

The Master said, "May not Shun be instanced as having governed efficiently without exertion? What did he do? He did nothing but gravely and reverently occupy his royal seat."

15-5

子張問行①。子曰:"言忠信,行篤敬,雖蠻貊之邦①,行矣! 言不忠信,行不篤敬,雖州里,行乎哉?立,則見其參於前也③;在輿,則見其倚於衡也④。夫然後行。"子張書諸紳⑤。

[注释]

　①子张问行:孔子的弟子子张问做一个人怎样才可以到处行得通。一说,子张问去异邦之道。　②蛮貊之邦:蛮,指南蛮。貊,读 mò,古称北狄。一说古代东北的少数民族。蛮貊之邦,即南蛮、北狄的邦国。　③立,则见其参于前也:站立时,(忠信、笃敬几个字)好像立在面前。④在舆,则见其倚于衡也:乘车时,(这几个字)好像傍倚于车前横木(衡木)上。意思是随其所在,常若有见。　⑤绅:腰间大带之下垂部分。

[白话文]

　子张问为人如何可以到处行得通。孔子说:"说话忠诚信实,行为笃实恭敬,即使到了蛮貊之邦,也是行得通的。如果说话不忠信,行为不笃敬,即使在自己家乡,能行得通吗?所以,你站着的时候,就好像看到忠信、笃敬几个字立在你面前;你乘车时,就好像看到这几个字傍倚于衡木上。能够这样,才能使自己到处行得通。"子张就把这些话写在腰间大带上了。

[英译文]

　Zi-zhang asked how a man should conduct himself, so as to be everywhere appreciated. The Master said, "Let his words be sincere and truthful, and his actions honourable and careful—such conduct may be practised among the rude tribes of the South or the North. If his words be not sincere and truthful, and his actions not honourable and careful, will be, with such conduct, be appreciated, even in his neighbourhood? When he is standing, let him see those two things, as it were, fronting him. When he is in a carriage, let him see them attached to the yoke. Then may he subsequently carry them into practice." Zi-zhang wrote these counsels on the end of his sash.

15-6

　子曰:"直哉史魚①!邦有道,如矢②;邦無道,如矢。君子哉蘧伯玉③!邦有道,則仕;邦無道,則可卷而懷之④。"

[注释]

　①史鱼:朱注:"史,官名。鱼,卫大夫,名鰌。"他是一个非常正直的史官,以敢谏而闻名,临终时遗命儿子不要"治丧正室",以劝谏卫灵公进用蘧伯玉、斥退弥子瑕,史称"尸谏"。　②矢:箭。　③蘧伯玉:参阅宪问篇第二十六章(14-26)注。因史鱼"尸谏",被卫灵公起用。　④卷而怀之:卷,收。怀,藏。卷而怀之,即收藏起来,喻隐居起来。

[白话文]

孔子说:"正直啊,史鱼! 国家政治清明时,他忠心任职,像箭一样正直;国家政治昏乱时,他正言直谏,也像箭一样正直。蘧伯玉是个君子呀! 国家政治清明时,他出来做官;国家政治昏乱时,他就收藏起自己的才能,隐居起来。"

[英译文]

The Master said, "Truly straightforward was the historiographer Yu. When good government prevailed in his state, he was like an arrow. When bad government prevailed, he was like an arrow. A superior man indeed is Qu Bo-yu! When good government prevails in his state, he is to be found in office. When bad government prevails, he can roll his principles up, and keep them in his breast."

15-7

子曰:"可與言而不與之言,失人;不可與言而與之言,失言。知者不失人,亦不失言。"

[白话文]

孔子说:"可以和他交谈而不和他谈,就会错失人才;不可以和他交谈却和他谈,就是失言。聪明人不会错失人才,也不会失言。"

[英译文]

The Master said, "When a man may be spoken with, not to speak to him is to err in reference to the man. When a man may not be spoken with, to speak to him is to err in reference to our words. The wise err neither in regard to their man nor to their words."

15-8

子曰:"志士、仁人,無求生以害仁,有殺身以成仁。"

[白话文]

孔子说:"志士、仁人,不会为了保全自己的生命而损害仁义,宁肯牺牲自己的生命来成全仁义。"

[英译文]

The Master said, "The determined scholar and the man of virtue will not seek to live at the expense of injuring their virtue. They will even sacrifice their lives to preserve their virtue complete."

15-9

子貢問爲仁。子曰："工欲善其事，必先利其器。居是邦也，事其大夫之賢者，友其士之仁者。"

[白话文]

子贡问如何实施仁。孔子说："工匠要做好他的工作，必须先要有快利的器具。在一个国家里要施行仁政也是这样，先要师事该国的贤大夫，结交当地有仁德的士人。"

[英译文]

Zi-gong asked about the practice of virtue. The Master said, "The mechanic, who wishes to do his work well, must first sharpen his tools. When you are living in any state, take service with the most worthy among its great officers, and make friends of the most virtuous among its scholars."

15-10

顏淵問爲邦①。子曰："行夏之時②，乘殷之輅③，服周之冕，樂則《韶》舞④。放⑤鄭聲，遠佞人。鄭聲淫，佞人殆⑥。"

[注释]

①颜渊问为邦：朱熹云："颜子王佐之才。"故问治天下之道。曰"为邦"者，谦辞。　②行夏之时：实行夏代的历法，即现在使用的农历。　③殷之辂：商（约公元前十七世纪初至前十一世纪）盘庚（帝名）迁都于殷，故商也称殷。辂，木车。殷所设计、使用的木车，朴实坚固。　④《韶》舞：《韶》，虞、舜时之乐曲，可伴舞。孔子认为它尽善尽美。一说"韶舞"是一种舞曲名。但据《荀子·乐论》"舞韶歌武"，可见"舞"、"歌"是动词，"韶"、"武"是名词。　⑤放：弃逐。　⑥佞人殆：佞人，巧言令色、阿谀谄媚之人。殆：读 dài，危害的意思。

[白话文]

颜渊问治国之道。孔子说："用夏代的历法（节气准，利农事），乘殷代的木车（朴实耐用），穿戴周朝的衣冠（文采、不奢侈），乐则采舜时的《韶》舞。弃去郑国的乐曲，远离巧言令色、阿谀奉承的佞人。因郑声放纵，佞人危险。"

[英译文]

Yan-yuan asked how the government of a country should be administered. The Master said, "Follow the seasons of Xia. Ride in the state carriage of Yin. Wear the ceremonial cap of Zhou. Let the music be the Shao with its pantomimes. Banish the songs of Zheng, and keep far from specious talkers. The songs of Zheng are licentious; specious talkers are dangerous."

15 – 11

子曰:"人無遠慮,必有近憂。"

[白话文]

孔子说:"做任何事如果没有深远的考虑,忧患就会随时临近。"

[英译文]

The Master said, "If a man take no thought about what is distant, he will find sorrow near at hand."

15 – 12

子曰:"已矣乎!吾未見好德如好色者也。"

[注释]

此章重出,参阅子罕篇第十七章(9-17)。

15 – 13

子曰:"臧文仲①其竊位者與?知柳下惠之賢而不與立也!"

[注释]

①臧文仲:即臧孙辰,鲁国大夫〔参阅公冶长篇第十七章(5-17)〕。齐孝公率兵侵鲁时,他建议鲁僖公召柳下惠,结果由柳下惠的弟弟展喜,受柳下惠的分析和意见,用词说服齐孝公退师。臧氏又世为司寇,柳下惠三黜士师〔参阅微子篇第二十二章(18-22)〕,而士师又正为臧氏属官。

[白话文]

孔子说:"臧文仲大概是个窃取官位的人吧?他明明知道柳下惠的贤能,却不推荐柳下惠同在公朝上治理国事。"

[英译文]

The Master said, "Was not Zang Wen-zhong like one who had stolen his situation? He knew the virtue and the talents of Liu Xia-hui, and yet did not procure that he should stand with him in court."

15 – 14

子曰:"躬自厚而薄責於人,則遠怨矣。"

[白话文]

孔子说:"多责备自己,少责备别人,那就不会招人怨恨。"

[英译文]

The Master said, "He who requires much from himself and little from others, will keep himself from being the object of resentment."

15 – 15

子曰:"不曰'如之何,如之何'者,吾末如之何也已矣。"

[白话文]

孔子说:"一个人处世办事该深思熟虑。如事先不想想怎么办、怎么办的人,我也不知道对他怎么办才好。"

[英译文]

The Master said, "When a man is not in the habit of saying, 'What shall I think of this? What shall I think of this?' I can indeed do nothing with him."

15 – 16

子曰:"群居終日,言不及義,好行小慧,難矣哉。"

[白话文]

孔子说:"一群人整天地聚在一起,没有一句正经话,喜欢耍弄小聪明,这种人如此下去,就难以长进了。"

[英译文]

The Master said, "When a number of people are together, for a whole day, without their conversation turning on righteousness, and when they are fond of carrying out the suggestions of a small shrewdness—theirs is indeed a hard case."

15 – 17

子曰:"君子義以爲質,禮以行之,孫以出之,信以成之。君子哉!"

[白话文]

孔子说:"君子用义作为一切行事的根本,依照礼节去进行,用谦逊的态度来表达,以诚信的实践来完成它,这真是个君子啊!"

[英译文]

The Master said, "The superior man in everything considers righteousness to be essential. He performs it according to the rules of propriety. He brings it forth in humility. He completes it with sincerity. This is indeed a superior man."

15 – 18

子曰:"君子病無能焉,不病人之不已知也。"

[白话文]

　　孔子说:"君子只愁自己无能力,不愁别人不知我。"

[英译文]

　　The Master said, "The superior man is distressed by his want of ability. He is not distressed by men's not knowing him."

15－19

　　子曰:"君子疾①没世②而名不称焉。"

[注释]

　　①疾:苦恼,担忧。　②没世:没,读 mò。没世,指离开人世。

[白话文]

　　孔子说:"君子担忧离开人世后还不被人称颂。"

[英译文]

　　The Master said, "The superior man dislikes the thought of his name not being mentioned after his death."

15－20

　　子曰:"君子求诸己①,小人求诸人。"

[注释]

　　①君子求诸己:本章承接前两章。"君子病无能焉,不病人之不己知",即"求诸己"之旨;"君子疾世而名不称",也是"求诸己"有为善之实。本章加以总结。求,责求的意思。

[白话文]

　　孔子说:"君子一切靠自己,小人则责求别人。"

[英译文]

　　The Master said, "What the superior man seeks, is in himself. What the mean man seeks, is in others."

15－21

　　子曰:"君子矜而不争,群而不党。"

[白话文]

　　孔子说:"君子庄矜自守,不与人争执,能合群而不结党营私。"

[英译文]

　　The Master said, "The superior man is dignified, but does not wrangle. He is sociable, but not a partizan."

15 – 22
子曰："君子不以言舉人,不以人廢言。"

[白话文]

孔子说:"君子观察人,不因他讲得好就认为他好而贸然举用,也不因他地位低或印象不好而抹杀他有道理的话。"

[英译文]

The Master said, "The superior man does not promote a man simply on account of his words, nor does he put aside good words because of the man."

15 – 23
子貢問曰:"有一言而可以終身行之者乎?"子曰:"其恕乎! 己所不欲,勿施於人。"

[白话文]

子贡问道:"有没有一句话可以作为终身奉行的?"孔子说:"那大概就是'恕'吧! 自己所不喜欢的,不要施加在别人身上。"

[英译文]

Zi-gong asked, "Is there one word which may serve as a rule of practice for all one's life?" The Master said, "Is not reciprocity such a word? What you do not want done to yourself, do not do to others."

15 – 24
子曰:"吾之於人也,誰毀誰譽①? 如有所譽者,其有所試矣! 斯民②也,三代③之所以直道而行也。"

[注释]

①谁毁谁誉:朱熹注:"毁者,称人之恶而损其真。誉者,扬人之善而过其实。夫子无是也。"意思是说,随便毁誉,皆非直道。　②斯民:现代(指孔子当时)的人。　③三代:夏、商、周。

[白话文]

孔子说:"我对于人,哪个可以随便毁之或誉之? 或有所赞誉的人,也是经过实际观察、考验的。现在的人,是经三代之治,尧之于舜,舜之于禹,皆行直道,亲自观察,不惑于人言。这样的人民能善其善,恶其恶,无所私曲,且容任意毁誉。"

[英译文]

The Master said, "In my dealings with men, whose evil do I blame, whose goodness do I praise, beyond what is proper? If I do sometimes exceed in praise, there must be ground for it in my examination of the individual. This people supplied the ground why the three dynasties pursued the path of straightforwardness."

15 – 25

子曰:"吾猶及史之闕文也,有馬者借人乘之,今亡矣夫!"

[白话文]

孔子说:"我尚能看到古代历史一些残缺的资料,像有马的人借给别人骑,今天连这种资料也没有了。"

[英译文]

The Master said, "Even in my early days, a historiographer would leave a blank in his text, and he who had a horse would lend him to another to ride. Now, alas! There are no such things."

15 – 26

子曰:"巧言^①亂德。小不忍^②,則亂大謀。"

[注释]

①巧言:朱注:"巧言,变乱是非,听之使人丧其所守。"意谓听了这些花言巧语,以致是非不清、正邪无辨、道德失守。 ②小不忍:朱注:"如妇人之仁、匹夫之勇皆是。"南怀瑾氏认为:处事的时候,"忍"字作决断用;对人的时候,"忍"应作"忍耐"、"包含"的意思。也就是说,该决断时应决断,不要以妇人之仁、姑息养奸而乱大局;该忍耐时应忍耐,不要以匹夫之勇、不明是非由委或心地狡窄而不能容忍、误了大事。

[白话文]

孔子说:"花言巧语会使人分不清是非而乱德;小处不忍,会败坏大事。"

[英译文]

The Master said, "Specious words confound virtue. Want of forbearance in small matters confounds great plans."

15 – 27

子曰:"衆惡之,必察焉;衆好之,必察焉。"

[白话文]

孔子说:"众人都说他不好,必须加以考察是否真的不好;众人都说他好,也要加以考察是否真的好。"

[英译文]

The Master said, "When the multitude hate a man, it is necessary to examine into the case. When the multitude like a man, it is necessary to examine into the case."

15 – 28

子曰:"人能弘道,非道弘人。"

[白话文]

孔子说:"人能发扬道,不是道发扬人。"

[英译文]

The Master said, "A man can enlarge the principles which he follows; those principles do not enlarge the man."

15 – 29

子曰:"過而不改,是謂過矣。"

[白话文]

孔子说:"有过错而不改正,这就是真正的过错。"

[英译文]

The Master said, "To have faults and not to reform them—this, indeed, should be pronounced having faults."

15 – 30

子曰:"吾嘗終日不食,終夜不寢,以思,無益,不如學也。"

[白话文]

孔子说:"我曾经整日不吃饭、整夜不睡觉,专心用来思考,结果却无益处。还不如踏踏实实地学习来得好。"

[英译文]

The Master said, "I have been the whole day without eating, and the whole night without sleeping—occupied with thinking. It was of no use. The better plan is to learn."

15 – 31

子曰:"君子謀道不謀食。耕也,餒^①在其中矣;學也,祿^②在其中矣。

君子憂道不憂貧。"

[注释]

①餧:读 něi,饥饿。　②禄:福气、俸禄。

[白话文]

孔子说:"君子用心追求的是修己治国之道,不是追求个人的生活衣食。耕田的目的是在于谋食,遇到荒年也难免挨饿。学道未必是为了生活衣食,学有所成,其中也会有福禄。作为一个君子,只忧道能否实行,不是愁个人的贫困。"

[英译文]

The Master said, "The object of the superior man is truth. Food is not his object. There is ploughing—even in that there is sometimes want. So with learning—emolument may be found in it. The superior man is anxious lest he should not get truth; he is not anxious lest poverty should come upon him."

15 - 32

子曰:"知及之①,仁不能守之,雖得之,必失之。知及之,仁能守之,不莊以涖之②,則民不敬。知及之,仁能守之,莊以涖之,動之③不以禮,未善也。"

[注释]

①知及之:知,同"智",包括知识、智谋等。及,达到。知及之,用智能、知识获得的(包括天下、政权、官位等)。　②不庄以涖之:庄,庄敬,慎重其事。涖,临、到。不庄以涖之,意即不能用庄敬认真的态度临事、临近民众。　③动之:朱注:"动之,动民也。犹曰鼓舞而作兴之云尔。"今则称"动员"。

[白话文]

孔子说:"用智能获取的东西,如果不能有仁德来保持它,即使得到了,也一定会失去它。用聪明才智取得官位,能用仁德来保持,如果不能用庄敬的态度去履行职责、不能尊重人民,那么人民也不会敬重他。靠聪明才智取得地位,用仁德来加以保持它,以庄敬的态度来履行职责,并以民为重,如果在动员中缺乏礼节,那也是不完善的。"

[英译文]

The Master said, "When a man's knowledge is sufficient to attain, and his virtue is not sufficient to enable him to hold, whatever he may have gained, he will lose again. When his knowledge is sufficient to attain, and he has virtue enough to hold fast, if he cannot govern with dignity, the people will not respect him. When his knowledge is sufficient to attain, and he has virtue enough to hold fast; when he governs also with dignity, yet if he try to move the people contrary to the rules of propriety—full excellence is not reached."

15-33

子曰:"君子不可小知而可大受也;小人不可大受而可小知也。"①

[注释]

①此为观人之法。知,我知之也。受,彼所受的任务。

[白话文]

孔子说:"对君子不可用小事的标准、要求来衡量他,却可以委以重大任务;对小人(庶民)不可以委以重大任务,但可以从小事中了解他,并发挥其所长。"

[英译文]

The Master said, "The superior man cannot be known in little matters; but he may be intrusted with great concerns. The small men may not be intrusted with great concerns, but he may be known in little matters."

15-34

子曰:"民之於仁也,甚於水火。水火,吾見蹈而死者矣,未見蹈仁而死者也。"

[白话文]

孔子说:"仁,对于人的重要性,远甚于水火。水火,是人生活中不可或缺的,但有时也会害人,我见过溺死或被烧死的人。至于为仁,彼此互爱,断无害人致死者。"

[英译文]

The Master said, "Virtue is more to man than either water or fire. I have seen men die from treading on water and fire, but I have never seen a man die from treading the course of virtue."

15-35

子曰:"當仁,不讓於師。"

[白话文]

孔子说:"面对仁德的事,对于老师也不用谦让。"

[英译文]

The Master said, "Let every man consider virtue as what devolves on himself. He may not yield the performance of it even to his teacher."

15－36

子曰:"君子貞^①而不諒^②。"

[注释]

　　①貞:忠于自己所信守的原则。　②谅:小信。参阅宪问篇第十八章(14-18)注。

[白话文]

　　孔子说:"君子坚持原则,不拘泥于不择是非轻重的小信。"

[英译文]

The Master said, "The superior man is correctly firm, and not firm merely."

15－37

子曰:"事君,敬其事而後其食。"

[白话文]

　　孔子说:"为人臣,供职于君主,要尽心力于职事,把待遇的事放在后头。"

[英译文]

The Master said, "A minister, in serving his prince, reverently discharges his duties, and makes his emolument a secondary consideration."

15－38

子曰:"有教無類。"

[白话文]

　　孔子说:"不论哪一类人,都可以给他以教育。"("有教无类"已成为全球教育名句。)

[英译文]

The Master said, "In teaching there should be no distinction of classes."

15－39

子曰:"道不同,不相爲謀。"

[白话文]

　　孔子说:"思想、目的不同,没有办法共同相谋。"

[英译文]

The Master said, "Those whose courses are different cannot lay plans for one another."

15 – 40

子曰："辞,达而已矣。"

[白话文]

孔子说："不论言辞、文辞,足以表达意思就可以了。"

[英译文]

The Master said, "In language it is simply required that it convey the meaning."

15 – 41

师冕①见,及阶。子曰:"阶也。"及席,子曰:"席也。"皆坐,子告之曰:"某在斯,某在斯。"师冕出。子张问曰:"与师言之道与?"子曰:"然。固相师之道也。"

[注释]

①师冕:一位名叫冕的乐师。古代的乐师一般由盲人来担任。

[白话文]

鲁国的一位盲人乐师冕来拜见孔子。孔子迎接了他,陪他一起走到台阶前对他说:"这是台阶。"走到坐席前,孔子又说:"这里是坐席。"等大家坐定,孔子向他介绍说:"某人在这儿,某人在这儿。"师冕辞别出去后,子张就问:"跟乐师谈话的方式就是这样的吗?"孔子说:"是啊! 这本来就是帮助盲人的方式。"

[英译文]

The Music-master, Mian, having called upon him, when they came to the steps, the Master said, "Here are the steps." When they came to the mat for the guest to sit upon, he said, "Here is the mat." When all were seated, the Master informed him, "So and so is here; so and so is here."

The Music-master, Mian, having gone out, Zi-zhang asked, "Is it the rule to tell those things to the Music-master?" The Master said, "Yes. This is certainly the rule for those who lead the blind."

季氏第十六

本篇凡十四章(16—1～16—14)。

16-1

季氏①將伐顓臾②。冉有、季路③見於孔子曰:"季氏將有事於顓臾。"孔子曰:"求! 無乃爾是過與? 夫顓臾,昔者先王以爲東蒙④主,且在邦域之中矣,是社稷⑤之臣也。何以伐爲?"冉有曰:"夫子⑥欲之,吾二臣者皆不欲也。"孔子曰:"求! 周任⑦有言曰:'陳力就列⑧,不能者止。'危而不持,顛而不扶,則將焉用彼相⑨矣? 且爾言過矣,虎兕⑩出於柙⑪,龜玉毀於櫝⑫中,是誰之過與?"冉有曰:"今夫顓臾,固⑬而近於費⑭。今不取,後世必爲子孫憂。"孔子曰:"求! 君子疾夫舍曰欲之而必爲之辭。丘也聞有國有家者⑮,不患寡而患不均,不患貧而患不安⑯。蓋均無貧,和無寡,安無傾。夫如是,故遠人不服,則脩文德以來之。既來之,則安之。今由與求也,相夫子,遠人不服而不能來也,邦分崩離析而不能守也,而謀動干戈於邦内。吾恐季孫之憂,不在顓臾,而在蕭牆之内⑰也。"

[注释]

①季氏:即季康子,参阅为政篇第十九章(2-19)注。 ②顓臾:读 zhuān yú,鲁国的附属小国,位于今山东费县西。 ③冉有、季路:冉有,即冉求,字子有。季路,即子路,字仲由。皆为孔子弟子,其时,都为季氏家臣。 ④东蒙:即蒙山,今山东蒙县南。 ⑤社稷:社,土神。稷,谷神。古代君主都要祭祀社、稷,后来就用社稷代表国家之称。 ⑥夫子:这里是指季康子。 ⑦周任:古代的一位著名史官。 ⑧陈力就列:陈力,贡献出力量。列,位、职位。就列,就位任职。 ⑨相:扶助盲人的人称相。这里作"辅臣"讲。 ⑩兕:读 sì,犀牛。 ⑪柙:读 xiá,关野兽的笼子。 ⑫櫝:读 dú,匣子。 ⑬固:坚固,这里指城郭坚固。 ⑭费:旧读 bì,季氏的私邑。 ⑮有国有家者:有国者,指诸侯国的国君。有家者,指卿大夫。家,是指宗族。 ⑯不患寡而患不均,不患贫而患不安:寡,指人口少。这两句中的"寡"、"贫"二字应对换,即"不患贫而患不均,不患寡而患不安"。此恐系竹简刻字之误。 ⑰萧墙之内:萧墙,屏风。萧墙之内,乃指鲁国当权者的内部。

[白话文]

季氏将要攻伐颛臾。冉有和季路来见孔子说:"季氏将要对颛臾用兵。"孔子说:"冉求,这不是你的过错吗? 颛臾,从前周先王曾授命它主持东蒙山的祭祀,而且地处鲁国境内,是鲁的臣属。为什么要攻打它呢?"冉有说:"季氏要这样做,我们两个家臣也都不愿意。"孔子说:"冉求,周任说过:'尽心尽力在自己的职位上,如果不能把事做好,就应该辞职。'拿那帮助盲人的人作比喻,如果任盲人走到危险的地方而不拉住他,盲人跌倒了又不扶起他,还要你干什么? 你还说攻伐颛臾是季氏的主张,这话更错了。试问老虎、犀牛从笼子里跑出来;神龟、宝玉毁坏在匣子里,要说这不是管理者的失职，又是谁的过错呢？"冉有说："颛臾的城郭坚固，又与季氏的邑地相近，如果不趁早攻取，会成为后代子孙的祸患。"孔子说："冉求，君子痛恨那不说自己的贪欲，还要另找借口来掩饰的人。我敢说有国有家的诸侯、大夫，不忧虑贫穷，只担心贫富不均；不忧虑人口稀少，只担心社会不安。如果财富分配均等，就无所谓贫穷；如果社会和谐，就不怕人口稀少；人民安定了，国家必不会颠覆。能够如此，如果远方的人还不归服，再修好礼乐教化去感召他们。来归以后，就使他们安定下来。现在，你们二人辅助季孙，远方的人不顺服，又没法招收他们来归化，国家弄得分崩离析，不能够保全，反而想在国内大动干戈。我怕季氏的忧患不在颛臾，而在于朝廷内部吧！"

[英译文]

The head of the Ji family was going to attack Zhuan-yu. Ran-you and Ji-lu had an interview with Confucius, and said, "Our chief, Ji, is going to commence operations against Zhuan-yu." Confucius said, "Qiu, is it not you who are in fault here? Now, in regard to Zhuan-yu, long ago, a former king appointed its ruler to preside over the sacrifices to the eastern Meng; moreover, it is in the midst of the territory of our state; and its ruler is a minister in direct connexion with the sovereign—what has your chief to do with attacking it?" Ran-you said, "Our master wishes the thing; neither of us two ministers wishes it." Confucius said, "Qiu, there are the words of Zhou-ren—when he can put forth his ability, he takes his place in the ranks of office; when he finds himself unable to do so, he retires from it. How can he be used as a guide to a blind man, who does not support him when tottering, nor raise him up when fallen? And further, you speak wrongly. When a tiger or rhinoceros escapes from his cage; when a tortoise or piece of jade is injured in its repository—whose is the fault?" Ran-you said, "But at present, Zhuan-yu is strong and near to Bi; if our chief do not now take it, it will hereafter be a sorrow to his descendants." Confucius said, "Qiu, the superior man hates that declining to say—I want such and such a thing, and framing explanations for the conduct. I have heard that rulers of states and chiefs of families are not troubled lest their people should be few, but are troubled lest they should not keep their several places; that they are not troubled with fears of poverty, but are troubled with fears of a want of contented repose among the people in their several places. For when the people keep their several places, there will be no poverty; when harmony prevails, there will be no scarcity of people; and when there is such a contented repose, there will be no rebellious upsetting. So it is—therefore, if remoter people are not submissive, all the influences of civil culture and virtue are to be cultivated to attract them to be so; and when they have been so attracted, they must be made contented and tranquil. Now, here are you, You and Qiu, assisting your chief. Remoter people are not submissive, and, with your help, he cannot attract them to him. In his own territory, there are divisions and downfalls, leavings and separations, and, with your help, he cannot preserve it. And yet he is planning these hostile movements within the state—I am afraid that the sorrow of the Ji-sun family will not be on account of Zhuan-yu, but will be found within the screen of their own court."

16-2

孔子曰:"天下有道,則禮樂征伐自天子出;天下無道,則禮樂征伐自諸侯出。自諸侯出,蓋十世希不失矣;自大夫出,五世希不失矣;陪臣執國命,三世希不失矣。天下有道,則政不在大夫。天下有道,則庶人不議。"

[白话文]

孔子说:"天下有道的时候,礼乐的制定、讨伐出征等大事,都是从天子那里做出决定和颁行的。天下无道的时候,礼乐、征伐的决定和颁行出自诸侯。由诸侯出者,不过传到十代,就很少有保持的;如果由大夫执掌国家政权,礼乐、征伐的决定出自大夫,传到五代能继续保持的就很少了;假使由陪臣(也就是大夫的家臣)执掌了政权,传到三代就很少有能保持的。天下有道,国家的政权不会落到大夫手中。天下有道,民众对政府不会议论纷纷。"

[英译文]

Confucius said, "When good government prevails in the empire, ceremonies, music, and punitive military expeditions proceed from the son of Heaven. When bad government prevails in the empire, ceremonies, music, and punitive military expeditions proceed from the princes. When these things proceed from the princes, as a rule, the cases will be few in which they do not lose their power in ten generations. When they proceed from the Great officers of the princes, as a rule, the cases will be few in which they do not lose their power in five generations. When the subsidiary ministers of the Great officers hold in their grasp the orders of the state, as a rule, the cases will be few in which they do not lose their power in three generations. When right principles prevail in the kingdom, gov-

ernment will not be in the hands of the Great officers. When right principles pre
vail in the kingdom, there will be no discussions among the common people."

16－3

孔子曰：“禄之去公室①五世②矣，政逮③於大夫四世④矣，故夫三桓⑤
之子孙微矣。”

[注释]

①禄之去公室：禄，指爵禄。赏授爵禄的权力应由公室(国家)操之。去公室，乃指君主大权
已旁落了。 ②五世：指国家政权从鲁宣公开始失去后，已经经历了五代——宣公、成公、襄公、
昭公、定公。 ③政逮：政，政权。逮，到、及。 ④于大夫四世：指国家政权落到大夫手中已经
四代——武子、悼子、平子、桓子。 ⑤三桓：指季孙氏、孟孙氏、叔孙三家贵族，皆出自桓公。
其中以季孙氏权力最大，但后来又被家臣阳虎篡夺，故曰微(式微)。

[白话文]

孔子说：“爵禄赏授的权力不在鲁国公室，已有五代了。国家政权落在大夫手
中，已有四代了。所以鲁桓公后代季孙、孟孙、叔孙三家子孙现在也衰微了。”

[英译文]

Confucius said, "The revenue of the state has left the ducal House now for
five generations. The government has been in the hands of the Great officers for
four generations. On this account, the descendants of the three Huan are much
reduced."

16－4

孔子曰：“益者三友，损者三友。友直、友谅①、友多闻，益矣；友便
辟②、友善柔③、友便佞④，损矣。”

[注释]

①谅：信用、诚实。 ②便辟：又写作“便嬖”，即因善于谄媚、逢迎而得宠的不正直的人。
③善柔：当面一套，背后一套，不诚实的人。 ④便佞：花言巧语、夸夸其谈而无真实见闻的人。

[白话文]

孔子说：“有益的朋友有三种，有害的朋友也有三种。结交正直的人、诚信的
人、博学多闻的人，是有益的；结交善于谄媚逢迎、不正直的人，结交当面一套、背后
一套、不诚实的人，结交夸夸其谈、无真实见闻的人，是有害的。”

[英译文]

Confucius said, "There are three friendships which are advantageous, and
three which are injurious. Friendship with the upright; friendship with the sin

cere; and friendship with the man of much observation—these are advantageous. Friendship with the man of specious airs; friendship with the insinuatingly soft; and friendship with the glib-tongued—these are injurious."

16-5

孔子曰:"益者三樂,損者三樂。樂節禮樂①,樂道人之善,樂多賢友,益矣。樂驕樂,樂佚②遊,樂宴樂③,損矣。"

[注释]

①乐节礼乐:前一个"乐"字读 lè,爱好的意思;后一个"乐"字读 yuè。乐节礼乐,即爱好用礼乐作为规矩,来节制言谈举止。　②佚:同"逸"。如"逸豫亡身"的逸,即表示纵情的快乐。③宴乐:以酒食吃喝为乐。

[白话文]

孔子说:"对人有益的爱好有三种,对人有害的爱好也有三种。爱好言谈以礼、乐来节制,爱好谈别人的优点、好处,爱好多交贤能的朋友,是有益的;爱好向人夸耀自己,显示骄傲为快乐,爱好纵情游玩,爱好以吃吃喝喝为乐,是有害的。"

[英译文]

Confucius said, "There are three things men find enjoyment in which are advantageous, and three things they find enjoyment in which are injurious. To find enjoyment in the discriminating study of ceremonies and music; to find enjoyment in speaking of the goodness of others; to find enjoyment in having many worthy friends—these are advantageous. To find enjoyment in extravagant pleasures; to find enjoyment in idleness and sauntering; to find enjoyment in the pleasures of feasting—these are injurious."

16-6

孔子曰:"侍於君子有三愆①:言未及之而言謂之躁;言及之而不言謂之隱;未見顏色而言謂之瞽②。"

[注释]

①愆:过失。　②瞽:瞎子,这里指不能察言观色。

[白话文]

孔子说:"陪侍君子说话容易有三失:不到该说话的时候就抢着说话,这就是浮躁;到该说话的时候又不说话,这就是隐匿;不看对方的脸色,不管该不该说而乱说话,这就是不懂得察言观色。"

[英译文]

Confucius said, "There are three errors to which they, who stand in the presence of a man of virtue and station are liable. They may speak when it does not come to them to speak—this is called rashness. They may not speak when it comes to them to speak—this is called concealment. They may speak without looking at the countenance of their superior—this is called blindness."

16 - 7

孔子曰："君子有三戒：少之時，血氣未定，戒之在色；及其壯也，血氣方剛，戒之在鬪；及其老也，血氣既衰，戒之在得。"

[白话文]

孔子说："君子有三件事要警戒：年轻时，血气未稳定，所以切忌贪恋女色；到了壮年，血气方刚，要戒之好勇争斗；到了老年，血气已衰颓，要警戒贪得无厌。"

[英译文]

Confucius said, "There are three things which the superior man guards against. In youth, when the physical powers are not yet settled, he guards against lust. When he is strong, and the physical powers are full of vigour, he guards against quarrelsomeness. When he is old, and the animal powers are decayed, he guards against covetousness."

16 - 8

孔子曰："君子有三畏：畏天命①、畏大人②、畏聖人之言③。小人不知天命而不畏也，狎④大人，侮聖人之言。"

[注释]

①天命：即天理，可以理解为自然和社会的规律。　②大人：指在上位的人，即国家的统治者。民主社会的领导人来自民选，同样应该得到民众的尊重和支持。　③圣人之言：圣人，指品格最高尚、智慧最高超的人。圣人之言，乃指圣人教人的道理。　④狎：轻慢、不庄重。

[白话文]

孔子说："君子有三项戒惧的事：天理不可违抗；敬畏有德行、在上位的人；理解和尊重圣人的话。小人未能意识到天命的存在，故毫无忌惮；对上位的人不庄重、心存轻慢，初则逢迎长恶，终乃作乱；侮慢圣人所说的话，甚至加以毁谤。"

[英译文]

Confucius said, "There are three things of which the superior man stands in awe. He stands in awe of the ordinances of Heaven. He stands in awe of great men. He stands in awe of the words of sages. The mean man does not know the ordinances of Heaven, and consequently does not stand in awe of them. He is disrespectful to great men. He makes sport of the words of sages."

16－9

孔子曰："生而知之者上也；學而知之者次也；困①而學之，又其次也；困而不學，民斯②爲下矣！"

[注释]

①困：困惑不懂。　②民斯：民，即人。斯，这、此。

[白话文]

孔子说："对于许多事物，一看就知道它的道理，好似生出来就知晓，这是上等资质的人；经过学习后知道，是次一等资质的人；遇到困惑不懂，才去学问求知，是又次一等资质的人；至于困惑不懂又不肯去学的人，终不能知，这就是最下等的人了。"

[英译文]

Confucius said, "Those who are born with the possession of knowledge are the highest class of men. Those who learn, and so, readily, get possession of knowledge, are the next. Those who are dull and stupid, and yet compass the learning, are another class next to these. As to those who are dull and stupid and yet do not learn—they are the lowest of the people."

16－10

孔子曰："君子有九思：視思明、聽思聰、色思温、貌思恭、言思忠、事思敬、疑思問、忿思難、見得思義。"

[白话文]

孔子说："君子须注意用心的事情有九项：看，须看得明白；听，要听清楚；（对人的）脸色表情要温和；容貌态度要谦恭；说话，要想到是否忠实诚恳；做事，要考虑做到严肃认真；有疑问，要想怎样把问题向知者请教清楚；发怒时，要想到后果如何；见有所得时，要想一想是否合乎义、可以取。"

[英译文]

Confucius said, "The superior man has nine things which are subjects with him of thoughtful consideration. In regard to the use of his eyes, he is anxious to see clearly. In regard to the use of his ears, he is anxious to hear distinctly. In regard to his countenance, he is anxious that it should be benign. In regard to his demeanour, he is anxious that it should be respectful. In regard to his speech, he is anxious that it should be sincere. In regard to his doing of business, he is anxious that it should be reverently careful. In regard to what he doubts about, he is anxious to question others. When he is angry, he thinks of the difficulties (his anger may involve him in). When he sees gain to be got, he thinks of righteousness."

16 – 11

孔子曰："見善如不及，見不善如探湯。吾見其人矣，吾聞其語矣。隱居以求其志，行義以達其道①。吾聞其語矣，未見其人也。"

[注释]

①隐居以求其志，行义以达其道："志"和"道"是一回事。隐居，功名利禄不足以动其心，是为保全志，求其所达之道。行义，为人处世奉行义理，以达其道，实行所求之志。

[白话文]

孔子说："见到好人好事，常感自己不及，因而努力为善，想及他。看见不善的人或事，犹如沸汤不能手探，赶快避开。我看到过这样的人，也听到过这样的话。隐居求以保全志向，奉行义理实行志向而达其道。我听到过这种话，但没有见到过这种人。"

[英译文]

Confucius said, "Contemplating good, and pursuing it, as if they could not reach it; contemplating evil, and shrinking from it, as they would from thrusting the hand into boiling water—I have seen such men, as I have heard such words. Living in retirement to study their aims, and practising righteousness to carry out their principles—I have heard these words, but I have not seen such men."

16 – 12

齊景公①有馬千駟②，死之日，民無德而稱焉。伯夷、叔齊③餓於首陽之下，民到於今稱之。其斯之謂與④？

[注释]

①齐景公：齐国国君，名杵臼。在位时，刑罚严峻，对人民剥削甚重。　②驷：四匹马称"驷"。　③伯夷、叔齐：参阅公冶长篇第二十二章(5-22)、述而篇第十四章(7-14)。　④其斯之谓与：此句似与上文脱节。宋儒提出颜渊篇第十章(12-10)最末的"诚不以富，亦只以异"(句山

223

《诗经·小雅》),应移置此句之前乃通。今仍从朱熹《集注》版所排原文。

[白话文]

　　齐景公有四千匹马,到他死时,人民对他没有什么可称道的。伯夷、叔齐虽然饿死在首阳山下(事情发生在周武王灭纣后),人们到现在还称道他们。就是说这种事呀!

[英译文]

　　The duke Jing of Qi had a thousand teams, each of four horses, but on the day of his death, the people did not praise him for a single virtue. Bo-yi and Shu-qi died of hunger at the foot of the Shou-yang mountain, and the people, down to the present time, praise them. Is not that saying illustrated by this?

16 – 13

　　陈亢^①問於伯魚^②曰:"子亦有異聞乎?"對曰:"未也。嘗獨立,鯉趨而過庭。曰:'學《詩》乎?'對曰:'未也。''不學《詩》,無以言。'鯉退而學《詩》。他日,又獨立,鯉趨而過庭。曰:'學禮乎?'對曰:'未也。''不學禮,無以立。'鯉退而學禮。聞斯二者。"陈亢退而喜曰:"問一得三。聞《詩》,聞禮,又聞君子之遠^③其子也。"

[注释]

　　①陈亢:即孔子弟子陈子禽。参阅学而篇第十章(1-10)。　②伯鱼:孔子的儿子,名鲤。他年轻早逝,他的儿子就是《中庸》作者子思。　③远:按司马光的说法,此远字"非疏远之谓",而是"谓其进见有说,接遇有礼,不朝夕嘻嘻相亵狎也",与弟子们无远近之分。

[白话文]

　　陈亢问伯鱼说:"你是不是从老师那里听得不同于大家的教诲?"伯鱼说:"没有。有一次家父一个人站在大厅上,我很快地走过厅堂,家父问我:'你学过《诗》没有?'我回答说:'没有。'家父说:'不学《诗》,就不懂得怎样把话说得得体。'我退下后就去学《诗》。过了些日子,家父又独立在大厅上,我很快地走过厅堂,家父说:'你学过礼没有?'我回答说:'没有。'家父说:'不学礼,如何立身处世?'我退回后便去学礼。我私下听到的就这两件事。"陈亢回去后高兴地说:"我问了一件事却知道了三件:知道了学《诗》的道理、学礼的道理,又知道了君子对自己的儿子没有偏私和厚爱。"

[英译文]

　　Chen-kang asked Bo-yu, "Have you heard any lessons from your father different from what we have all heard?" Bo-yu replied, "No. He was standing alone once, when I passed below the hall with hasty steps, and said to me, 'Have you learned the Odes?' On my replying 'Not yet', he added, 'If you do not learn the Odes, you will not be fit to converse with.' I retired and studied the Odes. Another day, he was in the same way standing alone, when I passed by below the hall with hasty steps, and said to me, 'Have you learned the rules of propriety?' On my replying 'Not yet', he added, 'If you do not learn the rules of propriety, your character cannot be established.' I then retired, and learned the rules of propriety. I have heard only these two things from him." Chen-kang retired, and, quite delighted, said, "I asked one thing, and I have got three things. I have heard about the Odes. I have heard about the rules of propriety. I have also heard that the superior man maintains a distant reserve towards his son."

16−14

邦君①之妻,君称之曰:"夫人。"夫人自称曰:"小童。"邦人称之曰:"君夫人。"称诸异邦曰:"寡②小君。"异邦人称之亦曰:"君夫人。"

[注释]

①邦君:指诸侯各国的国君。　②寡:寡德,谦辞。

[白话文]

诸侯各国国君的妻子,国君称她为"夫人";她自称为"小童";国人称她为"君夫人";于外邦讲话自称为"寡小君";外邦人也称她为"君夫人"。

[英译文]

The wife of the prince of a state is called by him Fu-ren. She calls herself Xiao-tong. The people of the state call her Jun Fu-ren, and to people of other states, they call her Gua Xiao-jun. The people of other states also call her Jun Fu-ren.

阳货第十七

本篇凡二十六章（17—1～17—26）。

17 - 1

陽貨①欲見孔子,孔子不見,歸孔子豚②。孔子時其亡也,而往拜之。遇諸塗③。謂孔子曰:"來! 予與爾言。"曰:"懷其寶而迷其邦④,可謂仁乎?"曰:"不可。""好從事而亟⑤失時,可謂知⑥乎?"曰:"不可。""日月逝矣,歲不我與。"孔子曰:"諾,吾將仕矣。"

[注释]

①阳货:又叫阳虎。一说货为名,虎为字。鲁国执政者季氏最信任的家臣,执国政。其人名声不佳,且势大凌主。最后杀害季桓子,事败奔齐,后又逃往晋国。 ②归孔子豚:归,同"馈",赠送。豚,读 tún,小猪,这里是指蒸熟的小猪。归孔子豚,即赠孔子一只蒸熟的小猪。 ③遇诸涂:诸,即"之于"二字的合音。涂,路。 ④怀宝迷邦:怀藏道德学问,不救邦国迷乱。 ⑤亟:数,屡次。 ⑥知:同"智"。

[白话文]

阳货想会晤孔子,想他出来从政,可是孔子不去见他,于是,他伺孔子不在家时送去了一只蒸熟的小猪。按照当时的礼俗,孔子非登门致谢不可,但他知道阳货的居心,也伺其不在家的时机去拜望他。不料两人正好在路上相遇。阳货对孔子说:"来! 我有话要跟你说。"随即说道:"一个人如果怀有高超的道德、才学,眼看邦道迷乱,不肯出来安邦治国,这可称得上是'仁'吗?"孔子说:"不可以。"阳货又说:"一个人如果想要出来为国家做事,却一次又一次地错过机会,这可称得上'智'吗?"孔子说:"不可以。"于是,阳货叹息地说:"日月像流水般逝去不复返,岁月也一年一年地使人老去,不会等我的。"用意是劝孔子及早为国出仕。孔子就答应道:"好! 我将出仕为政。"

[英译文]

Yang-huo wished to see Confucius, but Confucius would not go to see him. On this, he sent a present of a pig to Confucius, who, having chosen a time when Huo was not at home, went to pay his respects for the gift. He met him, however, on the way.

Huo said to Confucius, "Come, let me speak with you." He then asked, "Can he be called benevolent who keeps his jewel in his bosom, and leaves his country to confusion?" Confucius replied, "No." "Can he be called wise, who is anxious to be engaged in public employment, and yet is constantly losing the opportunity of being so?" Confucius again said, "No." "The days and months are passing away; the years do not wait for us." Confucius said, "Right. I will go into office."

17－2

子曰：“性①相近也，习②相远也。”

[注释]

①性：历来各家有性质、性情、性格、人性等不同的释读，James Legge 译为 Nature，本性。笔者认为，这里所说的“性”，确切地说应是指“人的本性”，是人之初，天生具有的本性。　②习：指人在后天所处的自然条件和社会环境中，通过对事物的接触感受所养成的性格、性情、习惯、品质，即所说的“习与性成”。

[白话文]

孔子说：“人与人天生的本性是相近似的，然而在后天的环境中，习于善则善，习于恶则恶，相异就远了。”

[英译文]

The Master said, "By nature, men are nearly alike; by practice, they get to be wide apart."

17－3

子曰：“唯上知與下愚不移①。”

[注释]

①上知、下愚：上知，即上智者，具有天赋的绝顶聪明的人。下愚，即下愚者，是绝顶呆笨的人，所谓“困而不学”者。这两种人，在人群中为数甚少，绝大多数是中等天资。《集注》引程子曰：“人性本善，有不可移者何也？语其性则皆善也，语其才则有下愚之不移。所谓下愚有二焉：自暴、自弃也。人苟以善自治，则无不可移，虽昏愚之至，皆可渐磨而进也。惟自暴者拒之以不信，自弃者绝之以不为，虽圣人与居，不能化而入也，仲尼之所谓下愚也。”

[白话文]

（本章紧接上章）但孔子又说：“唯有绝顶聪明的上智者和绝顶愚笨的人是不会改变的。”

[英译文]

The Master said, "There are only the wise of the highest class, and the stupid of the lowest class, who cannot be changed."

17－4

子之武城①，闻弦歌之聲，夫子莞爾②而笑曰：“割鷄焉用牛刀③？”子游④對曰：“昔者，偃也聞諸夫子曰：‘君子學道則愛人，小人學道則易使也。’”子曰：“二三子⑤！偃之言是也。前言戲之耳。”

[注释]

①武城：鲁国的一个县城，其时子游在那里做县令。　②莞尔：莞，读 wǎn。莞尔，微笑的样子。　③割鸡焉用牛刀：这是一个譬喻。乃指治天下，移风易俗，要用礼乐来教化人民；如今治理一个小小的县，何必要花这样大的力气呢？　④子游：孔子的弟子。姓言，名偃，子游是他的字，吴国人。　⑤二三子：指同到武城去的几个弟子。

[白话文]

孔子和几个弟子到了鲁国的武城，到处听到弦乐演奏和歌唱声，知道子游在这里推行礼乐教化百姓，内心暗喜，微笑地说："杀一只鸡何必要动用宰牛的大刀子？"譬喻治理这个小地方，不必实施如此宏大的礼乐教化。子游听后，疑惑地回答："从前我听老师说过：在上位的人学了礼乐，就会爱护百姓；百姓们学了礼乐，就容易听从号召、肯为国服务。"孔子便向弟子们说："你们几位听着，刚才言偃（子游）所说的话是正确的，我前面所说的话是和他开个玩笑罢了。"

[英译文]

The Master having come to Wu-cheng, heard there the sound of stringed instruments and singing. Well pleased and smiling, he said, "Why use an ox-knife to kill a fowl?" Zi-you replied, "Formerly, Master, I heard you say—when the man of high station is well instructed, he loves men; when the man of low station is well instructed, he is easily ruled." The Master said, "My disciples, Yan's words are right. What I said was only in sport."

17－5

公山弗擾①以費②畔③，召，子欲往。子路不説④，曰："末之也已，何必公山氏之之也⑤？"子曰："夫⑥召我者，而豈徒哉⑦？如有用我者，吾其爲東周乎？"

[注释]

①公山弗扰：公山氏，鲁国的公族。弗扰，其名，又作"不狃"，字子曳，为鲁国执政者季氏的家臣，曾与阳货共谋反叛季氏，事败后逃往齐国。　②费：季氏私邑，今山东费县的西南面。③畔：古同"叛"。　④说：同"悦"。　⑤末之也已，何必公山氏之之也：末，无。"末之"及"之也"两个"之"字，均作"往"字解。此句的意思是：道既不行，没有可往的地方去也就算了，何必要往公山氏那里去呢？　⑥夫：作代词，他；或作指示词，那、这。　⑦岂徒哉：徒，徒然。这里指那召我的人，岂徒然召我吗？

[白话文]

公山弗扰占据费城，发动叛变，召孔子去，孔子准备前去。子路不高兴，说："没有什么地方可去就算了，何必要往公山氏那里去呢？"孔子便说："那叫我去的人，难道会平白地召我去而没有什么用意吗？如果有人要重用我，我将使周文王、周武王的道在东方复兴。"

[英译文]

Gong-shan Fu-rao, when he was holding Bi, and in an attitude of rebellion, invited the Master to visit him, who was rather inclined to go.

Zi-lu was displeased, and said, "Indeed you cannot go! Why must you think of going to see Gong-shan?"

The Master said, "Can it be without some reason that he has invited me? If any one employ me, may I not make an eastern Zhou?"

17 - 6

子張問仁於孔子。孔子曰："能行五者於天下爲仁矣。""請問之。"曰："恭、寬、信、敏、惠。恭則不侮，寬則得衆，信則人任焉，敏則有功，惠則足以使人。"

[白话文]

子张问孔子怎样做才叫作仁。孔子说："能在天下实行五种美德，就可算是仁了。""哪五种？"孔子说："恭敬、宽厚、诚信、勤敏、施惠。对人恭敬则人们也会对他恭敬，不会招受侮慢；宽厚待人，则会获得众人的拥护；诚信交往、不失信于人，人们当然会信任他；勤敏于政、做事快捷、效率高，自然会有功绩；施惠于人民，泽被天下，则民心服而乐为之用。"

[英译文]

Zi-zhang asked Confucius about perfect virtue. Confucius said, "To be able to practise five things everywhere under Heaven constitutes perfect virtue." He begged to ask what they were, and was told, "Gravity, generosity of soul, sincerity, earnestness, and kindness. If you are grave, you will not be treated with disrespect. If you are generous, you will win all. If you are sincere, people will repose trust in you. If you are earnest, you will accomplish much. If you are kind, this will enable you to employ the services of others."

17 - 7

佛肸①召，子欲往。子路曰："昔者由②也聞諸③夫子曰：'親於其身爲不善者，君子不入也。'佛肸以中牟畔④，子之往也，如之何？"子曰："然，有是言也。不曰堅乎，磨而不磷⑤；不曰白乎，涅而不緇⑥。吾豈匏瓜⑦也哉？焉能繫⑧而不食？”

[注释]

　　①佛肸：人名。佛，读 bì；肸，读 xī。晋大夫赵氏的中牟（地名）宰。其时，据中牟，叛晋之赵简子，遣人来召请孔子。　②由：子路之名，仲由。　③诸：即“之于”二字的合音。　④中牟畔：中牟，为晋赵简子的食邑。畔，古同“叛”，这里乃指佛肸占据了中牟，发动叛变。　⑤磨而不磷：磷，读 lín，泛指损伤，这里指使其薄。磨而不磷，即磨不薄。　⑥涅而不缁：涅，读 niè，做黑色染料的矾石，即皂矾（又称绿矾，主要成分为硫酸亚铁）。缁，读 zī，黑色。涅而不缁，即用皂矾染也染不黑的意思。　⑦匏瓜：匏，读 páo。匏瓜，一年生草木，果实比葫芦大，不能食用，只能挂在壁上看看。　⑧系：系结（缚）。

[白话文]

　　佛肸遣人召请孔子，孔子准备前往。子路说：“过去，我曾听老师说过：‘其人如身为不善者（做坏事的人），君子是不会去他那里的。’如今佛肸占据中牟城而起兵叛乱，你却要去他那里，这又如何说呢？”孔子说：“是的，我说过这话。但是，我不是也说过，如果真正坚硬的东西，是怎么磨也磨不薄的；真正洁白的东西，涅染是染不黑的（言下之意是佛肸叛，吾前往察之，无损于我的坚毅和清白）。吾岂能像匏瓜那样，只是被悬挂着而不能食用呢？”

[英译文]

Bi-xi inviting him to visit him, the Master was inclined to go.

Zi-lu said, “Master, formerly I have heard you say, ‘When a man in his own person is guilty of doing evil, a superior man will not associate with him.’ Bi-xi is in rebellion, holding possession of Zhong-mou; if you go to him, what shall be said?”

The Master said, “Yes, I did use these words. But is it not said, that, if a thing be really hard, it may be ground without being made thin? Is it not said, that, if a thing be really white, it may be steeped in a dark fluid without being made black? Am I a bitter gourd! How can I be hung up out of the way of being eaten?”

17－8

　　子曰：“由也！女①闻六言六蔽②矣乎？”對曰：“未也。”“居③，吾語女。好仁不好學，其蔽也愚；好知④不好學，其蔽也蕩⑤；好信不好學，其蔽也賊⑥；好直不好學，其蔽也絞⑦；好勇不好學，其蔽也亂；好剛不好學，其蔽也狂。”

[注释]

①女:今作"汝",你。　②六言六蔽:六言,即仁、知、信、直、勇、刚,表示美德的六个字。蔽,多家释为弊,弊病、流弊、弊端。朱子《集注》曰:"蔽,遮掩也。"从之。六蔽,乃指上述六言者因"然徒好之而不学以明其理,则各有所蔽"(朱子语)。六蔽即愚、荡、贼、绞、乱、狂。　③居:坐下。　④好知:杨伯峻《论语译注》称:"爱耍聪明。"　⑤荡:放荡。　⑥贼:伤害、戕贼。　⑦绞:急切。

[白话文]

孔子问子路说:"由(子路)啊! 你听说过六言六蔽吗?"子路答:"没有。"孔子就叫子路坐下来说:"我告诉你。好仁的人,如果一味以仁爱待人而不好学以明理,就有类于愚人的可能;有才智的人不好学、爱耍聪明,就会沦于自恣放荡;与人交往讲诚信,固是美德,但不好学、缺乏观察识别能力,也有可能存在受骗上当以至于伤害自己的隐患;喜欢率直而不好学的人,常会过于急切,或多纠结;好勇不好学,易于酿成乱事;好刚不好学,必流而为愎,师心自用,则成狂妄。"

[英译文]

The Master said, "You! Have you heard the six words to which are attached six beclouding?" You replied, "I have not." "Sit down, and I will tell them to you." "There is the love of being benevolent without the love of learning—the beclouding here leads to a foolish simplicity. There is the love of knowing without the love of learning—the beclouding here leads to dissipation of mind. There is the love of being sincere without the love of learning—the beclouding here leads to an injurious disregard of consequences. There is the love of straightforwardness without the love of learning—the beclouding here leads to rudeness. There is the love of boldness without the love of learning—the beclouding here leads to insubordination. There is the love of firmness without the love of learning—the beclouding here leads to extravagant conduct."

17-9

子曰:"小子①何莫學夫②《詩》③?《詩》,可以興④、可以觀⑤、可以群⑥、可以怨⑦。邇⑧之事父,遠之事君;多識於鳥獸草木之名。"

[注释]

①小子:弟子。　②夫:这里作指示词,那、这。　③《诗》:即《诗经》。　④兴:激发情志。
⑤观:观察风俗、人情,了解民意,考见政治得失。故《汉书·艺文志》曰:"王者所以观风俗、知得失、自考正也。"　⑥群:诗教温柔敦厚,诵唱通于乐,乐以和为主,礼乐睦民,促进社会和谐。
⑦怨:诗所写哀怨之情,亦用以讽刺政治,但怨而不怒、哀而不伤,不务言理而言情,不务胜人而

感人。　⑧迩:近。

[白话文]

孔子对弟子们说:"弟子们! 你们为什么不学这《诗经》呢?《诗经》可以激发情志,可以考见政治得失,可以和睦人际、促进社会和谐,可以抒发忧怨。近,可以用来事奉父母;远,可以用来事奉国君。而且托物比兴,以物喻志,更可多认识一些鸟兽草木。"

[英译文]

The Master said, "My children, why do you not study the Book of Poetry? The Odes serve to stimulate the mind. They may be used for purposes of self-contemplation. They teach the art of sociability. They show how to regulate feelings of resentment. From them you learn the more immediate duty of serving one's father, and the remoter one of serving one's prince. From them we become largely acquainted with the names of birds, beasts, and plants."

17－10

子謂伯魚①曰:"女爲《周南》、《召南》②矣乎? 人而不爲《周南》、《召南》,其猶正牆面而立③也與④?"

[注释]

①伯鱼:孔子的儿子。　②《周南》、《召南》:《诗经》的地方民歌。大部分内容描写人与人的情感,亲切感人的生动画面,反映现实,抒发情怀。　③正墙面而立:面墙而立,比喻一无所见,寸步难行。　④与:同"欤",表示感叹,跟"啊"相同。

[白话文]

孔子对伯鱼说:"你读过《诗经》的《周南》、《召南》的诗篇吗? 人要是不学习《周南》、《召南》,就像面对着墙壁而立(至近之地,无所见,不能行)。"

[英译文]

The Master said to Bo-yu, "Do you give yourself to the Zhou-nan and the Zhao-nan. The man who has not studied the Zhou-nan and the Zhao-nan, is like one who stands with his face right against a wall. Is he not so?"

17－11

子曰:"禮云禮云,玉帛云乎哉? 樂云樂云,鐘鼓云乎哉?"

[白话文]

孔子说:"礼呀! 礼呀! (其本在于敬,)难道只是指玉帛之类的礼物而已吗? 乐呀! 乐呀! (其本在于和,)难道只是指钟鼓之类的乐器声而已吗?"

[英译文]

The Master said, "'It is according to the rules of propriety,' they say. 'It is according to the rules of propriety,' they say. Are gems and silk all that is meant by propriety?'It is music,'they say. 'It is music,'they say. Are bells and drums all that is meant by music?"

17－12

子曰:"色厲①而内荏②,譬諸小人③,其猶穿窬④之盗也與⑤?"

[注释]

①色厉:指面色威严。　②内荏:荏,读 rěn,虚弱。内荏,指内心虚弱。　③小人:指地位低的人,或作自称。也指人格、道德低下的人。　④穿窬:窬,读 yú,指从墙上爬过去。穿窬,钻洞和爬墙,指偷盗。　⑤与:同"欤",感叹词。

[白话文]

孔子说:"有一种人,表面上装得刚正无私、显得很威严,而内心却很虚弱。若用小人作比喻,就像钻洞爬墙的盗贼一样啊!"

[英译文]

The Master said, "He who puts on an appearance of stern firmness, while inwardly he is weak, is like one of the small, mean people—yes,is he not like the thief who breaks through, or climbs over, a wall?"

17－13

子曰:"鄉原①,德之賊也。"

[注释]

①乡原:乡,鄙俗。原,同"愿",老实、谨慎的样子。乡愿,指表面上老实谨慎、全乡人都以为是好人的人,实际上却是善于谄媚世俗,欺世盗名的伪君子。

[白话文]

孔子说:"那种善于谄媚世俗、伪装善良、是非面前不表态、貌似老实谨慎、却处处合流合污、欺世盗名的人,是窃取仁德之贼呀!"

[英译文]

The Master said, "your good, careful people of the villages are the thieves of virtue."

17－14

子曰:"道聽而塗①説,德之棄也。"

[注释]

①塗:同"途"。

[白话文]

孔子说:"道听途说,不辨别地人云亦云,这是自甘抛弃道德的行为。"

[英译文]

The Master said, "To tell, as we go along, what we have heard on the way, is to cast away our virtue."

17 - 15

子曰:"鄙夫①,可與事君也與哉? 其未得之也,患得之②;既得之,患失之。苟③患失之,無所不至矣!"

[注释]

①鄙夫:卑鄙之人。一说乡原一流人。　②患得之:应为"患不得之"。　③苟:读 gǒu,假使、如果。

[白话文]

孔子说:"卑鄙的人,怎么可以和他共同事奉君主(服务于朝廷)呢? 因为他心中只有官职利禄。当他没有得到职位时,则处心积虑,唯恐得不到职位;一旦得到了,又生怕失掉它。如果怕失去职位,他是无所不为的。"

[英译文]

The Master said, "There are those mean creatures! How impossible it is along with them to serve one's prince! While they have not got their aims, their anxiety is how to get them. When they have got them, their anxiety is lest they should lose them. When they are anxious lest such things should be lost, there is nothing to which they will not proceed."

17 - 16

子曰:"古者,民有三疾。今也,或是之亡也。古之狂也肆①,今之狂也蕩②;古之矜③也廉④,今之矜也忿戾⑤;古之愚也直⑥,今之愚也詐而已矣。"

[注释]

①肆:恣肆,不拘小节。　②荡:放荡、放纵。　③矜:读 jīn,骄矜自持。　④廉:廉洁,有棱角。　⑤忿戾:忿,同"愤"。忿戾,愤不服气,乖张暴戾。　⑥直:直率。

[白话文]

孔子说:"古时候人民中有三种病态,可现在的人,已不是那个样子了。古时,有的人狂妄，只是有点放肆、不拘小节；现在的狂妄之人，不但恣肆，而且放纵、放荡。古时，有的人骄矜自持，犹知正直自守，只是有棱角而露锋芒；现在矜持的人，不但自高自大，而且乖张凶暴。古时，有些人愚蠢，但还有直率的一面；今之愚蠢的人，只有欺诈作为而已。"

[英译文]

The Master said, "Anciently, men had three failings, which now perhaps are not to be found. The high-mindedness of antiquity showed itself in a disregard of small things; the high-mindedness of the present day shows itself in wild license. The stern dignity of antiquity showed itself in grave reserve; the stern dignity of the present day shows itself in quarrelsome perverseness. The stupidity of antiquity showed itself in straightforwardness; the stupidity of the present day shows itself in sheer deceit."

17－17

子曰："巧言令色，鲜矣仁。"

[注释]

此章重出，参阅学而篇第三章(1-3)。

17－18

子曰："恶①紫之夺朱②也，恶鄭聲③之亂雅樂④也，恶利口⑤之覆邦家者。"

[注释]

①恶：厌恶。 ②紫之夺朱：朱，大红，为正色；紫，是红和蓝合成的颜色。紫之夺朱，乃指紫色替代（夺取）了朱色（正色）的地位。 ③郑声：指郑国的音乐，是下流、奢靡之声。 ④雅乐：指周代之正乐。 ⑤利口：《集注》引范氏曰："利口之人，以是为非，以贤为不肖，以肖为贤。人君苟悦而信之，则国家之覆也不难矣。"

[白话文]

孔子说："颠倒紫色和大红色的地位，夺去大红色的光彩，这是我所厌恶的；以下流、奢靡的郑国音乐扰乱了周王的正统音乐，我也是厌恶的；我更厌恶那种只说不谏、颠倒是非的利嘴人，致使国家倾覆（即所谓'一言败邦'）。"

[英译文]

The Master said, "I hate the manner in which purple takes away the lustre of vermilion. I hate the way in which the songs of Zheng confound the music of the Ya. I hate those who with their sharp mouths overthrow kingdoms and families."

17－19

子曰:"予欲無言。"子貢曰:"子如不言,則小子^①何述焉?"子曰:"天何言哉^②? 四時行焉,百物生焉,天何言哉?"

[注释]

①小子:子贡自称。 ②哉:语气词,跟疑问词合用,表示疑问或反诘。

[白话文]

孔子说:"我不想再多说了。"子贡说:"如果老师不再说,那我们这群学生有什么可以传述的呢?"孔子回答说:"天,何尝讲过什么话? 一年四季照常运转,万物依然生长,天讲过什么话呢?"

[英译文]

The Master said, "I would prefer not speaking." Zi-gong said, "If you, Master, do not speak, what shall we, your disciples, have to record?" The Master said, "Does Heaven speak? The four seasons pursue their courses, and all things are continually being produced, but does Heaven say anything?"

17－20

孺悲^①欲見孔子,孔子辭以疾。將命者^②出户,取瑟而歌,使之聞之。^③

[注释]

①孺悲:鲁国人,曾学"士丧礼"于孔子。这次来见孔子而孔子不见的经过,历来各家多半同朱熹之注释,认为他有为人失礼之处,或有说其为人属乡原之流。笔者认为这些恐多属推断。孔子不见他的原因,一直未见经传。 ②命者:传话之人。 ③本章紧接上章,均记述了孔子实行"以不言而言,以不教诲而教诲"的一种教育方法。正如孟子所说:"教亦多术矣。予不屑之教诲也者,是亦教诲之而已矣!"〔参阅《孟子集注·告子章名(下)》〕

[白话文]

孺悲想会见孔子,孔子以生病为借口,不接见他。传话的人刚走出门,孔子便拿起瑟弹唱起来,使孺悲听到。

[英译文]

Ru-bei wished to see Confucius, but Confucius declined, on the ground of being sick, to see him. When the bearer of this message went out at the door, (the Master)took his lute and sang to it, in order that Bei might hear him.

17 - 21

宰我^①問："三年之喪，期已久矣。君子三年不爲禮，禮必壞；三年不爲樂，樂必崩。舊穀既没，新穀既升^②，鑽燧改火^③，期可已矣。"子曰："食夫稻，衣夫錦，於女安乎？"曰："安。""女安則爲之。夫君子之居喪，食旨^④不甘，聞樂不樂，居處不安，故不爲也。今女安，則爲之。"宰我出，子曰："予之不仁也！子生三年，然後免於父母之懷。夫^⑤三年之喪，天下之通喪也。予也有三年之愛於其父母乎？"

[注释]

①宰我：即宰予。参阅八佾篇第二十一章(3-21)注。 ②旧谷既没，新谷既升：旧的谷子已经吃完了，新的谷子已经登场了。 ③钻燧改火：古代钻木取火所用的木材，每季要改换不同的品种，一年轮遍。 ④食旨：旨，滋味美。食旨，吃美味的东西。 ⑤夫：助词。

[白话文]

宰我问："父母死后，要守丧三年的时间，实在太长了。君子三年不习礼仪会被败坏，三年不演奏音乐也会荒废。旧的谷子已吃完了，新的谷又已登场，钻火的燧木也轮换一遍了，看来守丧的时间一年也就可以了。"孔子说："在三年居丧期间吃米饭、穿锦衣，你安心吗？"答曰："心安。"孔子接着说："好吧！你既然心安，你就去做你的吧！一个有德行的君子，在居丧期间，吃美味的东西也不觉得甘美，听音乐不感到快乐，居住在家不觉得舒适，所以才不愿意那么做。现在你觉得心安，那就照你自己的想法去做吧！"宰我退出去后，孔子说："予（宰我）真是没仁德呀！子女出生三年，才能够脱离父母的怀抱。替父母守丧三年乃由此而来，天下都遵行。宰我有三年的爱心去报答父母之恩吗？"

[英译文]

Zai-wo asked about the three years, mourning for parents, saying that one year was long enough. "If the superior man," said he, "abstains for three years from the observances of propriety. Those observances will be quite lost. If for three years he abstains from music, music will be ruined. Within a year the old grain is exhausted, and the new grain has sprung up, and, in procuring fire by friction, we go through all the changes of wood for that purpose. After a complete year, the mourning may stop." The Master said, "If you were, after a year, to eat good rice, and wear embroidered clothes, would you feel at ease?" "I should," replied Wo.

The Master said, "If you can feel at ease, do it. But a superior man, during the whole period of mourning, does not enjoy pleasant food which he may eat, nor derive pleasure from music which he may hear. He also does not feel at ease, if he is comfortably lodged. Therefore he does not do what you propose. But now you feel at ease and may do it."

Zai-wo then went out, and the Master said, "This shows Yu's want of virtue. It is not till a child is three years old that it is allowed to leave the arms of its parents. And the three years' mourning is universally observed throughout the empire. Did Yu enjoy the three years' love of his parents?"

17－22

子曰："飽食終日，無所用心，難矣哉! 不有博奕①者乎? 爲之猶賢乎已②!"

[注释]

①博奕:博,古时掷采行棋的局戏。奕,即今之围棋。 ②犹贤乎已:犹,尚且。贤,超过。已,止。犹贤乎已,尚且比什么都不做的好。

[白话文]

孔子说："整天吃饱了饭,没有一件事肯用心,这种人是难有所作为的呀! 不是有掷采行棋和下围棋的游戏吗? 就是做做这些,尚且比什么都不做的好。"

[英译文]

The Master said, "Hard is it to deal with him, who will stuff himself with food the whole day without applying his mind to anything good! Are there not gamesters and chessplayers? To be one of these would still be better than doing nothing at all."

17－23

子路曰："君子尚勇乎?"子曰："君子義以爲上。君子有勇而無義爲亂,小人有勇而無義爲盜。"①

[注释]

①本章所称之君子、小人,乃指在上位者和平民。《集注》曰:"君子为乱,小人为盗,皆以位言者也。"

[白话文]

子路说："君子(在上位的人)崇尚勇敢吗?"孔子说："君子把义看得最重要。一个在上位的人如果有勇而无义,就会犯上作乱,危害国家;而一般百姓如果只有勇而不讲义,就会成为盗。"

[英译文]

Zi-lu said, "Does the superior man, esteem valour?" The Master said, "The superior man holds righteousness to be of highest importance. A man in a superior situation, having valour without righteousness, will be guilty of insubordination; one of the lower people, having valour without righteousness, will commit robbery."

17 – 24

子貢曰：“君子亦有惡①乎？”子曰：“有惡。惡稱人之惡者，惡居下流②而訕③上者，惡勇而無禮者，惡果敢而窒④者。”曰：“賜也，亦有惡乎？”“惡徼⑤以爲知者，惡不孫⑥以爲勇者，惡訐⑦以爲直者。”

[注释]

①恶：本章除了“称人之恶”的“恶”字读è，作善恶的“恶”解，其余的“恶”字均作憎恶、厌恶的“恶”解。　②居下流：指地位在下的。　③讪：读shàn，讥讽、谤毁。　④窒：窒塞不通，这里指不通事理。　⑤徼：读jiǎo，伺察。英文译为pry，亦窥探之意。　⑥孙：今作“逊”，谦让。　⑦讦：读jié，揭人隐私，使人难堪。

[白话文]

子贡说：“君子也有所憎恶的人吗？”孔子说：“有的。憎恶专说人家坏处的人；憎恶那种居下位而喜欢讪谤上位的人；憎恶那种徒凭勇猛而不讲礼节的人；憎恶那种有决断果敢而不通事理的人。”孔子接着又问：“赐（子贡）！你也有憎恶的人吗？”子贡回答说：“我憎恶那种专门暗中窥探别人而自炫其能，自以为聪明的人；憎恶那种不知谦让而自以为勇敢的人；憎恶那种喜欢揭露别人隐私，使人难堪而自以为正直的人。”

[英译文]

Zi-gong said, "Has the superior man his hatreds also?" The Master said, "He has his hatreds. He hates those who proclaim the evil of others. He hates the man who, being in a low station, slanders his superiors. He hates those who have valour merely, and are unobservant of propriety. He hates those who are forward and determined, and, at the same time, of contracted understanding."

The Master then inquired, "Ci, have you also your hatreds?" Zi-gong replied, "I hate those who pry out matters, and ascribe the knowledge to their wisdom. I hate those who are only not modest, and think that they are valorous. I hate those who make known secrets, and think that they are straightforward."

17 - 25

子曰："唯女子與小人爲難養也。近之則不孫,遠之則怨。"

[白话文]

孔子说："只有女子和小人难以对待。亲近了,就不知谦逊,忘乎所以;疏远一些,则又会抱怨。"

[英译文]

The Master said, "Of all people, girls and servants are the most difficult to behave to. If you are familiar with them, they lose their humility. If you maintain a reserve towards them, they are discontented."

17 - 26

子曰："年四十①而見惡②焉,其終也已!"

[注释]

①年四十:不惑之年(参阅为政篇)应是到了懂得道理、是非之年龄。　②见恶:恶,厌恶。见恶,被人厌恶。

[白话文]

孔子说："一个人如果到了四十岁(左右)仍无才德而被人厌恶,那么这个人就止于此而已了。"

[英译文]

The Master said, "When a men at forty is the object of dislike, he will always continue what he is."

微子第十八

本篇凡十一章(18−1〜18−11)。

18－1

微子①去之，箕子②爲之奴，比干③谏而死。孔子曰："殷有三仁④焉。"

[注释]

①微子：名启，殷纣王庶兄，因纣无道，屡谏不听，故跑到别处去了。　②箕子：殷纣王之叔父，名胥馀，因进谏被囚禁，贬为奴隶。　③比干：殷纣王之叔，因苦谏不听，为纣王所杀。④三仁：指微子、箕子、比干三人。他们均出于至诚恻怛之心，不忍国之陷于危亡，人民困于水火，忠心进谏而遭如此下场。史称"三仁"。

[白话文]

〔商（殷）纣王暴虐无道，〕微子屡谏不听，弃官而去；箕子也因劝谏被囚，又被贬为奴隶；比干更因苦谏，被纣王当廷剖腹而死。三人均因看到纣王暴虐、国之将危、人民处于水深火热之中而不惜牺牲个人爵禄、生命。所以孔子赞叹："殷有三位仁人啊！"

[英译文]

The viscount of Wei-zi withdrew from the court. The viscount of Ji-zi became a slave to Zhou. Bi-gan remonstrated with him and died. Confucius said, "The Yin dynasty possessed these three men of virtue."

18－2

柳下惠①爲士师②，三黜③。人曰："子④未可以去乎？"曰："直道而事人，焉往而不三黜？枉道而事人，何必去父母之邦？"

[注释]

①柳下惠：鲁国贤人，姓展，名获，字禽。惠是他的私谥。柳下是他的居地。　②士师：狱官。　③黜：读 chù，罢免官职。　④子：指柳下惠。

[白话文]

柳下惠任鲁国的狱官，三次被罢黜（一次为鲁君所黜，一次为藏文仲因意见不合而黜免，一次为夏公弗忌亦因意见不合黜免）。有人对他说："你何不去其他国做官？"柳下惠深感世道衰微，无处不一样。他说："如果以正直之道为人做事，到哪里去不会被革职呢？如果用枉道去为人做事，其他国家不会被捕革职，本国也不会被革职，何必要离开父母之邦呢？"

[英译文]

Liu Xia-hui being chief criminal judge, was thrice dismissed from his office. Some one said to him, "Is it not yet time for you, Sir, to leave this?" He replied,

"Serving men in an upright way, where shall I go to, and not experience such a thrice-repeated dismissal? If I choose to serve men in a crooked way, what necessity is there for me to leave the country of my parents?"

18－3

齐景公待孔子，曰："若季氏①，则吾不能，以季、孟②之间待之。"曰："吾老矣，不能用也。"③孔子行。

[注释]

①季氏：鲁国上卿，掌全国政权者。 ②孟：鲁国下卿，当时不掌政权。 ③齐景公为如何待遇孔子与臣僚谈了两次，本章分两节叙述，可见不在同一时。前节称安排季、孟之间的规格待之，未尝不可；而后节以自己年老（当时景公六十岁）为托词而反悔前言。

[白话文]

齐景公和臣僚讨论怎样待遇孔子，说："要像鲁国待季氏那样去待孔子，我做不到；但也不能像待孟氏那样，所以想安排在季氏、孟氏之间的职位、规格。"后来又说："我老了，不能用孔子了。"孔子听闻之后，就离开了齐国。

[英译文]

The duke Jing of Qi, with reference to the manner in which he should treat Confucius, said, "I cannot treat him as I would the chief of the Ji family. I will treat him in a manner between that accorded to the chief of the Ji, and that given to the chief of the Meng family." He also said, "I am old; I cannot use his doctrines." Confucius took his departure.

18－4

齐人归女乐①，季桓子②受之，三日不朝。孔子行。

[注释]

①齐人归女乐：时定公十四年，孔子在鲁国任司寇之职，参与政事，齐国因惧鲁国强盛起来，对齐国有威胁，故用黎弥之献计，选八十名会歌舞的美女送给鲁君。归，同"馈"。 ②季桓子：名斯。鲁国大夫，掌全国政权。

[白话文]

齐国送给鲁国许多会歌舞的美女，季桓子接受后，连续三天不上朝廷处理政事。孔子见了这种情形，觉得政事办不成，便离开了鲁国。

[英译文]

The people of Qi sent to Lu a present of female musicians, which Ji Huan-zi received, and for three days no court was held. Confucius took his departure.

18-5

楚狂接舆①歌而过孔子,曰:"凤兮! 凤兮! 何德之衰②? 往者不可谏,来者犹可追。已而! 已而! 今之从政者殆而!"孔子下,欲与之言,趋而辟③之,不得与之言。

[注释]

①接舆:人名,姓接,名舆。一说接舆不是真实姓名,是以事命名,如看门的称"晨门",执拐杖的称"丈人"。这"接舆"就是接孔子舆(车)的人。近人沈知方《四书广解》引《高士传》称:姓陆,名通,字接舆。多从之。他是楚国的一个狂士。 ②凤兮! 凤兮! 何德之衰:凤,是古代人们心目中的圣鸟。天下有道时出现,无道时则隐。这里是歌者(接舆)以凤喻孔子。说他在天下无道的今天却不隐去,是不是德行衰败了。 ③辟:同"避"。

[白话文]

楚国狂人接舆从孔子的车前经过,同时唱道:"凤呀! 凤呀! 你的德行是不是衰败了? 为何不隐居起来? 过去的无法挽回,不用多说了;未来的还是可以补救(现在隐居还来得及)。算了吧! 算了吧! 现在从政的人都很危险。"孔子听了便下车,想要和接舆谈谈,但接舆很快避开了,孔子无法和他谈话。

[英译文]

The madman of Chu, Jie-yu, passed by Confucius, singing and saying, "O Feng! O Feng! How is your virtue degenerated! As to the past, reproof is useless; but the future may still be provided against. Give up your vain pursuit. Give up your vain pursuit. Peril awaits those who now engage in affairs of government." Confucius alighted and wished to converse with him, but Jie-yu hastened away, so that he could not talk with him.

18-6

长沮、桀溺①耦而耕②,孔子过之③,使子路问津④焉。长沮曰:"夫执舆者⑤为谁?"子路曰:"为孔丘。"曰:"是鲁孔丘与?"曰:"是也。"曰:"是知津矣。"问于桀溺。桀溺曰:"子为谁?"曰:"为仲由。"曰:"是鲁孔丘之徒与?"对曰:"然。"曰:"滔滔者天下皆是也,而谁以易之⑥? 且而⑦与其从辟人之士⑧也,岂若从辟世之士⑨哉?"耰⑩而不辍。子路行以告。夫子怃然曰:"鸟兽不可与同群,吾非斯人之徒与而谁与⑪? 天下有道,丘不与易也。"

[注释]

①长沮、桀溺:是两位不知其真实姓名、避世而隐于农的士人。沮,读 jǔ。桀,读 jié。溺,

读 ní。　②耦而耕：两人并耕。　③孔子过之：时值孔子自楚返蔡，途经于此。　④津：过渡处。
⑤执舆者：拿着车上驾驭牲口用的缰绳者。　⑥滔滔者天下皆是也，而谁以易之：滔滔者，形容大
水滚滚，弥漫无际。比喻时局祸乱，到处都是，谁可以改变它呢？　⑦而：在这里作"汝"字解。
⑧辟人之士：见人之无道而避之者，言者乃指孔子。　⑨辟世之士：举世之无道而避者，言者指
自己。　⑩耰：读 yōu，古代一种碎土、平整田地用的农具。也指播种后用耰翻土、盖土的动作。
⑪鸟兽不可与同群，吾非斯人之徒与而谁与：鸟飞兽走，二者不能合为群。人也各有其志，岂可
因世道混乱而绝人弃世以为自洁？推行大道不与天下人在一起又与谁在一起呢？

[白话文]

　　长沮、桀溺二人一起在田里耕作，孔子经过，让子路来询问他们渡口在何处。
长沮先问子路："车上拿着缰绳的是谁？"子路说："是孔丘。"长沮又问："是鲁国的孔
丘吗？"子路说："是的。"长沮就说："那他应该知道渡口在哪儿！"子路就去问桀溺。
桀溺反问说："你是谁？"子路说："我是仲由。"桀溺又问："是鲁国孔丘的徒弟吗？"
子路答："是的。"桀溺于是说："今天像滔滔洪水的祸乱，天下到处都是，又有谁能
改变这种局势呢？况且，像你这样跟从着避开无道者的'辟人之士'（指孔子），还不
如跟从避世隐居的'辟世之士'（指言者自己）。"说完，仍然不停地翻土。子路回到
孔子身边把经过报告给孔子。孔子失望地说："鸟能高飞，兽会远走，二者不能合
群。人各有志，为推行大道，不和天下人在一起又与谁在一起呢？如果政治清明、
天下太平、人民安乐，我就不会和你们一起来改革它了。"

[英译文]

Chang-ju and Jie-ni were at work in the field together, when Confucius passed by them, and sent Zi-lu to inquire for the ford.

Chang-ju said, "Who is he that holds the reins in the carriage there?" Zi-lu told him, "It is Kong-qiu." "Is it not Kong-qiu of Lu?" asked he. "Yes," was the reply, to which the other rejoined, "He knows the ford." Zi-lu then inquired of Jie-ni, who said to him, "Who are you, Sir?" He answered, "I am Zhong-you." "Are you not the disciple of Kong-qiu of Lu." asked the other. "I am," replied he, and then Jie-ni said to him, "Disorder, like a swelling flood, spreads over the whole empire, and who is he that will change its state for you? Than follow one who merely withdraws from this one and that one, had you not better follow those who have withdrawn from the world altogether?" With this he fell to covering up the seed, and proceeded with his work, without stopping.

Zi-lu went and reported their remarks, when the Master observed with a sigh, "It is impossible to associate with birds and beasts, as if they were the same with us. If I associate not with these people, with mankind, with whom shall I associate? If right principles prevailed through the empire, there would be no use for me to change its state. "

18－7

子路從而後,遇丈人①,以杖荷蓧②。子路問曰:"子見夫子乎?"丈人曰:"四體不勤,五穀③不分。孰爲夫子?"植其杖而芸④。子路拱而立。止子路宿,殺雞、爲黍⑤而食之,見其二子焉。明日,子路行以告。子曰:"隱者也。"使子路反⑥見之。至,則行矣。子路曰:"不仕無義。長幼之節,不可廢也;君臣之義,如之何其廢之? 欲潔其身,而亂大倫⑦。君子之仕也,行其義也;道之不行,已知之矣。"

[注释]

①丈人:老人。 ②以杖荷蓧:杖,拐杖。荷,背负。蓧,《说文》作"筱",竹制的耘草器。以杖荷蓧,即用杖挑着蓧,背负着。 ③五谷:稻、梁、麦、黍、稷。 ④芸:同"耘",耘田去杂草。⑤为黍:做饭。 ⑥反:同"返"。 ⑦大伦:父子有亲,君臣有义,夫妇有别,长幼有序,朋友有信。

[白话文]

子路跟从孔子行,远落于后,遇见一位老人,用拐杖挑着除草用的竹器。子路便问:"请问,看见我的老师了吗?"老人说:"四体不勤,五谷不分,我知道你的老师是谁?"说罢,将杖插在田里,就去耘田除草。子路则拱着手站立在那里。天晚了,老人留子路到家住宿,并杀鸡、做饭来招待,又叫他的两个儿子来拜见子路。

翌日,子路辞去赶上孔子,向孔子报告了这件事。孔子说:"他是一位隐士。"当即叫子路返回去拜见他。子路到了他家,老人已出去了。子路便对他的两个儿子说:"不愿出仕(做官)是不合乎义的。长幼之间的礼节不可废除,君臣之间的义又如何可以废除呢? 看到官场恶浊,为洁身自好而不出仕,却乱了大伦(君臣之义)。君子出仕不是为了利禄,是行其义,实行他应该做的事。至于大道之不实现,我是知道的。"

[英译文]

Zi-lu, following the Master, happened to fall behind, when he met an old man, carrying across his shoulder on a staff a basket for weeds. Zi-lu said to him, "Have you seen my master, Sir?" The old man replied, "Your four limbs are unaccustomed to toil; you cannot distinguish the five kinds of grain—who is your master?" With this, he planted his staff in the ground, and proceeded to weed.

Zi-lu joined his hands across his breast, and stood before him.

The old man kept Zi-lu to pass the night in his house, killed a fowl, prepared millet, and feasted him. He also introduced to him his two sons.

Next day, Zi-lu went on his way, and reported his adventure. The Master said, "He is a recluse." and sent Zi-lu back to see him again, but when he got to the place, the old man was gone.

Zi-lu then said to the family, "Not to take office is not righteous. If the relations between old and young may not be neglected, how is it that he sets aside the duties that should be observed between sovereign and minister? Wishing to maintain his personal purity, he allows that great relation to come to confusion. A superior man takes office, and performs the righteous duties belonging to it. As to the failure of right principles to make progress, he is aware of that."

18－8

逸民①：伯夷、叔齊、虞仲、夷逸、朱張、柳下惠、少連。子曰："不降其志，不辱其身，伯夷、叔齊與？"謂："柳下惠、少連，降志辱身矣；言中倫，行中慮，其斯而已矣。"謂："虞仲、夷逸，隱居放言②，身中清，廢中權。我則異於是，無可無不可③。"

［注释］

①逸民：隐逸而不出仕，有才德的士人。本章所列七名，伯夷、叔齐、柳下惠均已见前；虞仲，《集注》认为，即泰伯之弟仲雍，但多异议；夷逸、朱张，不见经传，身世已不可知；少连，《集注》亦曰"事不可考"，然《记》（礼祀）称其"善居丧，三日不怠，三月不解，期悲哀，三年忧"，则行中虑，亦可见矣。　②隐居放言：隐居者，无功名利禄之图，敢于客观、公正地放言评论世事。　③无可无不可：孔子自述对待出仕的态度，异于逸民的有可有不可。孟子谓"孔子可以仕则仕，可以止则止，可以久则久，可以速则速"。

［白话文］

有才德而隐居的人有：伯夷、叔齐、虞仲、夷逸、朱张、柳下惠、少连。孔子说："不屈降自己的意志，不屈辱自己的身份，大概只有伯夷和叔齐两人吧！"又评论柳下惠、少连说："他们两人虽然降志辱身，但他们的言论合乎伦理，行为经过思虑，如此而已。"又说："虞仲、夷逸隐居起来，敢于放言论世，又能独善其身，保持自身清白，放弃官职，以免祸患，合乎权变的道理，识时务者也。"最后，自我评说："我跟他们都不一样，我是无可无不可的（不一定主张进，不一定主张退。道义上需要进，则乱世亦进；道义上应该退，则治世亦退）。"

［英译文］

The men who have retired to privacy from the world have been Bo-yi, Shu-qi, Yu-zhong, Yi-yi, Zhu-zhang, Liu Xia-hui and Shao-lian.

The Master said, "Refusing to surrender their wills, or to submit to any taint in their persons—such, I think, were Bo-yi and Shu-qi. It may be said of Liu Xia-hui, and of Shao-lian, that they surrendered their wills, and submitted to taint in their persons, but their words corresponded with reason, and their actions were such as men are anxious to see. This is all that is to be remarked in them. It may be said of Yu-zhong and Yi-yi, that, while they hid themselves in their seclusion, they gave a license to their words; but, in their persons, they succeeded in preserving their purity, and, in their retirement, they acted according to the exigency of the times. I am different from all these. I have no course for which I am predetermined, and no course against which I am predetermined."

18 - 9

大師摯①適②齊,亞飯干③適楚,三飯繚適蔡,四飯缺適秦,鼓方叔④入於河,播鼗武⑤入於漢,少師陽⑥、擊磬襄⑦入於海。

[注释]

①大师摯:大,读 dài。大师,鲁国乐官的领导人。摯,大师之名。　②适:去,往。　③亚饭干:亚饭,和后文的"三饭"、"四饭"都是古代分管天子和诸侯吃饭时所奏乐章的乐官之称。亚饭名干,下文的缭、缺分别是三饭、四饭的乐官人名。　④鼓方叔:敲鼓的乐官,名方叔。　⑤播鼗武:播,摇动。鼗,读 táo,两边系有小槌的小鼓。播鼗的乐官,名武。　⑥少师阳:少师,亦乐官,名阳。　⑦击磬襄:磬,读 qìng,古代的一种打击乐器。击磬,亦乐官,名襄。

[白话文]

(鲁国的音乐教化衰微。)乐官长摯逃到齐国去了,二饭乐师干逃到了楚国,三饭乐师缭逃到了蔡国,四饭乐师缺逃到了秦国,鼓手方叔逃到了河内,摇小鼓的武逃到了汉中,副乐官阳和击磬的襄逃到海岛去了。(从此鲁国的音乐教化更为衰败。)

[英译文]

The grand music-master, Zhi, went to Qi. Gan, the master of the band at the second meal, went to Chu. Liao, the band-master at the third meal, went to Cai. Que, the band-master at the fourth meal, went to Qin. Fang-shu, the drum-master, withdrew to the north of the river. Wu, the master of the hand-drum, withdrew to the Han. Yang, the assistant music-master, and Xiang, master of the musical stone, withdrew to an island in the sea.

18－10

周公①謂魯公曰："君子不施②其親,不使大臣怨乎不以。故舊無大故,則不棄也。無求備於一人。"

[注释]

①周公:即周公旦。受封于鲁,自己仍相成王,由他的儿子伯禽到鲁国去做君主。这段话是周公告诉伯禽任人用事应该注意的问题。　②施:同"弛",放松。有的版本将施用为"弛"字。也有作"用"字解。

[白话文]

周公对鲁公说:"一个有才德的君主,在任人用事方面不要放松对亲人的要求,不要任人唯亲;不要使大臣抱怨不受重视;老人旧属如果没有大的错误,就不要抛弃他们;不要对人求全责备。"

[英译文]

The duke of Zhou addressed his son, the duke of Lu, saying, "The virtuous prince does not neglect his relations. He does not cause the great ministers to repine at his not employing them. Without some great cause, he does not dismiss from their offices the members of old families. He does not seek in one man talents for every employment."

18－11

周有八士①:伯達、伯适②、仲突、仲忽、叔夜、叔夏、季隨、季騧③。

[注释]

①周有八士:周之兴,有赖于贤人哲士之辅助。所列八士,即反映了当时人才之盛,亦说明了当局者善于用人——选贤与能。　②适:读 kuò,不是"适"的简化字。　③騧:读 guā。

[白话文]

周朝有八位贤士:伯达、伯适、仲突、仲忽、叔夜、叔夏、季随、季騧。

[英译文]

To Zhou belonged the eight officers: Bo-da, Bo-kuo, Zhong-tu, Zhong-hu, Shu-ye, Shu-xia, Ji-sui, Ji-gua.

子張第十九

本篇凡二十五章(19—1～19—25)。

19-1

子张曰:"士①见危致命,见得思义,祭思敬、丧思哀,其可已矣。"

[注释]

①士:古代贵族中最低一级的人称士,读书人(相当于现代所称的知识分子)以及具有某种品质或某种技能的人亦称为士。

[白话文]

子张说:"一个士人,遇到国家危急的时候,便肯献出生命;有利可得时,要考虑是否正当;祭祀时,应考虑到恭敬;居丧时,要考虑到是否尽了哀悼心。能够这样做,也就可以了!"

[英译文]

Zi-zhang said, "The scholar, trained for public duty, seeing threatening danger, is prepared to sacrifice his life. When the opportunity of gain is presented to him, he thinks of righteousness. In sacrificing, his thoughts are reverential. In mourning, his thoughts are about the grief, which he should feel. Such a man commands our approbation indeed."

19-2

子张曰:"执德不弘,信道不笃①,焉能为有? 焉能为亡②?"

[注释]

①笃:厚实,一心一意。 ②亡:同"无"。

[白话文]

子张说:"执守德行却不能发扬宏大,信仰道义又三心二意,这种人有没有都无足轻重。"

[英译文]

Zi-zhang said, "When a man holds fast to virtue, but without seeking to enlarge it, and believes in right principles, but without firm sincerity, what account can be made of his existence or non-existence?"

19-3

子夏之门人问交①于子张。子张曰:"子夏云何?"对曰:"子夏曰:'可者与之,其不可者拒之。'"子张曰:"异乎吾所闻:君子尊贤而容众,嘉善而矜②不能。我之大贤与,于人何所不容? 我之不贤与,人将拒我,如之何其拒人也?"

[注释]

①交:交友之道。　②矜:怜悯、怜惜。

[白话文]

　　子夏的学生向子张请教交朋友的道理。子张说:"你的老师(子夏)怎么说呢?"答道:"我的老师说:'可交往的就交往,不可交往的就拒绝他。'"子张说:"这和我所听说的不同。君子应当尊敬贤人,而且能容纳众人,夸奖善良的人,怜悯能力差的人。我若是一个大贤人,我对别人有什么不能容纳呢? 我如果不是个贤人,别人也将拒绝我,我又怎么说得上拒绝别人呢?"

[英译文]

　　The disciples of Zi-xia asked Zi-zhang about the principles that should characterize mutual intercourse. Zi-zhang asked, "What does Zi-xia say on the subject?" They replied, "Zi-xia says, 'Associate with those who can advantage you. Put away from you those who cannot do so.'" Zi-zhang observed, "This is different from what I have learned. The superior man honours the talented and virtuous, and bears with all. He praises the good, and pities the incompetent. Am I possessed of great talents and virtue? Who is there among men whom I will not bear with? Am I devoid of talents and virtue? Men will put me away from them. What have we to do with the putting away of others?"

19－4

　　子夏曰:"雖小道①,必有可觀者焉;致遠恐泥②,是以君子不爲也。"

[注释]

①小道:指一技一艺的学问和技能。　②泥:滞陷不通。

[白话文]

　　子夏说:"虽然只是一种小技艺,也必定有它可取之处。但是对从事远大事业者来说,任重道远,如果太专注这些小技艺,恐会影响前进,所以君子不愿这样做。"

[英译文]

　　Zi-xia said, "Even in inferior studies and employments there is something worth being looked at; but if it be attempted to carry them out to what is remote, there is a danger of their proving inapplicable. Therefore, the superior man does not practise them."

19－5

子夏曰："日知其所亡^①，月無忘其所能，可謂好學也已矣！"

[注释]

① 亡：同"无"，这里指自己所未有的。

[白话文]

子夏说："每天学习一些过去所不懂的知识，每月复习，使自己学到的知识不忘记。能这样做的人，可以说是好学的人了！"

[英译文]

Zi-xia said, "He, who from day to day recognises what he has not yet, and from month to month does not forget what he has attained to, may be said indeed to love to learn."

19－6

子夏曰："博學而篤志^①，切問^②而近思^③，仁在其中^④矣！"

[注释]

①笃志：意志坚定。　②切问：提出的问题要切实、明确，不要泛问。　③近思：思考问题要有个中心，从现实出发，加以类推，不做虚无缥缈、不切实际的空想。　④仁在其中：《中庸》有"力行近乎仁"句。《集注》曰："四者（按：指博学、笃志、切问、近思）皆学问思辨之事耳，未及乎力行而为仁也。然从事于此，则心不外驰，而所存自熟，故曰'仁在其中矣'。"

[白话文]

子夏说："一个人能够广博地学习知识，有自己的坚定意志，提出的问题明确、切实，思考问题从实际出发。这样，仁德就在其中了。"

[英译文]

Zi-xia said, "There are learning extensively, and having a firm and sincere aim; inquiring with earnestness, and reflecting with self-application—virtue is in such a course."

19－7

子夏曰："百工居肆^①以成其事，君子學以致其道。"

[注释]

①肆：工场。

[白话文]

子夏说："各种工匠在工场里专心致志地完成作业。作为一个人格高尚的人也要像他们那样，不受外诱，专心力学，以深造其道。"

[英译文]

　　Zi-xia said, "Mechanics have their shops to dwell in, in order to accomplish their works. The superior man learns, in order to reach to the utmost of his principles."

19－8

　　子夏曰："小人之過也，必文①。"

[注释]

　　①文：掩饰。

[白话文]

　　子夏说："小人对自己的过错一定会加以掩饰。"

[英译文]

　　Zi-xia said, "The mean man is sure to gloss his faults."

19－9

　　子夏曰："君子有三變：望之儼然，即之也温，聽其言也厲。"

[白话文]

　　子夏说："君子给人的感觉有三种变相：一时望见他，觉得容貌举止十分庄重；和他接近后，又觉得温和可亲；听到他的讲话，却感到义正辞严。"

[英译文]

　　Zi-xia said, "The superior man undergoes three changes. Looked at from a distance, he appears stern; when approached, he is mild; when he is heard to speak, his language is firm and decided."

19－10

　　子夏曰："君子①信而後勞其民；未信，則以爲厲②己也。信而後諫；未信，則以爲謗己也。"

[注释]

　　①君子：这里指在上位的人。　　②厉：虐待。

[白话文]

　　子夏说："在上位的人，首先必须获得人民的信任，然后才去使唤他们；如果没有取得信任，人民必以为是虐政，是坑害他们。作为下位者对待上位的人，也必须先取得信任而后才去进谏，否则，就会以为你在毁谤他。"

[英译文]

Zi-xia said, "The superior man, having obtained their confidence, may then impose labours on his people. If he has not gained their confidence, they will think that he is oppressing them. Having obtained the confidence of his prince, one may then remonstrate with him. If he have not gained his confidence, the prince will think that he is vilifying him."

19－11

子夏曰：“大德不踰閑^①；小德出入可也。”

[注释]

①闲：读 xián，栅栏（养马的圈），范围，界限。

[白话文]

子夏说：“一个人在大的道德操守上是不可以超越规矩界限的；至于行为上的小节，偶然出入一些也是可以的。”

[英译文]

Zi-xia said, "When a person does not transgress the boundary-line in the great virtues, he may pass and repass it in the small virtues."

19－12

子游曰：“子夏之門人小子，當灑掃、應對、進退，則可矣，抑末也。本之則無，如之何？”子夏聞之曰：“噫！言游過矣！君子之道，孰先傳焉？孰後倦焉？譬諸草木，區以別矣。君子之道，焉可誣也？有始有卒者，其惟聖人乎！”

[白话文]

子游说：“子夏的学生们，做些洒扫庭院、应对客人和进退礼节的事，那是可以的，但是这些都是琐屑末节，没有学到根本的学问，怎么可以呢？”子夏听到后说：“唉！言游（子游姓言）错了，君子的学问，哪一些先传授？哪一些后传授？好比花草树木，是有区别的。如果不量其深浅，不问其生熟，不能分别对待，这是歪曲了君子的教学之道，怎么可以呢？能够按照固定的次序，有始有终地进行教育，大概只有圣人能做得到吧！”

[英译文]

Zi-you said, "The disciples and followers of Zi-xia, in sprinkling and sweeping the ground, in answering and replying, in advancing and receding, are sufficiently accomplished. But these are only the branches of learning, and they are left ignorant of what is essential. How can they be acknowledged as sufficiently taught?"

Zi-xia heard of the remark and said, "Alas! Yan-you is wrong. According to the way of the superior man in teaching, what departments are there which he considers of prime importance, and delivers? What are there which he considers of secondary importance, and allows himself to be idle about? But as in the case of plants, which are assorted according to their classes, so he deals with his disciples. How can the way of a superior man be such as to make fools of any of them? Is it not the sage alone, who can unite in one the beginning and the consummation of learning?"

19－13

子夏曰："仕而優①則學,學而優則仕。"

[注释]

①优:余裕。如有余裕的时间,有余力。

[白话文]

子夏说:"一个出任官职的人,如果有余力和时间,就应当学习知识,充实和提高自己;一个从事学问的人,如有余力,也应当出仕,将学问付诸实践。"

[英译文]

Zi-xia said, "The officer, having discharged all his duties, should devote his leisure to learning. The student, having completed his learning, should apply himself to be an officer."

19－14

子游曰："喪,致乎哀而止。"

[白话文]

子游说:"一个人在居丧时,表达了内心的哀悼就可以了。"

[英译文]

Zi-you said, "Mourning, having been carried to the utmost degree of grief, should stop with that."

19－15

子游曰："吾友張①也,爲難能也! 然而未仁。"

[注释]

　　①张：即同学子张,姓颛孙,名师,陈国人。

[白话文]

　　子游说:"我友子张,是一位难能可贵的人,然而还没有达到仁的境界。"

[英译文]

　　Zi-you said, "My friend Zhang can do things which are hard to be done, but yet he is not perfectly virtuous. "

19－16

　　曾子曰:"堂堂①乎張也,難與并爲仁矣。"

[注释]

　　①堂堂:形容仪表庄严大方,亦形容有志气、有气魄。

[白话文]

　　曾子说:"子张为人,堂堂正正,但难以共同相勉为仁。"

[英译文]

　　The philosopher Zeng said, "How imposing is the manner of Zi-zhang. It is difficult along with him to practise virtue. "

19－17

　　曾子曰:"吾聞諸①夫子:'人未有自致②者也,必也親喪乎!'"

[注释]

　　①诸:"之于"的合音。　②自致:自发而尽量。

[白话文]

　　曾子说:"我听老师讲过:'人的真挚之情,在平时没有无端而自发地尽情表达的。要是有的话,必是在父母去世时。'"

[英译文]

　　The philosopher Zeng said, "I heard this from our master—men may not have shown what is in them to the full extent, and yet they will be found to do so, on occasion of mourning for their parents. "

19－18

　　曾子曰:"吾聞諸夫子:'孟莊子①之孝也,其他可能也;其不改父之臣,與父之政,是難能也。'"

[注释]

①孟庄子:鲁国的大夫,姓仲孙,名速,乃孟献子(即仲孙蔑)的儿子。鲁襄公十九年(公元前五百九十四年),孟献子卒,孟庄子接位,继续任用了乃父的家臣,并因循其政。

[白话文]

曾子说:"我听老师说过:'孟庄子的孝行,在其他方面,别人都做得到。至于他仍旧任用了他父亲的一班旧臣,继续沿袭他父亲所制定的政治措施,则是别人难以做到的了。'"

[英译文]

The philosopher Zeng said, "I have heard this from our master—the filial piety of Meng Zhuang-zi, in other matters, was what other men are competent to, but, as seen in his not changing the ministers of his father, not his father's mode of government, it is difficult to be attained to."

19 - 19

孟氏①使陽膚②爲士師③,問於曾子。曾子曰:"上失其道,民散久矣。如得其情,則哀矜而勿喜。"

[注释]

①孟氏:鲁国家臣。　②阳肤:曾子的学生。　③士师:狱官。

[白话文]

孟氏任命阳肤做狱官,阳肤来问曾子。曾子告诫他说:"如今,上位的人久已失去了治民之道,民心离散很久了,种种犯罪行为也由之而发生。你去当狱官,在办案时如果查出了犯罪行为的实情,要有同情的心哀其罹刑,怜其无知或有所不得已,切不可因查出实情沾沾自喜。"

[英译文]

The chief of the Meng family having appointed Yang-fu to be chief criminal judge, the latter consulted the philosopher Zeng. Zeng said, "The rulers have failed in their duties, and the people consequently have been disorganized, for a long time. When you have found out the truth of any accusation, be grieved for and pity them, and do not feel joy at your own ability."

19 - 20

子貢曰:"紂①之不善,不如是之甚也。是以君子惡居下流②,天下之惡皆歸焉。"

[注释]

①纣:商(殷)朝的末代君主,名辛,纣是他的谥号,相传是个暴君。　②恶居下流:恶,读 wù,讨厌、憎恨。下流,指水系的下游。江河中的污浊最后都会汇集到这里。君子恶居下流,乃谓不愿置身下流,恐所有的污浊坏事都揽在自己身上。

[白话文]

子贡说:"纣王的作恶,并不像后世传说的那么严重。(正因为他做了坏事,所以一切恶名归集到他的身上。)故君子憎恶居于下流,恐天下的恶名都归到他身上了。"

[英译文]

Zi-gong said, "Zhou's wickedness was not so great as that name implies. Therefore, the superior man hates to dwell in a low-lying situation, where all the evil of the world will flow in upon him."

19－21

子贡曰:"君子之过也,如日月之食焉。过也,人皆见之;更也,人皆仰之。"

[白话文]

子贡说:"君子也会有过错的,如同日蚀和月蚀一样。过错发生时,人人都看得到;更改了过错,人人都景仰他。"

[英译文]

Zi-gong said, "The faults of the superior man are like the eclipses of the sun and moon. He has his faults, and all men see them; he changes again, and all men look up to him."

19－22

卫公孙朝①问於子贡曰:"仲尼焉②学?"子贡曰:"文武之道③,未坠於地,在人。贤者识④其大者,不贤者识其小者。莫不有文武之道焉。夫子焉不学? 而亦何常师之有?"

[注释]

①公孙朝:卫国的大夫。　②焉:副词,哪里、怎么。　③文武之道:周文王、周武王所制定的礼乐教化。　④识:读 zhì,文字记录。

[白话文]

卫国公孙朝问子贡:"仲尼的学问渊博精深,是哪里学来的?"子贡说:"周文王、周武王之道还没有被丢失,仍流传在人间。贤能的人记录了它的重大内容,不贤能的人也记录了细小的部分。文王、武王之道无处不在,老师到处都能学习。又何必要有一个固定的老师呢?"

[英译文]

Gong Sun-chao of Wei asked Zi-gong, "From whom did Zhong-ni get his learning?"

Zi-gong replied, "The doctrines of Wen and Wu have not yet fallen to the ground. They are to be found among men. Men of talents and virtue remember the greater principles of them, and others, not possessing such talents and virtue, remember the smaller. Thus, all possess the doctrines of Wen and Wu. Where could our master go that he should not have an opportunity of learning them? And yet what necessity was there for his having a regular master?"

19－23

叔孫武叔①語大夫於朝曰:"子貢賢於仲尼。"子服景伯②以告子貢。子貢曰:"譬之宮牆③,賜之牆也及肩,窺見室家之好。夫子之牆數仞④,不得其門而入,不見宗廟之美,百官之富。得其門者或寡矣!夫子之云,不亦宜乎?"

[注释]

①叔孙武叔:叔孙氏,名州仇,武是谥号。鲁国的大夫,是一个竭力诋毁孔子的人。 ②子服景伯:亦为鲁国大夫,又是子贡的同学。子服氏,名何,字伯,景是谥号。 ③宫墙:古时,天子和上大夫,所居房屋均可称宫。宫墙,即其房屋的围墙。 ④仞:长度七尺为一仞。

[白话文]

叔孙武叔在朝廷上对诸大夫说:"子贡比他的老师仲尼还要贤明。"子服景伯听到此话转告子贡。子贡说:"就拿墙垣作比喻吧!我的墙只有肩膀那么高,人人都很容易从墙外看到屋内美好的陈设。而我们老师的墙有数仞(几十尺)高,如果找不到门进去,就看不见宗庙之美、百官房舍之富丽。可是,能得其门而入的人是很少的。武叔老夫子这样说不是很自然吗?"

[英译文]

Shu-sun Wu-shu observed to the great officers in the court, saying, "Zi-gong is superior to Zhong-ni."

Zi-fu Jing-bo reported the observation to Zi-gong, who said, "Let me use the comparison of a house and its encompassing wall. My wall only reaches to the shoulders. One may peep over it, and see whatever is valuable in the apartments. The wall of my master is several fathoms high. If one do not find the door and enter by it, he cannot see the ancestral temple with its beauties, nor all the officers in their rich array. But I may assume that they are few who find the door. Was not the observation of the chief only what might have been expected?"

19 – 24

叔孫武叔毀仲尼。子貢曰：“無以爲也！仲尼不可毀也。他人之賢者，丘陵也，猶可踰也；仲尼，日月也，無得而踰焉。人雖欲自絶，其何傷於日月乎？多見其不知量也。”

[白话文]

叔孙武叔毁谤仲尼。子贡说：“没有用的，仲尼是毁谤不了的。别的贤人，好比丘陵，人们还是能爬越过去的；仲尼呢，就好像太阳、月亮，没有人攀得上去。纵使有人想拒绝太阳、月亮的光辉，（任你如何诋毁他，）于日月有什么伤害呢？适足以见得他不自量力罢了！”

[英译文]

Shu-sun Wu-shu having spoken revilingly of Zhong-ni. Zi-gong said, "It is of no use doing so. Zhong-ni cannot be reviled. The talents and virtue of other men are hillocks and mounds, which may be stepped over. Zhong-ni is the sun or moon, which it is not possible to step over. Although a man may wish to cut himself off from the sage, what harm can he do to the sun or moon? He only shows that he does not know his own capacity."

19 – 25

陳子禽①謂子貢曰：“子爲恭也，仲尼②豈賢於子乎？”子貢曰：“君子一言以爲知，一言以爲不知，言不可不慎也。夫子之不可及也，猶天之不可階而升也。夫子之得邦家者③，所謂立④之斯立，道⑤之斯行，綏⑥之斯來，動⑦之斯和⑧。其生也榮，其死也哀。如之何其可及也？”

[注釋]

①陈子禽：参阅学而篇第十章(1-10)注。 ②仲尼：本章及以前称孔子字，乃据古礼，弟子辈对师长可称字号，不能称名。 ③夫子之得邦家者：指老师若能得国而为诸侯，得家而为大夫来治理的话。 ④立：近人沈知方从《皇疏》注为立之以礼。 ⑤道：导之以教。 ⑥绥：安抚。 ⑦动：《集注》曰：“谓鼓舞也。” ⑧和：《集注》曰：“于变时雍。”句出《尚书·虞书·尧典》，乃称天

下臣民都友好和睦。

[白话文]

　　陈子禽对子贡说:"你对老师仲尼这样恭敬谦逊,他真的比你贤能吗?"子贡说:"君子说一句话,就会显示出他的明智;同样,说一句话,也可显示出他的不明智。所以说话不可不谨慎。老师的不可比及,好像天一样,是不能用阶梯爬上去的。我们的老师如果能担任诸侯之政,管理卿大夫之事,去治理邦国,其于人民立以礼则人立;导之以教则人民自然会跟着走;安抚天下,安抚人民,则人民就会前来归顺;鼓舞民心,同心协力,人民也因此而友好和睦。老师在世的时候光荣备至,人人尊重;去世之后,人人都悲哀伤痛。像我这样的人,怎能及得上老师呢?"

[英译文]

　　Chen Zi-qin addressing Zi-gong, said, "You are too modest. How can Zhong-ni be said to be superior to you?"

　　Zi-gong said to him, "For one word a man is often deemed to be wise, and for one word he is often deemed to be foolish. We ought to be careful indeed in what we say. Our master cannot be attained to, just in the same way as the heavens cannot be gone up to by the steps of a stair. Were our master in the position of the ruler of a state or the chief of a Family, we should find verified the description which has been given of a sage's rule—he would plant the people, and forthwith they would be established; he would lead them on, and forthwith they would follow him; he would make them happy, and forthwith multitudes would resort to his dominions; he would stimulate them, and forthwith they would be harmonious. While he lived, he would be glorious. When he died, he would be bitterly lamented. How is it possible for him to be attained to?"

堯曰第二十

本篇凡三章(20－1～20－3)。

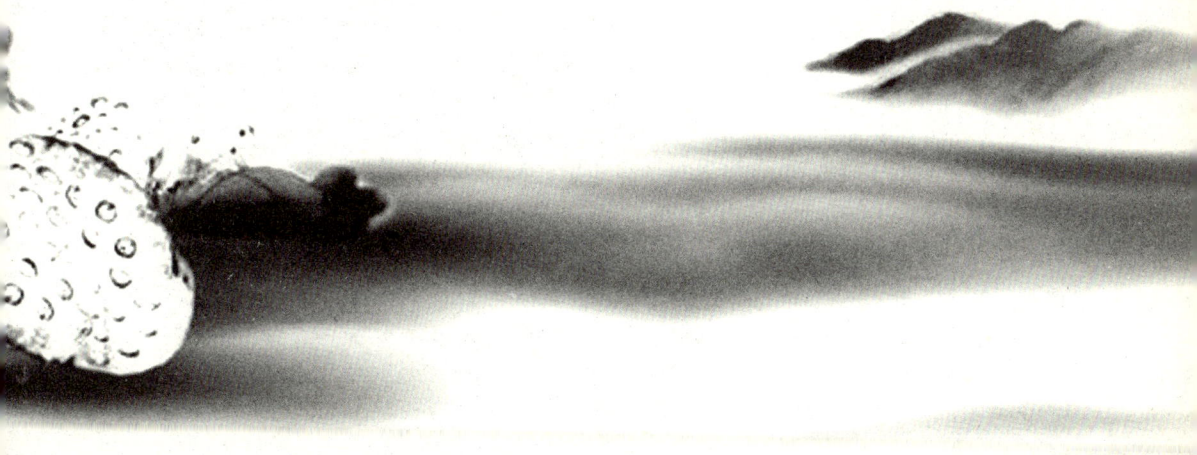

20-1

尧①曰："咨！尔舜②！天之历数③在尔躬④，允执其中⑤。四海困穷，天禄永终⑥。"

舜亦以命禹⑦。

曰⑧："予小子履⑨，敢用玄牡⑩，敢昭告⑪于皇皇后帝⑫，有罪不敢赦。帝臣⑬不蔽⑭，简⑮在帝心。朕⑯躬有罪，无以万方。万方有罪，罪在朕躬。"

周⑰有大赍⑱，善人是富。"虽有周亲，不如仁人。百姓有过，在予一人。"

谨权量，审法度⑲，修废官⑳，四方之政行焉；兴灭国，继绝世，举逸民，天下之民归心焉。所重民，食、丧、祭㉑。宽则得众，信则民任焉，敏则有功，公则说㉒。

[注释]

①尧：中国五帝时期（约公元前二十六世纪至前二十一世纪）的一位帝者。名放勋，在位七十年，传位给舜（参阅《尚书·尧典》）。这里是在他传位给舜时所讲的话。　②舜：名重华，在位五十年。　③历数：即历法。为尧帝组织了羲和二氏，观察研究日月星辰、一年四季运行变化之规律，制定法则，授之于民，应用于农业生产和生活，并认为这是天数，不可违。而帝王相继承的次序，也是天数。　④躬：身体，人身。　⑤允执其中：允，公平，得当。《集注》曰："信也。"执，执守，执行。中，不偏不倚，无太过、无不及。　⑥四海困穷，天禄永终：四海之人困穷，则君禄亦永绝了。应戒之。　⑦舜亦以命禹：舜，后来传位给禹，建立夏朝。舜在传位时，也将尧对他所讲的话告诫给禹（参阅《尚书·大禹谟》）。　⑧曰：因"曰"字前无主语，故这一节是谁所说，有两种不同解释。有人将此节紧接编排于"舜亦以命禹"句之下，认为是舜所说。但较多的版本认为是商汤所说，排版也另起一行。《集注》曰："'曰'上当有汤字。"考《尚书·汤诰》载汤推翻夏桀后发表的文告，与本节所述文字大同小异，均收载于文告之中。故当从。　⑨履：汤名。　⑩玄牡：黑公牛。　⑪昭告：明白地报告。　⑫皇皇后帝：在天上的上帝，一切的主宰。　⑬帝臣：人间的帝皇君臣，都是上帝的臣仆。　⑭蔽：遮盖。　⑮简：古代用竹简记录，故简作为"记"字解。　⑯朕：帝王自称。秦始皇后专作天子的自称。　⑰周：商汤传位二十九代至纣，暴虐无道，被武王推翻，建立了周朝。　⑱赍：赏赐。这里是指周建立了政权就大赍天下。《尚书·武成》有"散鹿台之财，发钜桥之粟，大赍于四海"句。　⑲谨权量，审法度：权，秤锤。量，升、斗。法度，礼乐制度等。谨权量，审法度，乃指谨慎、精细地统一规定度、量、衡的标准，审定各种礼乐制度。　⑳修废官：修，同"修"。本句意指整治那些形同虚设，起不到好的作用之政府机构和冗员；修复建立那些亟有必要而却遭到废除的官职。　㉑所重民，食、丧、祭：由于有些版本所置标点符号不同——如《集注》曰："所重：民、食、丧、祭。"亦有的版本为："所重民食，丧祭。"故解释各有所

异。据《尚书·武成》"重民五教,唯食丧祭"句,似解读为"注重人民的食、丧、祭三件事"较当。
㉒说:同"悦"。

[白话文]

尧让位给舜时说:"唉! 舜呀! 天的历数决定帝位传承在你身上了。你要诚实执守,不偏不倚,无太过与不及,好好治理百姓。如果天下百姓陷于困苦贫穷,天赐你的禄位也将永远终止。"

舜让位给禹时,也以这话告诫禹。

夏禹受天子位后,传到第十六代的桀,暴虐无道,被商汤推翻。汤在讨伐时向上天祷告说:"我小子履,谨用黑色的牡牛作祭品,明白地禀告皇天上帝,桀有罪,我不敢随便地赦免他。天下的帝皇君臣都是上帝的臣仆,我不敢有所遮盖隐瞒。你早已简阅,记在心里。我自己若有罪,不要牵涉到万方百姓。万方百姓有罪,罪责在我身上。"

汤建立了商朝,传位二十九代至纣,也是个无道之君。武王伐,纣亡,建立周王朝,大规模地赏赐天下,善良的人都富裕起来了。周武王说:"纣虽然有很多至亲,却不如我有仁德的贤人。百姓如果有过错,责任在我一个人。"

谨慎、精细地规定了度、量、衡的标准,审定了各种礼乐制度,整治了政府机构,修复了被废置的官职和职责,政令就会在全国通行。复兴被灭亡的国家,接继已被断绝沿袭的后代,举用隐逸的贤士,能这样做,天下的百姓就会心悦诚服。教化人民,重视人民的食、丧、祭三件大事。宽厚,会得到民众的拥护;诚信,会得到人民的信任;勤敏工作,会取得很好的功绩;公平,则百姓喜悦、心服。

[英译文]

Yao said, "Oh! Shun, the Heaven-determined order of succession now rests in your person. Sincerely hold fast the due mean. If there shall be distress and want within the four seas, the heavenly revenue will come to a perpetual end."

Shun also used the same language in giving charge to Yu.

Tang said, "I, the child Lu, presume to use a dark-coloured victim, and presume to announce to you, O most great and sovereign God, that the sinner I dare not pardon, and your ministers, O God, I do not keep in obscurity. The examination of them is by your mind, O God. If, in my person, I commit offences, they are not to be attributed to you, the people of the myriad regions. If you in the myriad regions commit offences, these offences must rest on my person. "

Zhou conferred great gifts, and the good were enriched. "Although he has his near relatives, they are not equal to my virtuous men. The people are throwing blame upon me, the one man. "

He carefully attended to the weights and measures, examined the body of the laws, restored the discarded officers, and the good government of the kingdom took its course. He revived states that had been extinguished, restored families whose line of succession had been broken, and called to office those who had retired into obscurity, so that throughout the kingdom the hearts of the people turned towards him. What he attached chief importance to, were the food of the people, the duties of mourning, and sacrifices. By his generosity, he won all. By his sincerity, he made the people repose trust in him. By his earnest activity, his achievements were great. By his justice, all were delighted.

20 - 2

　　子張問於孔子曰：“何如斯①可以從政矣？”子曰：“尊五美，屏②四惡，斯可以從政矣！”子張曰：“何謂五美？”子曰：“君子惠而不費，勞而不怨，欲而不貪，泰而不驕，威而不猛。”子張曰：“何謂惠而不費？”子曰：“因民之所利而利之，斯不亦惠而不費乎？擇可勞③而勞之，又誰怨？欲仁而得仁④，又焉貪？君子無衆寡，無大小，無敢慢⑤，斯不亦泰而不驕乎？君子正其衣冠，尊其瞻視，儼然人望而畏之，斯不亦威而不猛乎？”子張曰：“何謂四惡？”子曰：“不教而殺謂之虐；不戒視成謂之暴⑥；慢令致期謂之賊⑦；猶之與人也，出納之吝謂之有司⑧。”

［注释］

　　①斯：这，此；于是；就。　②屏：屏除。　③择可劳：选择可以劳役之事，可以劳役之时。④欲仁而得仁：即求仁得仁。参阅述而篇第十四章(7-14)中，孔子答子贡伯夷、叔齐之事问。⑤慢：玩忽职守，怠慢。　⑥不戒视成谓之暴：戒，同“诫”。暴，《集注》曰：“谓卒遽而无渐。”事前不告诫，要马上拿出成果。　⑦慢令致期谓之贼：致期，到期。玩弄法令，先慢其令，后限期要完成。缓于前而急于后，以误其民而刑之，是贼害也。　⑧有司：指官吏。

［白话文］

　　子张向孔子请教：“如何才可以从事政治呢？”孔子说，“尊重五种美德，屏除四种恶政，如是，可以从政了。”子张再问：“什么是五种美德？”孔子说：“在位的人，对人民施惠而自己却无所耗费；劳役人民而人民没有怨言；追求仁义而不贪求财物；神态安详而无骄矜之色；表情威严而无凶猛之感。”子张又问：“什么叫对人施惠而自己却无耗费呢？”孔子说：“就人民可以得利的方面，帮助他们去实现，使人民获得利益，这不是给他们恩惠而自己又不耗费吗？选择可以通过人民劳役来完成的事，选择合适的时间，动员组织人民劳役，还有谁会怨恨呢？欲追求仁义而得到仁义，怎么能叫贪财图利呢？君子处事，不论对多数人或是少数人，不论其地位高低和事情的大小，都认真对待，不敢怠慢，这不是泰而不骄的行为吗？君子衣冠整齐，目光端正，使人望之而有敬畏感，这不是威而不猛吗？"子张又问："四种恶政是什么呢？"孔子说："没有对人民进行教育，人民一旦犯罪就严刑峻罚，加以杀戮，这就叫虐；不事先申诫，马上便要成果，这叫暴；玩弄法令，拖延时间下达任务，又要克期完成，结果造成耽误却责罪于下，这叫贼；赐予人，或应该属于人民的东西，在发放（落实）时却显得十分吝啬，像某些管钱的小吏那样，结果造成'人亦不怀其惠'，体会不到政策，事莫大焉！"

［英译文］

Zi-zhang asked Confucius, "In what way should a person in authority act in order that he may conduct government properly?" The Master replied, "Let him honour the five excellent, and banish away the four bad, things —then may he conduct government properly." Zi-zhang said, "What are meant by the five excellent things?" The Master said, "When the person in authority is beneficent without great expenditure; when he lays tasks on the people without their repining; when he pursues what he desires without being covetous; when he maintains a dignified ease without being proud; when he is majestic without being fierce." Zi-zhang said, "What is meant by being beneficent without great expenditure?" The Master replied, "When the person in authority makes more beneficial to the people the things from which they naturally derive benefit—is not this being beneficent without great expenditure? When he chooses the labours which are proper, and makes them labour on them, who will repine? When his desires are set on benevolent government, and he secures it, who will accuse him of covetousness? Whether he has to do with many people or few, or with things great or small, he does not dare to indicate any disrespect—is not this to maintain a dignified ease without any pride? He adjusts his clothes and cap, and throws a dignity into his looks, so that, thus dignified, he is looked at with awe—is not this to be majestic without being fierce?" Zi-zhang then asked, "What are meant by the four bad things?" The Master said, "To put the people to death without having instructed them—this is called cruelty. To require from them, suddenly, the full tale of work, without having given them warning—this is called oppression. To issue orders as if without urgency, at first, and, when the time comes, to insist on them with severity—this is called injury. And, generally, in the giving pay or rewards to men, to do it in a stingy way—this is called acting the part of a mere official."

20 - 3

子曰:"不知命①,無以爲君子也;不知禮,無以立也;不知言,無以知人也。"

[注释]

①不知命:命,指"天命"。《论语》虽几次提到命、天命,但未展开阐述,且子罕篇中列入"罕言"。朱熹解释天命谓:"天命即天道之流行而赋于物者。乃事物所以当然之故。"今学者南怀瑾称之为"时代的趋势"。李零说,命有性命之命和命运之命,人对命多少有一点影响力,但最终不能操控。笔者认为天命即自然之理,也有称天理者。用现代通俗的话来说,是不能以人的意志为转变的人(社会)和自然的规律。不知命,即不知自然之理。不能顺天应时,违反自然和社会规律,就会给国家和人民带来祸殃。

[白话文]

孔子说:"不懂得天命,便不能成为一个有才德的君子;不懂得礼节,就不能立足于社会;不懂得分辨人言的是非,就无法了解别人。"

[英译文]

The Master said, "Without recognising the ordinances of Heaven, it is impossible to be a superior man. Without an acquaintance with the rules of Propriety, it is impossible for the character to be established. Without knowing the force of words, it is impossible to know men."

图书在版编目（CIP）数据

论语今译:汉、英/孙芝斋编注. —杭州:浙江大学出版社，2008.11

ISBN 978-7-308-06299-2

Ⅰ.论… Ⅱ.孙… Ⅲ.①儒家②论语－译文－汉、英 Ⅳ.B222.24

中国版本图书馆 CIP 数据核字（2008）第 159655 号

论语今译(汉英对照)

孙芝斋　编注

责任编辑	王长刚
文字编辑	葛玉丹
封面设计	陈　辉
出版发行	浙江大学出版社
	（杭州天目山路 148 号　邮政编码 310028）
	（E-mail:zupress@mail.hz.zj.cn）
	（网址:http://www.zjupress.com
	http://www.press.zju.edu.cn）
	电话:0571－88925592，88273066（传真）
经　销	浙江省新华书店
排　版	杭州中大图文设计有限公司
印　刷	杭州浙大同力教育彩印有限公司
开　本	787mm×1092mm　1/16
印　张	17.5
字　数	305 千
版 印 次	2008 年 11 月第 1 版　2008 年 11 月第 1 次印刷
书　号	ISBN 978-7-308-06299-2
定　价	30.00 元